INSIGHT.xla

Business Analysis Software for Microsoft Excel

Sam L. Savage

Stanford University

Duxbury Press

An Imprint of Brooks/Cole Publishing Company

I⟨T⟩P® An International Thomson Publishing Company

Pacific Grove • Albany • Belmont • Bonn • Boston • Cincinnati • Detroit • Johannesburg • London
Madrid • Melbourne • Mexico City • New York • Paris • Singapore • Tokyo • Toronto • Washington

Sponsoring Editor: *Curt Hinrichs*
Project Development Editor: *Cynthia Mazow*
Marketing Team: *Marcy Perman, Jean Thompson*
Editorial Assistant: *Rita Jaramillo*
Production Editor: *Nancy L. Shammas*
Manuscript Editor: *Robin Gold*
Interior Design: *Robin Gold*

Interior Illustration: *Lotus Art*
Design Editor: *E. Kelly Shoemaker*
Cover Design: *Bay Graphics Design, Inc.*
Art Editor: *Jennifer Mackres*
Typesetting: *Forbes Mill Press*
Printing and Binding: *Malloy Lithographing, Inc.*

Foreword

Professor Savage concedes up front that the use of spreadsheets for business analysis has some weaknesses (as compared to statistical and optimization packages, simulation languages, and handcrafted programs). He then proceeds to demonstrate a remarkably wide range of spreadsheet capabilities for statistical analysis, discrete-event simulation, and optimization, partly through skillful use of basic capabilities of spreadsheets—specifically Excel—and partly through add-ins supplied with *INSIGHT.xla*.

Along the way, Professor Savage provides valuable advice concerning the use of various analysis methods. Rarely has such sound theory been provided in such an entertaining manner. *INSIGHT.xla* is a must read for those who analyze business problems, are comfortable with Excel, and are not otherwise supplied with all the statistical, simulation, and optimization tools needed for analysis.

Harry Markowitz
Nobel Laureate in Economics

About the Author

After receiving his Ph.D. in computer science from Yale University, Sam Savage spent a year at General Motors Research Laboratory. He joined the faculty of the University of Chicago Graduate School of Business in 1974 where he taught regular classes until 1990. He then developed a popular executive seminar series on Management Science in Spreadsheets.

In 1985, he led the development of the first widely marketed spreadsheet optimization package, What's*Best!®*, which won *PC Magazine*'s Technical Excellence Award. In its 1992 review of his work, *OR/MS Today* stated, "Savage is on the forefront of a movement that is about to change how management science is being taught."

Dr. Savage is currently in the School of Engineering at Stanford University, where he teaches courses in Analytical Modeling in Spreadsheets and directs a program to promote industry/university relations. He consults and lectures extensively to business and government agencies and is the founder and president of AnalyCorp Inc. (www.AnalyCorp.com), a firm that develops executive education programs and software for improving business analysis.

Dr. Savage's home page is www-leland.stanford.edu/ ~ savage.

Dedicated to Russell, Jacob and Daryl, and to the memory of my parents.

"I have never let my schooling interfere with my education"

MARK TWAIN

Preface

Two decades ago, I started teaching Management Science to MBA students. I soon discovered that only about 10 percent of them understood the material, and of those, only 10 percent went on to apply it. There was a fundamental problem in the way Management Science was taught to business students: The approach was so abstract and mathematical that an *algebraic curtain* separated Management from Management Science.

Since then, three revolutions have reshaped the technology and process of decision making. First, the explosive proliferation of microcomputers set the stage for computational rather than algebraic solutions. Second, the electronic spreadsheet created a common analytical vernacular for millions of managers. Third, the Internet is now integrating decision makers, data, and analytical tools in ways never before possible. Today, better business decisions in such diverse areas as risk management, resource allocation, and finance are being guided by analytical spreadsheet models without abstract mathematical formulations. The algebraic curtain is coming down fast.

INSIGHT.xla provides decision makers with intuition into practical problem solving through concrete examples, concepts, and tutorials based on a set of Excel add-ins. No previous training in mathematics or statistics is required; however, I have assumed that the user can create and copy simple spreadsheet formulas.[1] For those with statistics or mathematics experience, it is hoped that this package will rekindle the embers of abstract knowledge.

---

1. For those who cannot, put this package down and go out and learn. Basic spreadsheet skills are more important in today's business environment than most analytical skills.

INSIGHT.xla has been designed for both the classroom, and individual use in the workplace. In the classroom, *INSIGHT.xla* can be used to teach Quantitative Analysis, Management Science, Operations Research, and Production and Operations Management. Instructors may wish to use it in conjunction with a traditional textbook. However, I have used pre-released versions as the sole text and courseware in university classes and executive education seminars. In the workplace, *INSIGHT.xla* can be used on an as-needed basis, and I hope that it serves as a guide in the development of analytic solutions to business and engineering problems.

Most of the sections stand alone, so the material can be covered in any order. Chapter 1 introduces some important general spreadsheet skills such as scaleable formulas and data tables. Chapter 2 introduces Monte Carlo simulation as a method of modeling uncertainty. In particular, random variables and diversification are explored experientially. Chapter 3 extends simulation to general spreadsheet models with uncertain inputs. Examples include inventory lot size, bidding problems, and stock options among others. Chapter 4 covers discrete event simulation for modeling waiting lines and Markov chains for analyzing evolving systems such as competitive markets and populations in health care systems. Chapter 5 is concerned with forecasting, and covers regression and time-series analysis. Chapter 6 introduces decision trees and the value of information. A spreadsheet-based probability wheel is used to introduce subjective probability. Chapter 7 is devoted to simple optimization models such as product mix, blending, transportation and staffing. Chapter 8 describes integrated, integer, and stochastic models including portfolio optimization.

Forty-five years ago my father, L. J. Savage, wrote in his preface to *The Foundations of Statistics* that when reading technical material, "Pencil and paper are nearly indispensable; for there are always figures to be sketched and steps in the argument to be verified by calculation." Instead of pencil and paper, today I recommend a computer with a blank worksheet for the same purpose.

Acknowledgments

This work grew out of a series of executive seminars on Management Science in Spreadsheets that I initiated through the University of Chicago, Graduate School of Business in 1990. I am indebted to John P. Gould, then dean, whose support enabled the seminar series and its spin-offs to get off the ground. I also owe a great deal to Linus Schrage, who has supplied me for decades with insights into everything from linear programming to simulation.

Since 1990, I have been associated with Stanford University's School of Engineering where I have benefited from continual interaction with the faculty. In particular Peter Glynn, Gerd Infanger, Ross Shachter, and Arthur

Veinott have all left their mark on this work. The forecasting routines are based on the ideas of Everette Gardner at the University of Houston who is a master of the spreadsheet in his own right. I have also been influenced by Ben Ball of MIT who adheres to the uncommon notion that applied mathematics should actually be applied to something.

David Empey and Anton Rowe provided inspired programming in Visual Basic and C as well as many design improvements along the way.

Valuable comments on early drafts of the software and manuscript were provided by Robert L. Armacost, University of Central Florida; David Ashley, University of Missouri; Mark N. Broadie, Columbia University; George D. Brower, Moravian College; Jim Collier, Southern Arkansas University; Byron Finch, Miami University of Ohio; Samuel B. Graves, Boston College; Tom Groleau, Bethel College; Victoria Mabin, University of Wellington; Richard H. McClure, Miami University of Ohio; Pierre Ndilikilikesha, Duke University; Stephen G. Powell, Dartmouth College; Robert M. Saltzman, San Francisco State University; Ken Saydan, University of North Carolina; Carl Schultz, University of New Mexico; Rick L. Wilson, Oklahoma State University; Wayne Winston, Indiana University; and Martin Young, University of Michigan. Alexander Tonsky of Pacific Telesis suggested some nice enhancements to the queuing models.

In terms of getting the package out the door, Curt Hinrichs of Duxbury Press combined persistence with patience to maintain momentum through thick and thin. Copy editing and suggestions from Rebecca Lee and Charles Seiter filled in numerous holes and smoothed off some rough edges. Robin Gold of Forbes Mill Press did the final layout and made numerous detail improvements to the flow.

An enjoyable source of wisdom came from my uncle, I. R. Savage, whose detailed comments yielded many improvements throughout. Finally, to my wife Daryl, who read through the entire manuscript I say, thanks, and no more books (at least for a while).

Contents

1 **Analytical Modeling in Spreadsheets** **1**

Introduction 2
    The Technology of Decision Making 2
    Analytical Models 3

Tutorial: A Manufacturing Example 3
    Understanding the Elements of a Worksheet Model 4
    Separation of Data and Formulas 4
    Making Sure the Model is Scalable 6
    Experimenting with the Model 7

The Voices of Experience 12

The Pros and Cons of Spreadsheet Modeling 15
    First the Cons 15
    Now the Pros 16

2 **The Building Blocks of Uncertainty: Random Variables** **17**

Introduction 18
    From Manhattan Project to Wall Street 18
    SIM.xla 19

Tutorial: Estimating Profit with Monte Carlo Simulation 19
  An Example: Uncertain Profit 19
  Monte Carlo Simulation: The Basic Steps 21

The Building Blocks of Uncertainty 28
  Uncertain Numbers: Random Variables 29
  Averages of Uncertain Numbers: Diversification and
  the Central Limit Theorem 36
  Important Classes of Uncertain Numbers: Idealized Distributions 42
  Uncertain Numbers and Bad Outcomes: Risk Management 50
  Conclusion 51

3 **The Buildings of Uncertainty:**
     Functions of Random Variables   52

The Building Blocks of Uncertainty 52

Introduction 53

Tutorial: Estimating Inventory Costs Given Uncertain Demand 54
  An Inventory Problem 54
  Simulating the Cost 55
  Simulation Results 59

The Buildings of Uncertainty 61
  Worksheet Models Based on Uncertain Numbers:
  Functions of Random Variables 61
  Experimenting Under Uncertainty: Parameterized Simulation 66
  Uncertain Numbers That Are Related to Each Other: Statistical
  Dependence 75
  How Many Trials Are Enough? Convergence 89
  Sensitivity Analysis: The Big Picture 90
  Conclusion 92

4 **Uncertainties That Evolve Over Time   93**

Introduction 94
  Systems That Evolve Over Time 94
  QUEUE.xla and Q_NET.xla 95

Simulation Through Time: Discrete-Event Simulation 95
  A Fixed Time Incremented Simulation of a Forest Fire 96
  Queuing Models 98
  Classifying Queues 99
  Fixed- versus Event-Incremented Time 100
  Queuing Networks 103

Markov Chains 109
    An Example: Market Share 109
    MARKOV.xls 110
    A Remarkable Property of Markov Chains 112
    Modifying the Transition Matrix to Evaluate Replacement Strategy 115
    Conclusion 117

5   **Forecasting 118**

Introduction 119
    Causal Forecasting 119
    Time Series Analysis 120
    Regression in Excel and FORECAST.XLA 122

Tutorials: Regression and Time Series Analysis 123
    Regression: Estimating Sales Based on Advertising Level 123
    Time Series Analysis: Predicting Future Sales Based
    on Past History 128

The Importance of Errors 133
    Errors Generated by Regression 134
    Errors Generated by Time Series 138

Explanation of Regression and Exponential Smoothing 142
    Regression 142
    Exponential Smoothing 143

6   **Decision Trees 148**

Introduction 149
    An Example: Ice Cream and Parking Tickets 149
    Good Decisions Versus Good Outcomes 151
    TREE.XLA 151

Tutorial: Building a Decision Tree 152
    Experimental Drug Development 152
    Building a Decision Tree with TREE.XLA 152

Decision Analysis: Basic Concepts 157
    Utility 158
    Probability 160
    Expected Value 162
    Decision Forks 163

Uncertainty Forks   167
Sensitivity Analysis   166
Value of Information   169
State Variables   173
Mustering the Courage of Your Convictions   180

7   Overview of Optimization   182

Introduction 183

Tutorial: Maximum Profit 185
How Many Boats to Produce?   185
The ABCs of Optimization   188
Interacting with the Model: What's Best If   193
The D's of Optimization: Dual Values   194

Basic Optimization Examples 196
Product Mix   197
Blending   197
Staff Scheduling   200
Transportation   205
Network Flow Models   207
Conclusion   212

8   Extensions of Optimization   213

Extending the Application of Optimization 214
Integer Variables   214
Combining Optimization Models: An Object Oriented Approach   221
Optimization Under Uncertainty   230
Nonlinear Optimization   233

Common Errors in Optimization Models 238
Linear and Nonlinear Formulas   238
Improper Constraints   240
Local Maxima or Minima in Nonlinear Optimization   240

The Basics of Optimization Theory 241
Optimizing a Simplified BOAT Problem   241
Linear versus Nonlinear Problems   246
More on Dual Values   248
Conclusion   250

Appendixes

A   Queuing Equations: QUEUE.xla and Q_NET.xla   251

B   Two-Parameter Exponential Smoothing for Estimating Trends   255

C   Software Command Reference   259
    SIM.XLA 259
    QUEUE.XLA and Q_NET.XLA 268
    FORECAST.XLA 272
    TREE.XLA 276
    Optimization Software 280

References 287

Index   289

Fundamental Concepts

SUMPRODUCT   7

Random Variables   29

Continuous and Discrete Random Variables   30

Histograms   33

The Cumulative Graph   34

The Mean, Mode, and Median   35

The Variance and Standard Deviation   35

Diversification and Variance Reduction   38

The Central Limit Theorem   40

The Normal Distribution   43

A Function of Random Variables   62

Linear Model   62

The Average of a Function of Random Variables   63

Statistical Dependence   76

Covariance   82

Correlation   83

Correlated Investments   85

How Time Is Advanced in Discrete-Event Simulation   97

M/M/1 Queues   99

Relation Between Poisson and Exponential Distributions   101

Markov Chains   110

Markov Chain Equilibrium   113
Dependent and Independent Variables   125
Stationary Random Variable   129
Random versus Systematic Errors   134
The Formulas of Linear Regression   143
Probability   160
Subjective Definition of Probability   161
Expected Value   163
Decision Trees   164
Tableau   243
Feasible Region   243
Contours   244
Corner Solutions 244
Dual Values   249

Exercises

EXERCISE 1.1
Experimenting with the Assumptions
   of the Production Model   11

EXERCISE 1.2
Documenting and Auditing the
   Model   11

EXERCISE 1.3
Pure Aesthetics   11

EXERCISE 2.1
Test Your Intuition on Random
   Variables   30

EXERCISE 2.2
Test Your Intuition on Random
   Variables Again   36

EXERCISE 2.3
The Distribution of the Maximum of Two
   Uniform Random Variables   41

EXERCISE 2.4
Simulating Dice   41

EXERCISE 2.5
Creating Histograms Using
   = FREQUENCY   41

EXERCISE 2. 6
Creating Simulations From Data
   Tables   42

EXERCISE 2.7
Using the Histogram Command from the
   Data Analysis Tools   42

EXERCISE 2.8
Test Your Intuition about
   Investments   45

EXERCISE 3.1
Test Your Intuition about Point
   Estimates   55

EXERCISE 3.2
Increasing the Bins of a Histogram   60

EXERCISE 3.3
Estimating Project Duration   64

EXERCISE 3.4
A Pro Forma Cash Flow Statement   64

EXERCISE 3.5
Estimating Production Quantity   65

EXERCISE 3.6
Estimating Overtime Expenses   65

EXERCISE 3.7
Create One of Your Own   66

EXERCISE 3.8
The Optimal Staffing Level   70

EXERCISE 3.9
Competitive Bidding   70

EXERCISE 3.10
Option Pricing   73

EXERCISE 3.11
Determining the Optimal Number
of Seats to Sell   81

EXERCISE 3.12
The Correlation of the Hypothetical
Weather Data   83

EXERCISE 4.1
Explaining the Formula for the Spread
of Fire   97

EXERCISE 4.2
The Average Number of Cars Waiting
at a Toll Booth   98

EXERCISE 4.3
Simulating a Queue   103

EXERCISE 4.4
Simulating Parallel Queues   105

EXERCISE 4.5
A More Realistic Simulation of
Parallel Queues   105

EXERCISE 4.6
Modeling an Assembly Line   106

EXERCISE 4.7
Service at a Bank   107

EXERCISE 4.8
Air Traffic Control   108

EXERCISE 4.9
Solving for Markov Chain
Equilibria   113

EXERCISE 4.10
Machine Replacement   116

EXERCISE 4.11
Health Care Screening   116

EXERCISE 5.1
Accounting for the Two Peaks in
Champagne Sales   130

EXERCISE 5.2
Linking Forecasting to a Simulation
Model   133

EXERCISE 5.3
Forecasting Freight   133

EXERCISE 5.4
A Simulation Based on a Regression   138

EXERCISE 5.5
Minimizing Mean Squared Error in
Time Series Analysis   140

EXERCISE 5.6
Simulating Future Periods of a Time
Series Based on Confidence
Intervals   141

EXERCISE 6.1
Umbrella Problem   150

EXERCISE 6.2
Fastest Route   151

EXERCISE 6.3
The Probability of Effectiveness   157

EXERCISE 6.4
Utility for Ice Cream   159

EXERCISE 6.5
Utility for the Umbrella   159

EXERCISE 6.6
Utility for Fastest Route   159

EXERCISE 6.7
Course Grade   162

EXERCISE 6.8
Thumb Tacks   162

EXERCISE 6.9
Expected Values   163

EXERCISE 6.10
The Ice Cream Example's
    Decision Tree   165

EXERCISE 6.11
Experimenting with Probability
    Estimates   166

EXERCISE 6.12
The Probability of Getting a Ticket,
    Revisited   169

EXERCISE 6.13
Friend's Information   170

EXERCISE 6.14
Expressway Hotline   170

EXERCISE 6.15
Experimenting with the Probability
    of a Gusher   178

EXERCISE 6.16
Toy Manufacturing   178

EXERCISE 7.1
Boat Market Limitations   194

EXERCISE 7.2
Determining the Profitability of a New
    Boat Type   196

EXERCISE 7. 3
Manufacturing Athletic Shoes   197

EXERCISE 7.4
Optimizing a Blending Model   200

EXERCISE 7.5
Blending Feedmix   200

EXERCISE 7.6
Staff Scheduling   202

EXERCISE 7.7
Generalizing STAFF.XLS: Covering
    Problems   203

EXERCISE 7.8
The Cutting Stock Problem   204

EXERCISE 7.9
Transportation Between Steel Mills
    and Plants   207

EXERCISE 7.10
Disaster Relief   207

EXERCISE 7.11
Maximum Flow Through a
    Network   211

EXERCISE 7.12
Minimum Cost at Maximum Flow   212

EXERCISE 7.13
Shortest Path Problem   212

EXERCISE 7.14
The SUMIF Formula   212

EXERCISE 8.1
Using Binary Integer Variables for
    Boolean Logic   220

EXERCISE 8.2
Integer Production Amounts   224

EXERCISE 8.3
Additional Motors   224

EXERCISE 8.4
Combining a Production and
    Transportation Model   228

EXERCISE 8.5
Generating a Trade-Off Curve   232

EXERCISE 8.6
Parameterized Portfolio
    Optimization   237

EXERCISE 8.7
Visual Basic Macro for Parameterized
    Portfolio Optimization   237

EXERCISE 8.8
Optimizing BOAT.XLS   241

EXERCISE 8.9
Corner Solutions for Large Sailboats   245

EXERCISE 8.10
Reduced Cost on Large Sailboats   249

EXERCISE 8.11
Dual Value Ranges   250

Analytical Modeling in Spreadsheets

I hear, I forget
I see, I remember
I do, I understand

CHINESE PROVERB

The unprecedented strategic and operational problems of World War II ushered in an analytical approach to decision making that was based on mathematical models of the real world.

Today, people who enter their own formulas into an electronic spreadsheet are doing mathematical modeling whether they know it or not. It requires only a small further step to build analytical models that can significantly aid in decision making.

It is not enough to hear about analytical models, or to merely see models that have been developed by someone else. As the proverb suggests, you will only understand analytical models by building them on your own.

This chapter introduces some aspects of spreadsheet modeling that are important in the analytical techniques that appear in subsequent chapters.

OVERVIEW

Introduction

This section contains instructions for installing the INSIGHT software, followed by a brief introduction to the technology of decision making and analytical modeling.

Tutorial: A Manufacturing Example

We start with the problem of modeling the manufacture of boats from a set of limited raw materials. Within this context, the concepts of scalable models and data tables are introduced.

The Voices of Experience

We present observations of several experienced model builders.

The Pros and Cons of Spreadsheet Modeling

The pros and cons of modeling in this environment are briefly summarized.

Introduction

To install INSIGHT, place the INSIGHT Disk 1 in your floppy drive, then run SETUP. This program will then step you through the complete installation of INSIGHT onto your hard disk.

The Technology of Decision Making

The unprecedented strategic and operational problems of World War II ushered in an analytical approach to decision making, known as operations research, based on mathematical models of the real world.

After the war, the approach was adapted to the needs of general industry, and the field of management science emerged. Such techniques as simulation, forecasting, decision analysis, and linear programming were adopted by industry in the 1960s and 1970s to solve problems in manufacturing, transportation, marketing, and finance. As the power and cost of computers skyrocketed and plummeted, respectively, the field continued to grow. Layers of programmers and mathematicians still formed an "algebraic curtain," however, separating most managers from management science.

In the 1980s, millions adopted the electronic spreadsheet as the quantitative tool of choice. Mathematical modeling, once the exotic domain of the theoretician was now the vernacular of management. Many analytical methods of the past migrated quickly to this new interactive environment. The algebraic curtain was coming down.

As we approach the end of the 1990s, the field is poised for yet another revolution as the Internet ties together decision makers, data, and analytical techniques. INSIGHT introduces some of the primary analytical models on which the technology of decision making is based.

Analytical Models

An analytical model approximates the real world but gives us the freedom to experiment. As an example, PROFIT = REVENUE – EXPENSE is a very simple analytical model of almost any business. A more complex model might be used to help you forecast future sales, allocate scarce resources among competing projects, or make a decision to acquire another firm.

The reasons people build analytical models of management situations before making managerial decisions are much the same reasons people build models of airplanes before making engineering decisions:

- It is much less costly to make mistakes in a model than in the real world.

- A model can yield insights into real world problems. For example, the Wright brothers gained critical knowledge about aerodynamics by experimenting with kites and small models of wings.

- A model allows you to apply tools not available in the real world. For the Wright brothers, the tool was the wind tunnel that allowed them to experiment with different wing cross sections in search of an optimal design.

- The discipline of building a model forces us to better understand the relationships being modeled and the data required for analysis.

Tutorial: A Manufacturing Example

As an example, we will start with a manufacturing model that will be expanded in a later chapter to demonstrate mathematical optimization. A manufacturer produces two types of fiberglass boats: a large sailboat, with a profit per unit of $1,200 and a motor boat with a profit per unit of $1,000.

Although many raw materials are required to manufacture the boats, three are currently in short supply: sailcloth, used only for the sailboat; glass fiber, used in both boats; and engines, used only in the motor boat. The boats' profit, raw material requirements, and quantity of raw materials on hand are specified in BOAT.xls, shown in the following figure:

	A	B	C	D	E
1			Large Sailboat	Motor Boat	
2	Production Quantity		0	0	
3	Profit Per Unit		$1,200	$1,000	
4					
5					
6			Large Sailboat	Motor Boat	
7	Raw Materials		Requirements by product		On Hand
8	Sailcloth		4	0	400
9	Glass Fiber		8	4	1000
10	Engines		0	1	120

Starting with BOAT.xls, which you should open now, we will construct a production planning model of this situation.

Understanding the Elements of a Worksheet Model

Worksheet models contain two fundamental types of elements:

- Numbers that might or might not be under managerial control
- Formulas that specify functional relationships between the numbers

BOAT.xls contains all the numbers needed for this model (don't confuse it with BOATS.xls, which will be used in later chapters). In the following tutorial, you will fill in formulas for total profit and quantities of resources used for a given level of production.

Separation of Data and Formulas

Profit

The total profit is found by summing the profit per unit multiplied by the associated production quantity. A possible formula for profit is $= C2*1200 + D2*1000$. However, this is not a good approach. If the profit per unit changes, the formula must be modified.

A better plan is to keep the data and formulas *separate* with the formula $= C2*C3 + D2*D3$. Enter this in cell B4 of the worksheet. Type "Total Profit" into cell A4. Now if the profit numbers change, they can simply be updated in cells C3 and D3. As a general rule, data should never be typed directly into a formula.

Note: Always test formulas after entering them. This not only verifies your model as it is being built, but also results in a bit of gratification when you see it work correctly. Type the number 1 into cell C2, and total profit should be $1,200. Now type 1 into cell D2 and profit should rise to $2,200 as shown in the following figure:

B4	▼		=C2*C3+D2*D3	
	A	B	C	D
1			Large Sailboat	Motor Boat
2	Production Quantity		1	1
3	Profit Per Unit		$1,200	$1,000
4	Total Profit	$2,200		

Resource Utilization

Total usage of sailcloth is calculated by using a formula similar to the one for profit: =C$2*C8+D$2*D8. Enter this formula in cell B8 and the label "Used" in B7. The $ signs before the row number indicate an absolute reference that allows the formula to be copied to cells B9:B10, yielding the remaining materials' total usage. Copy the formula now by selecting cell B8, placing the cursor over the small black square in the lower right corner of the cell, and dragging down to B10. The worksheet should appear as shown in the following figure:

B8	▼		=C$2*C8+D$2*D8		
	A	B	C	D	E
1			Large Sailboat	Motor Boat	
2	Production Quantity		1	1	
3	Profit Per Unit		$1,200	$1,000	
4	Total Profit	$2,200			
5					
6			Large Sailboat	Motor Boat	
7	Raw Materials	Used	Requirements by product		On Hand
8	Sailcloth	4	4	0	400
9	Glass Fiber	12	8	4	1000
10	Engines	1	0	1	120

As always, test the model by changing the input cells and verifying that you are getting the right results.

Making Sure the Model is Scalable

This worksheet gives correct values for profit and resource utilization if positive production quantities are entered in cells C2 and D2. But what if the manufacturer introduces additional types of raw materials or boats?

Additional Types of Materials

The model can be expanded to include an additional material type by adding new information in columns A, C, D, and E of row 11 and then copying the formula in cell B10 to B11.

Additional Types of Boats and the SUMPRODUCT Formula

You can insert a column in the worksheet for the new boat type with the **Insert Column** command, then profit and requirement data can be entered. However, *all the formulas would need to be modified!* Not only is this very tedious, but it is also likely to introduce errors into the model.

A more scalable model can be achieved using the SUMPRODUCT formula. The profit formula C2*C3 + D2*D3 can be replaced by the formula = SUMPRODUCT(C2:D2,C3:D3).

SUMPRODUCT performs exactly the same calculation, however, it has the advantage of automatically including additional columns inserted between C and D. The calculations for resource utilization should similarly be changed to SUMPRODUCT formulas. Don't forget to use $ signs on the arguments ($C$2:$D$2) so you can copy the formula correctly. A convenient way to apply $ signs to the correct arguments is to press the F4 key while you edit the formula. Save your model before proceeding.

Range Names

It is useful to give names to certain ranges of cells in your model. In this case we will name cells C2:D2 QUANTITY, cells C3:D3 PROFIT_PER_UNIT, and cell B4 TOTAL_PROFIT.

This can be done by selecting the range, then invoking the **Insert Name Define** command and typing the desired name. Another way is to select the range, type the name into the name box in the left of the formula bar, and press the Enter key.

■ FUNDAMENTALS 1-1 ■ ■ ■ ■ ■ ■ ■ ■ ■ ■ ■ ■ ■

SUMPRODUCT

- *SUMPRODUCT* is an important formula in analytical modeling. It is known mathematically as the *vector inner product* of the ranges C2:D2 and C3:D3.

- *SUMPRODUCT* is an example of a *scalable* formula. That is, the formula need not be modified to handle problems of different sizes. Any formula that takes a range of cells as an argument has this property. Other common scalable formulas are SUM, MAX, and MIN.

Name box ──────▶ | QUANTITY ▾ | | 1 | |

	A	B	C	D
1			Large Sailboat	Motor Boat
2	Production Quantity		1	1
3	Profit Per Unit		$1,200	$1,000

Once you have defined range C2:D2 as QUANTITY, name the range C3:D3 as PROFIT_PER_UNIT, and B4 as TOTAL_PROFIT. At this point you can either click on the little triangle to the right of the name box or press the F5 key to see all the names currently in the sheet.

Names can be used in formulas, either by typing them or, more conveniently, by using the F5 key or the name box and selecting the desired name off the list. Edit the formula for profit to use range names. It should now appear as shown in the following equation:

=SUMPRODUCT (QUANTITY,PROFIT_PER_UNIT)

Experimenting with the Model

Feasibility Checking

Although this model is simple, it can nonetheless yield important insights. As we experiment with various production figures, we must remember to check that our production figures are feasible. That is, we must not consume more raw materials than we have on hand. We can use logical formulas that compare the quantity of raw materials used with the quantity on hand. Enter the formula = E8 > = B8 in cell F8. This formula returns the logical value TRUE if cell E8 (the quantity of sailcloth) is greater than or equal to cell B8 (the amount used), and FALSE otherwise. Copy cell F8 to

F9:F10 and enter the label "Feasible" in cell F7. Your model should appear as shown in the following figure:

F8	▼		=E8>=B8	
B	**C**	**D**	**E**	**F**
7 **Used**	Requirements by product		**On Hand**	Feasible
8 4	4	0	400	TRUE
9 12	8	4	1000	TRUE
10 1	0	1	120	TRUE

"What If" Analysis

Given a spreadsheet model such as this, you can experiment with the inputs by hand. This is often known as "what if" analysis. Start by setting both boat production quantities to zero. Now how many sailboats can you produce? By trying various guesses in cell C2, you will find that a maximum of 100 sail boats can be produced before sail cloth is depleted. This results in profit of $120,000 and leaves 1000 – 800 = 200 units of glass fiber and 120 engines. Now, increase production of motor boats to 50, and glass fiber will be depleted. This should result in a $170,000 profit and a remaining inventory of 120 – 50 = 70 engines. Because all sail cloth and glass fiber have been exhausted, it is not possible to increase the production of either type of boat, but we have a healthy profit. It is tempting to stop here, but next we will apply a more analytical approach.

Data Tables

Data tables require a bit of setup but provide a more thorough form of analysis. You might have used spreadsheets for years without ever having used this powerful command. A data table allows you to repeatedly evaluate a particular formula within the model while systematically varying one or two input cells on which the formula depends.

We will now set up a data table to repeatedly calculate profit while varying the production quantities of both types of boat.

The Formula That Drives the Table. Because the table will have narrow columns, we will express profit in 000's so that the numbers will fit. To accomplish this, divide total profit by 1000. The formula in cell B4 should now look like the following equation:

=SUMPRODUCT (QUANTITY,PROFIT_PER_UNIT)/1000

Also, we must only print the profit value if the production quantities are feasible, that is, if all the cells F8:F10 are TRUE. This is expressed in Excel as AND(F8:10). We will now enter the formula that drives the table. This formula, which should be entered in G6, will return the total profit in thousands for every combination of production quantities that is feasible. Otherwise, it will return a blank. This will require an IF statement, the general syntax of which is

=IF(logical_test, value_if_true, value_if_false).

In our case the logical test is that the production quantities are feasible. That is, AND(F8:F10) is TRUE. The value if true is TOTAL_PROFIT; the value if false is blank, or " ". The formula to type into G6 is thus

= IF(AND(F8:F10),TOTAL_PROFIT," ")

Test the formula by changing the production quantities in cells C2 and D2.

Specifying the Quantities to Evaluate.   Now that the formula is in place, we must specify the production quantities that we want to evaluate in the table.

The production quantities of sailboats will be stored in row 6 starting in column H. We will experiment with all numbers and from 0 through 150 in increments of 5. Start by placing 0 in cell H6 and 5 in I6.

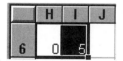

Next select cells H6 and I6 and drag the small box in the lower right corner of the selected region to column AL while holding down the mouse key. This should result in the array of values as shown in the following figure.

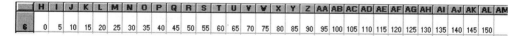

H	I	J	K	L	M	N	O	P	Q	R	S	T	U	V	W	X	Y	Z	AA	AB	AC	AD	AE	AF	AG	AH	AI	AJ	AK	AL	AM
0	5	10	15	20	25	30	35	40	45	50	55	60	65	70	75	80	85	90	95	100	105	110	115	120	125	130	135	140	145	150	

The production quantities of motor boats will be stored in column G starting in row 7. This time we will start at 150 and go to 0. Start by placing 150 in cell G7 and 145 in G8. Again select the two cells. Then drag them to row 37. Now you should have the numbers 0 to 150 in increments of 5, running from H6 to AL6, and the numbers 150 to 0, in decrements of 5, running from G7 to G37.

STEPS: **USING THE DATA TABLE COMMAND**

1   Select the entire range of the table (G6:AL37). Then invoke the **Data Table** command. The Data Table dialog box appears.

2

Place the cursor in the **Row Input** field of the dialog box, then click on cell C2. That is, C2 is the cell into which the row of sail boat quantities at the top of the table will be plugged.

3

Place the cursor in the **Column Input** field and click on cell D2. The dialog box should appear as shown below.

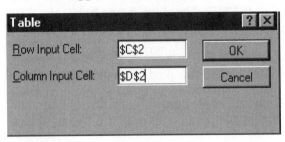

Click **OK**, and the entire table will be filled in.

4

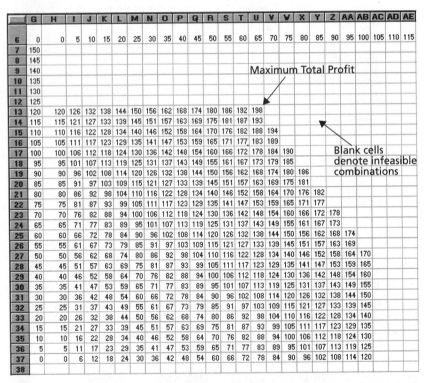

This table provides a great deal of information. Among other things it shows that a profit of $198,000 is possible by producing 65 sailboats and 120 motor boats. Notice that this occurs at a corner of the area of feasible production figures.

EXERCISE 1.1

Experimenting with the Assumptions of the Production Model

a. Suppose the number of engines available were only 100 units. What would be the maximum profit, and for what production quantities would it occur?

b. Return the number of engines to 120. Now suppose that the profit per unit of motor boats were less than $800. How low can it go before additional production quantities give the same total profit as 65 sailboats and 120 motor boats? What production quantities maximize total profit if the profit per unit for motor boats drops still further?

EXERCISE 1.2

Documenting and Auditing the Model

Documentation is especially important for models that will be used by more than one person. Because the formulas in a worksheet model are hidden, it is easy to lose track of the flow of the calculations.

a. Use the **Insert Notes** command to place a note in cell F8 that explains the meaning of the TRUE or FALSE that appears there. Merely moving the cross shaped cursor over the cell will cause the note to appear.

b. The auditing tools track the flow of calculations. Place the cursor in cell G6, the formula that drives the table. Then repeatedly invoke the **Tools Auditing Trace Precedents** command. You will see the cells that G6 depends on, the cells that they depend on, and so on. Next bring up the auditing toolbar, shown below, with the **Tools Auditing Show Auditing Toolbar** command.

It is useful to keep this auditing tool bar on screen when you are either creating a new model, or investigating a model created by someone else. These tools automate the generation of worksheet flow diagrams defined in Savage [1992].

EXERCISE 1.3

Pure Aesthetics

The file 3DGRAPH.xls uses a data table to graph an arbitrary function of two variables. Cells K28 and L28 are named X and Y respectively. The function of X and Y is typed into K26, creating the graph. It is shown in the following figure for F(X,Y) = X^2+Y^2.

Make sure that your spreadsheet's calculation is set to automatic under **Tools Options**. Open the file and start by changing the formula to X^2+Y^3. Then make as aesthetically pleasing a picture as you can by trying different functions of X and Y in cell K26.

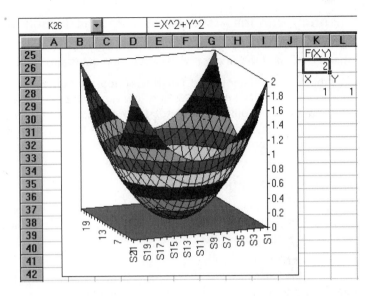

The Voices of Experience

The previous tutorial has walked you through the development of a small analytical model. As in any pursuit, however, there is no substitute for experience. What follows are a number of observations made by experienced analytical modelers that offer a useful perspective for the beginner.

The Five Stages of Model Development—Donald Knuth

Donald Knuth, a Stanford computer scientist, discovered that computer program development generally goes through five stages. I have paraphrased these as they apply equally to analytical modeling in general:

1. Decide what you want the model to do.

2. Decide how to build the model.

3. Build the model.

4. Debug the model.

5. Trash stages 1 through 4 and start again, now that you know what you really wanted in the first place.

Once you realize that stage 5 is inevitable, you become more willing to discard bad models early rather than to continually patch them up.

"Spreadsheets are Dimensionally Arthritic" —Arthur Geoffrion

Arthur Geoffrion, a UCLA Management Scientist has investigated the properties of modeling environments. By Geoffrion's criteria the biggest drawbacks of the spreadsheet involve scaling a small prototype model to industrial size. For example, in the boat production model of the tutorial, if we had not been careful, it would have been difficult to add new types of boats.

A more serious problem is that spreadsheet models are fundamentally two dimensional. Suppose we wanted to model production in each of 12 consecutive months. This requires adding a new dimension to the model for time. Conceptually we could do this by making 11 more copies of the original model. Now suppose we need to model production in two separate plants. We must make two copies of the 12 models we have already made. I refer to changing the dimensionality of a model as *hyperscaling*. Now imagine adding a new boat type to all 24 sub models described and you will understand what Geoffrion means by dimensional arthritis.

Three things that can reduce dimensional arthritis are

1. Keep data separate from formulas. This will prevent you from having to modify the model when the data changes.

2. Use scalable range formulas such as SUMPRODUCT that can expand with your model. If you are successful in this regard, your small initial models can be expanded more easily to address larger scale problems.

3. Use multiple worksheets to represent a third dimension beyond rows and columns.

"A Pencil is a Crutch, a Calculator is a Wheelchair, and a Computer is an Ambulance"—Gene Woolsey

Gene Woolsey, a professor of Economics and Business at the Colorado School of Mines points out that the mechanical act of calculation is not the same as thinking about a problem and can even interfere with the thought process. There is not time to build an analytical model to back up every business decision, and you must usually rely on intuition. Perhaps the greatest value to be derived from analytical modeling is the extent to which it improves your intuition.

"All Models Are Wrong, Some Models Are Useful" —W. Edward Deming

Deming, the father of modern quality control, is reputed to have made this remark. It reminds us that even the best analytical model is a little like telling a lie. And what's worse than telling a lie? Telling multiple lies. With this in mind you can appreciate the importance of simplicity in model building.

The "Inter Ocular Trauma Test" of Joe Berkson

Even if you learn something important from an analytical model, it is not of much use if you can't communicate the result to others. Joe Berkson, a bio-statistician at the Mayo Clinic stressed the use of graphs. For a result to be really useful the graph must pass the *Inter Ocular Trauma Test*. That is, it must hit you between the eyes. Spreadsheets have extensive graphing facilities that should be used to communicate results.

"Clear and Precise Seeing Becomes as One with Clear and Precise Thinking"—Edward Tufte

Now that we are on the subject of graphics, Edward Tufte, a Yale professor, has made a career of studying effective visual display. A scatter plot similar to the one in the following figure appears in his book *Visual Explanations*.[1] Although you don't yet know what this chart represents, make a guess at the *y* value that would correspond to the *x* value indicated by the question mark.

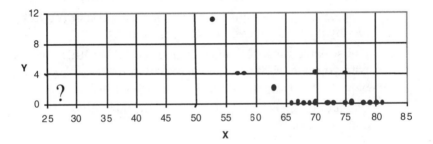

We might reasonably expect a high value of *y*, perhaps a good deal higher than any observed so far.

Now for the story that goes with this graph as related by Tufte: Before the launch of the ill-fated space shuttle Challenger, there was concern that unusually low temperatures at Cape Canaveral might cause O-Rings in the booster rockets to leak, leading to catastrophic failure. Analysts attempting to resolve this issue shortly before the launch had access to extensive data on O-Ring damage in previous launches. According to Tufte, although this data was studied in detail, it was never used to create a simple scatter plot of temperature versus the degree of O-Ring damage. If this had been done, the analysts would have observed the previous chart, where *x* and *y* represent the temperature and O-Ring damage respectively observed in previous

---

1. Edward Tufte, *Visual Explanations*, Graphics Press, 1996.

launches and the question mark denotes the predicted temperature for the Challenger launch. Given the prior concern over O-Ring problems at low temperature, this chart might have convinced those in charge to postpone the launch. Instead, the Challenger exploded because of O-Ring failure, killing all on board.

"It's Dumb to Be Too Smart"—Sam L. Savage

Faced with determining the effect of temperature on O-Ring performance, we could create a complex statistical model resulting in confidence intervals and R^2 coefficients. You would have to be pretty smart both to develop such a model and to interpret its results. A relatively dumb person could have created and understood the scatter plot that passes Berkson's Inter Ocular Trauma Test and thus saved the Challenger.

Someone who builds a mathematical model can get carried away with all the clever things that can be done with it. The model becomes a safe little world, free from anxiety and office politics, rewarding in its own right. This often results in a very clever model that has little to do with reality. Resist the temptation to be too smart in building a model. Take small model building steps interspersed with healthy doses of reality.

The Pros and Cons of Spreadsheet Modeling

Spreadsheets have both strengths and weaknesses. Here we summarize the pros and cons of using this environment for analytical modeling.

First the Cons

Documentability. Spreadsheet models are notoriously difficult to document because all the formulas are hidden. The cell Notes and Auditing Tools can mitigate this problem, but errors often slip through anyway.

Scalability. Before typing a formula into a spreadsheet model, you should ask yourself how it will scale if the quantity of data changes. Range formulas such as SUM and SUMPRODUCT help you scale your model.

Hyperscalability. I use the term hyperscaling to describe the addition of new dimensions to a model. Because spreadsheets are fundamentally two dimensional, adding new dimensions requires copying models multiple times. This is awkward at best and a show stopper at worst.

The cons are summarized in the following figure:

Now the Pros

The pros of spreadsheet models are shown in the following figure. Despite their drawbacks, spreadsheets have overwhelmingly become the analytical vernacular of management.

2

The Building Blocks of Uncertainty: Random Variables

The only certainty is that nothing is certain.

PLINY THE ELDER, A ROMAN SCHOLAR

Some 2000 years later, it's a safe bet Pliny the Elder was right. Everyone must deal with uncertainty.

■ What will the temperature be this afternoon?

■ What will the price of my favorite stock be tomorrow?

■ What number will show up the next time I roll a pair of dice?

In the case of the dice, you can learn a lot about the outcomes by throwing them hundreds of times while recording the results. This is the basic idea behind a computer procedure known as Monte Carlo simulation, which uses the computer to throw a bunch of random inputs into a model. The result is somewhat analogous to shaking a ladder before climbing it, to determine how stable it is.

OVERVIEW

Introduction

This section contains a short introduction to simulation and instructions for installing and running SIM.xla, a Monte Carlo simulation add-in for Excel.

Tutorial: Estimating Profit with Monte Carlo Simulation

The concept of Monte Carlo simulation is introduced in the context of estimating profit given uncertain demand and production costs. We are also introduced to the boss who, when faced with uncertainty, always demands "a number."

The Building Blocks of Uncertainty

This section introduces the basic building blocks for modeling uncertainty and risk. Simulation is used throughout to provide an experiential understanding of such fundamental concepts as random variables, the Central Limit Theorem, distributions, and risk management.

Introduction

From Manhattan Project to Wall Street

Developed during the Manhattan (Atomic Bomb) Project in the 1940s, Monte Carlo simulation involves feeding a large number of random inputs into a model while recording the range of outputs. The random inputs are analogous to rolls of dice or spins of a roulette wheel at a casino, hence the name.

As early as 30 years ago, simulation was suggested as an analytical tool for business by David Hertz (1979) while Simon, Atkinson, and Shevokas had proposed it as an intuitive technique for teaching statistics (1976). Efron and Tibshirani and others have used simulation to expand the theoretical scope of statistics (1993).

Today, commercial software packages such as @RISK™ (AR) and Crystal Ball® (CB)[1] have brought sophisticated Monte Carlo simulation to spreadsheets, adding to its popularity in areas as diverse as accounting, finance, logistics, marketing, operations management, risk management, and strategy.

---

1. @RISK is trademarked by Palisade Corporation. Crystal Ball is a registered trademark of Decisioneering, Inc.

SIM.xla

SIM.xla is a simple Monte Carlo simulation package for Excel 5.0 and higher. It is easy to install and learn, and as a Visual Basic Add-in, is at home in either Windows® or Macintosh® environments. A larger version of SIM.xla is available for purchase from www.AnalyCorp.com.

Running SIM.xla. Launch Excel and open SIM.xla from the File menu. A simulate menu will be added to the Excel menu bar.

Auto Load Option. If you want SIM.xla to load every time you launch Excel, follow these steps:

1. Select **Add-ins** from the **Tools** menu in Excel.
2. Select SIM.xla from list of add-ins and click **OK**.

A **Simulate** menu will be added to the Excel menu bar. ***NOTE:*** While SIM.xla is loaded, the Excel Edit Undo command will be disabled. When you close SIM.xla, this feature will be restored.

You can later go back and deselect SIM.xla from the **Add-in** menu to prevent Excel from loading it automatically.

Tutorial: Estimating Profit with Monte Carlo Simulation

An Example: Uncertain Profit

A firm is introducing a product into a new market. Imagine that as marketing manager, you are trying to estimate the profit that will result from the product introduction. The items on which profit depends are

- Sales in units.
- Price per unit.
- Unit cost: The marginal cost per unit of production, marketing, and sales.
- Fixed costs: Fixed overhead, advertising, and so on. These are known to be $30,000.

The calculation for profit is as follows:

$$\text{Profit} = \text{Sales} * (\text{Price} - \text{Unit Cost}) - \text{Fixed Cost}$$

Market Scenarios

Because this is a new market, there is significant uncertainty. It is generally believed that either a low or high volume market can occur with equal likelihood: If there is a low volume market, sales of roughly 60,000 units are expected at a price of $10 per unit. If there is a high volume market, the good news is that your company's sales are expected to be roughly 100,000 units.

The bad news is that under this scenario, the market is so hot that it brings in competitors. This, in turn, drives the expected price down to $8 per unit. These market scenarios are summarized in the following table:

	Market Scenarios		
	Low Volume	High Volume	Average
Probability	50%	50%	
Units	60,000	100,000	80,00
Price	$10	$8	$9

Unit Cost

The VP of production believes that the cost per unit will be $7.50. But you have been advised that depending on the cost of raw materials and actual production experience, this cost might be as low as $6.00 or as high as $9.00. This uncertainty is summarized in the following table.

Low	Most Likely	High	Average
$6.00	$7.50	$9.00	$7.50

Enter the Boss

Typically, managers entrusted to work on problems like these have bosses who ask questions such as the following:

The Boss: What is the profit going to be for the new product?

You: I'm not sure what profit's going to be because I don't know what sales or prices or costs are going to be.

The Boss: What are we paying you for? GIVE ME A NUMBER. I want it now, 15 minutes at the latest!

So back you go to your desk to come up with a number.

Enter the Worksheet

Luckily you have been building a worksheet model called PROFIT.xls to help you answer this question. Open this file now, as well as SIM.xla, and follow this example on your own computer.

The boss needs the number now, so you do the simplest thing that comes to mind. You plug in averages of all the uncertain inputs in cells B5:B7 and fixed cost, the one number you are certain of, in cell B8 as shown in the following figure:

	A	B	C	D	E	F	G
1	PROFIT.XLS						
2					Market Scenarios		
3	Financials				Low Volume	High Volume	Average
4				Prob.	50%	50%	
5	Sales in Units	80,000		Units	60,000	100,000	80,000
6	Price per Unit	$ 9.00		Price	$10	$8	$9
7	Unit_Cost	$ 7.50					
8	Fixed_Costs	$ 30,000		Unit Cost Scenarios			
9				Low	Most Likely	High	Average
10	Profit	$90,000		$ 6.00	$ 7.50	$ 9.00	$ 7.50

=Sales * (Price – Unit_Cost) – Fixed_Cost

Great! Profit is $90,000, you have a number for the boss and 14 minutes to spare. Actually that 14 minutes will provide plenty of time to refine your answer with Monte Carlo simulation as described in the next section.

Monte Carlo Simulation: The Basic Steps

The basic steps of running a Monte Carlo simulation are

1. Build a model of the uncertain situation
2. Specify the simulation setting
3. Run the simulation and examine the results

These steps will now be discussed in detail in the context of the PROFIT example. The first step in creating a simulation is to model the uncertainty you face. In general, this constitutes the bulk of the work and comprises two parts: the worksheet and the uncertain inputs. Once you have developed the model, you will specify the settings for the simulation.

The Worksheet

The worksheet must reflect the relationships between the various numbers of the model, regardless of whether those numbers are certain or uncertain. This step has already been carried out in PROFIT.xls and consists of the formula for Profit in cell B10 shown earlier.

The Uncertainties

The uncertainties are modeled by formulas in the spreadsheet that output random numbers each time they calculate.

STEPS: MODELING MARKET SCENARIOS

We will start by modeling the market scenario uncertainty.

1 In cell D11 enter the formula =RAND(). This is a built-in Excel function that produces numbers randomly between, but not including, 0 and 1. Such a function is known as a random number generator.

2 Press the calculate key (the F9 key in Windows or Command-= in Macintosh) a few times to see how it behaves. Cell D11 is just as likely to be greater than or less than .5. We will say that the high volume scenario has occurred when d11 is greater than .5, and the low volume scenario has occurred otherwise.

3 In cell B5, type the formula =IF($D$11 > 0.5,F5,E5), then copy it down one cell to B6. Use the **Edit Paste Special Formulas** command to avoid altering the formatting of cell B6. These formulas have the effect of plugging the high or low volume numbers into cells B5 and B6 with equal probabilities. Press the calculate key a few times to make sure it really works. The model should appear as shown below, although the exact numbers will depend on the RAND() function.

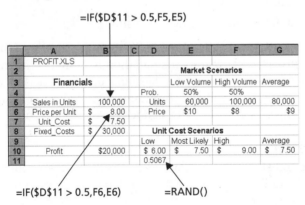

=IF($D$11 > 0.5,F5,E5)

=IF($D$11 > 0.5,F6,E6)   =RAND()

STEPS: MODELING UNIT COST

When you have estimates of a low, most likely, and high value for an uncertainty, it is often reasonable to use a random number generator with what is known as a Triangular Distribution. In this example, the number appearing in the cell will take on random values between $6.00 and $9.00 but not with equal likelihood. The most likely value is $7.50, with linearly decreasing probability as the values go to the extremes.

1

If you have not yet loaded SIM.xla, do so now. Then with the cursor in the Unit Cost cell B7, click on the function icon. The Function Wizard menu will appear.

function
icon

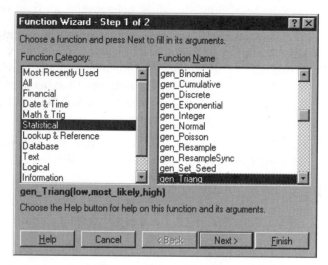

2

Select *Statistical* from the left menu, *gen_Triang* from the right menu, and click **Next.** The following dialog box opens.

3

Fill in the **low, most_likely,** and **high** values as shown in the previous figure and click **Finish.** As an alternative to entering numbers, you can place the cursor in the boxes in the dialog box, then click on the cell in the spreadsheet in which the desired number is stored, cells D10, E10, and F10 in this case.

Unlike the market uncertainty that was modeled to give two discrete possibilities, high volume or low volume, unit cost can have a continuum of outcomes in our model. **Note:** Uncertainties come in both discrete and continuous varieties, and either or both can appear in a model.

4

Press the calculate key a few times to be sure all the uncertain input cells are functioning. At first this appears to be a big step backwards. At least before you introduced uncertainties into your worksheet you had a number to give the boss. Now the model behaves like a can of worms.

At this stage you could perform a Monte Carlo simulation by pressing the calculate key a few hundred times while a friend with a clipboard records the values of profit in cell B10. By analyzing the hundreds of profit values on the clipboard, you could estimate the likelihood of losing money, making more than $10,000, making more than $20,000, and so forth, given that you decide to introduce the new product.

Fortunately, two people and a clipboard can be replaced today by a Visual Basic macro (SIM.xla) as we will see in the next step. Save your changes to PROFIT.xls before continuing.

STEPS: **SPECIFYING THE SETTINGS FOR MONTE CARLO SIMULATION**

Now that you have completed the model you must specify the simulation settings.

1

Select **<u>R</u>un Simulation** from the **Simulate** menu to open the following dialog box:

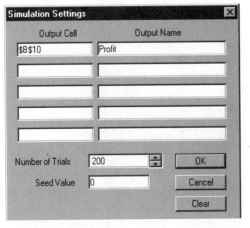

2

Click on cell B10 to specify the cell containing the profit formula as an **Output Cell.**

3

Type "Profit" in the box to the right of output cell.

4

Specify 200 **Trials** by either typing the number or clicking on the small arrows to the right of the field.

5

Click **OK** to run the simulation. This is equivalent to pressing the calculate key 200 times while keeping track of each resulting profit.

Simulation Output

Statistics. You will see a count of the number of trials on the status bar until the simulation is finished, then the statistics of the simulation are displayed in a workbook called SIMSTATS.xls. Observe the average profit.

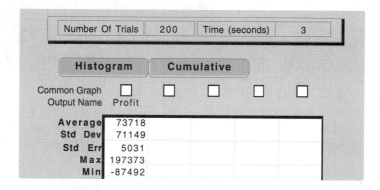

Uh Oh! Although results will vary from run to run, the average value of profit for the 200 trials will almost surely be less than the $90,000 you were about to tell the boss. In fact, it is probably less than $70,000!

There is also a lot of variability. Look at the maximum and minimum values of profit that occurred in the 200 trials. The minimum value is probably quite negative, meaning there is a chance you could lose a lot of money. How are you going to explain that to the boss?

The Histogram. Click on the Histogram button to view the percentage of trials that fall into various intervals or *bins*. The following dialog box appears:

Click **OK** to select a five-bin histogram. The histogram will be created on its own tab in the SIMSTATS workbook. This graph shows the relative likelihood of profit falling into different ranges. The number under each bar represents the right edge of that bar.

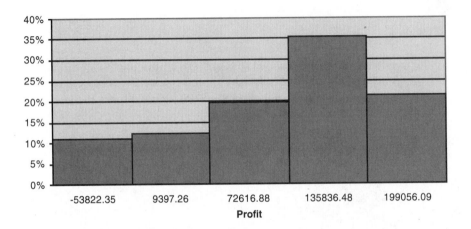

Notice that there is about a 20% chance of being between about $135,000 and $200,000, but a 10% chance of losing more than $50,000.

The Cumulative Graph. Click the **Statistics** tab, then the **Cumulative** button to create the cumulative graph. This shows the percentage of times that profit was less than or equal to the amount shown on the horizontal axis. The average, in this case $73,718, is shown by a vertical line.

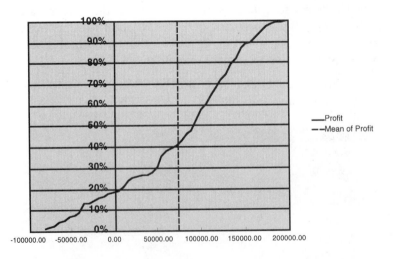

Thus the likelihood of losing money is determined by locating 0.00 on the horizontal axis, then going up to the curve and over to the vertical axis to read the percent of trials that are less than 0, or about 23% in this case. In fact, about 10% of the time you can expect to lose about $60,000 or more.

Back to the Boss

Once you are proficient in using simulation, the previous analysis could easily have been done in 10 minutes, allowing you to get back to the boss 4 minutes early. Let's listen in.

You:	Well, Boss, if you average out all the things that might happen with this product, you should expect a profit of about $73,000. But that doesn't tell the whole story.
The Boss:	What do you mean "not the whole story"? I told you I want a number.
You:	Well, the $73,000 average includes a 10% chance that we lose over $60,000. Look at this. (You hold up the cumulative graph). If it's a number you want for profit, here are all the numbers between –$150,000 and $200,000 with the probability that profit will be less than or equal to any of them.
The Boss:	You mean there's over one chance in five of losing money?
You:	Right, but also an equal chance of making more than $140,000. You're the one who has to decide whether or not to go ahead with the new product. You need to evaluate these trade-offs.
The Boss:	I guess you're right. Maybe we should run a simulation taking into account our entire product line to better analyze the total profit picture.

We flash forward one year and, unfortunately, the product has lost money. We first tune in on what would have happened if you hadn't bothered to run the simulation.

The Boss:	You told me we would make $90,000 and we lost money! You're fired!

Consider the scenario in which you ran the simulation.

You:	I'm sorry the product lost money.
The Boss:	Well, I knew the kind of risk we were facing and decided to take the gamble.

Of course, the boss might not really want to know. A manager who is aware that something undesirable can occur is responsible for doing something to prevent it. Thus managers might have incentives to keep themselves in the dark, and as far from cumulative probability graphs as possible. If you want to keep your own boss ignorant of legitimate risks, it's your business, but don't do so without considering the consequences.

Back to the Model

In a real problem, of course, you must justify how you model the uncertainties. More important than the detail regarding an individual uncertainty, however, is figuring out which ones to model in the first place. For example suppose you were estimating the economic output of an oil well in the Gulf of Mexico. You could spend months modeling the uncertain costs of drilling, the uncertain quantity and quality of oil produced, and the uncertain price of crude at time of delivery. But the precision of all this work is meaningless if you have neglected to take into account the chance that a tanker could collide with the platform causing a massive oil spill. When building a simulation model, think big.

The Building Blocks of Uncertainty

Now that the concept of Monte Carlo simulation has been introduced as a tool for dealing with uncertain events, we will get back to basics and examine the fundamental building blocks of uncertainty. These include the following:

- **Uncertain Numbers: Random Variables.** Everyone must deal with numbers they are not certain of. Simulation will be used to demonstrate some of the most basic concepts regarding uncertain numbers, or *random variables* as they are technically called.

- **Averages of Uncertain Numbers: Diversification.** As uncertain numbers are averaged together, uncertainty is reduced. This is known as *diversification* and is an important manifestation of the *Central Limit Theorem*.

- **Some Important Classes of Uncertain Numbers: Idealized Distributions.** There are several important classes of idealized uncertain numbers. The most important of these are *normal* random variables.

- **Uncertain Numbers and Bad Outcomes: Risk Management.** Uncertainty is an objective feature of the universe. Risk is in the eye of the beholder; it depends on what you are afraid of. Risk management is the attempt to minimize the undesired outcomes of uncertainty.

■ **FUNDAMENTALS 2-1** ■ ■ ■ ■ ■ ■ ■ ■ ■ ■ ■ ■

Random Variables

Numbers you don't know yet are called *random variables*. We will also refer to them as *uncertain numbers*.

Uncertain Numbers: Random Variables

Everyone must deal with numbers they are not certain of. We will use Monte Carlo simulation to demonstrate some of the most basic concepts regarding uncertain numbers, or *random variables* as they are technically called.

Your firm's future sales, costs, and project durations are all numbers you don't know yet. While you grapple with this array of uncertainties, your boss, introduced in the previous tutorial, is likely to come in and demand "a number" for next year's profit. This section is devoted to developing a constructive response to such situations.

A Simple Example with a Spinner

As a simple example, consider the number pointed to by a game board spinner like the one simulated in SPINNER.xls. This random variable is also built into every worksheet as the function = RAND(), which behaves just like a spinner, outputting a different number between 0 and 1 every time it calculates.

Type = RAND() into a blank workbook and press the calculate key (the F9 key in Windows and Command- = in Macintosh) a few times to see how it behaves.

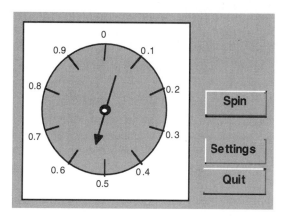

■ **FUNDAMENTALS 2-2** ■ ■ ■ ■ ■ ■ ■ ■ ■ ■ ■ ■ ■

Continuous and Discrete Random Variables

A random variable such as the outcome of a spinner is known as a *continuous* random variable because it can take on all values between two extreme values. A random variable, such as the outcome of rolling dice is known as a *discrete* random variable because it can take on only distinct values.

To attach more meaning to the spinner example, imagine that your company's profit for next year displayed the same degree of uncertainty as if someone twirled the spinner and then multiplied the result by $1 million. To make it more interesting, suppose further that if profit is less than $200,000, you will be laid off.

EXERCISE 2.1

Test Your Intuition on Random Variables

Before running a simulation to analyze profit, test your intuition by trying to answer the following questions:

a. If you faced this same situation repeatedly, what would profit be on average?

b. What is the likelihood of getting laid off?

c. What should you tell the boss when he demands "a number" for profit?

d. Starting with the following diagram, create a bar graph that shows the percentage of times profit in millions is likely to fall between 0 and .2, .2 and .4, and so forth.

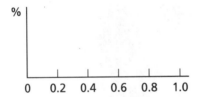

Quickly jot down your answers on a piece of paper, including a sketch for part d, passing over those questions for which you have no ready answer. We will now run a simulation to answer these questions.

Building the Model: Simulation Setting and Output

The first step in creating a worksheet simulation is to model the uncertainty you face. In general, this constitutes the bulk of the work but in this case there is not much to it. To model profit in millions, simply type = RAND() into a cell in a blank workbook, such as B2. Press the calculate key a few times to observe the results. This single cell is the whole model.

STEPS: SPECIFYING SIMULATION SETTINGS

1 Select **Run Simulation** to bring up the following dialog box. Specify the cell containing the profit formula as the first **Output Cell**.

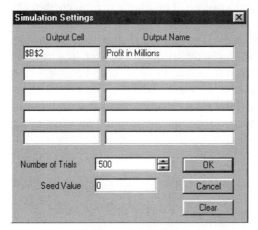

2 Specify 500 trials by either typing the number or clicking on the small arrows to the right of the field.

3 Click **OK** to run the simulation.

Statistics. Let's now examine the simulation we just created. Although results will vary from run to run, the average value over the 500 trials will be close to .5 million as shown in the following figure. The remaining statistics will be discussed in later examples.

| Number Of Trials | 500 | Time (seconds) | 3 |

| Histogram | Cumulative |

Common Graph ☐ ☐ ☐ ☐ ☐
Output Name fit in Millions

Average	0.5017
Std Dev	0.2941
Std Err	0.0132
Max	0.9983
Min	0.0005

Click on the histogram button. The graph will be created on its own tab in the SIMSTATS workbook. This shows that roughly equal numbers fell into each of the five intervals 0–.2, 2.–.4, and so forth. If enough trials were run, the bars would be perfectly uniform. In fact, the technical term for RAND() is a *uniform* random variable. This is the shape you should have drawn in question d in the previous exercise. Yet a surprising number of people draw something that is clearly higher in some places than others, indicating that the arrow of the spinner is more likely to stop in some places than in others.

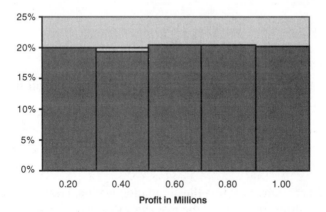

Now on to question 1b: What is the likelihood of getting laid off? Remember that if a number less than .2 is spun, you're on the street. Select the **Statistics** tab of the SIMSTATS worksheet, then click on the **Cumulative** button. The likelihood that the output cell will be less than any particular number can be read from the cumulative graph, which is created on its own sheet.

■ **FUNDAMENTALS 2-3** ■ ■ ■ ■ ■ ■ ■ ■ ■ ■ ■ ■

Histograms

A random variable can be thought of as a shape known as a *histogram*, which reflects the likelihood that the number will take on different values.

The intervals covered by the bars are called *bins*. The histogram can have any shape, as long as the bars total 100%. If you think of the bars as blocks of wood sitting on a board, then the *average*, also known as the *mean* or *expected value* of the random variable, is the point at which the board would balance.

The more trials you run and the more bins you add, the greater the accuracy of the picture of the random variable. If you were to run an extremely large number of trials with extremely narrow bins, your histogram would approach the *probability distribution*, which displays all possible outcomes of the random variable.

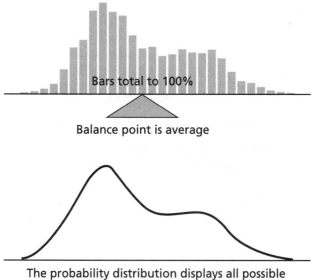

Bars total to 100%

Balance point is average

The probability distribution displays all possible
outcomes of the random variable

■ **FUNDAMENTALS 2-4** ■ ■ ■ ■ ■ ■ ■ ■ ■ ■ ■ ■

The Cumulative Graph

The *cumulative graph* allows us to read the probability that the output cell is less than or equal to any particular number. This may be the most useful way to express an uncertainty to your boss.

_Profit in Millions
__Mean of Profit in Millions

The Cumulative Graph. The cumulative graph shows the percentage of trials that were less than or equal to the amount shown on the horizontal axis. The average is shown by a vertical line (in this case at .5).

The likelihood of getting laid off is found by locating 0.2 on the horizontal axis, then going up to the diagonal line and over to the vertical axis to read the percent of trials that were less than .2, or 20%.

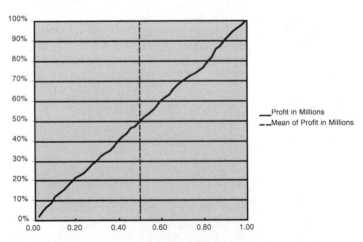

■ **FUNDAMENTALS 2-5** ■ ■ ■ ■ ■ ■ ■ ■ ■ ■ ■ ■ ■

The Mean, Mode, and Median

The *mean* of a random variable can be thought of as the balance point of its histogram. Related concepts are the *mode*, the place with the tallest bar, and the *median*, the bar with equal weight to its right and left. In general the mean, mode, and median will be different unless the histogram is symmetric.

■ **FUNDAMENTALS 2-6** ■ ■ ■ ■ ■ ■ ■ ■ ■ ■ ■ ■ ■

The Variance and Standard Deviation

Several measures of the spread or degree of uncertainty of a random variable have been defined. A common calculation used to represent the degree of uncertainty is the *variance,* σ^2. This is calculated by subtracting the average from the random variable, squaring it, and taking the average of that.

Because we are squaring the numbers, the variance ends up in squared units. Thus you might have a stock portfolio with expected earnings of $10,000 with the variance in earnings equal to 1 million square dollars. Because squared units are not intuitive, the square root of the variance, known as the *standard deviation,* σ, is often used.

How about question 1c: What do you tell the boss when you are asked for "a number" for profit? As discussed in the tutorial, the cumulative graph provides *all* the possible numbers on the horizontal axis, so that one can immediately determine the likelihood that profit will be less than or equal to any particular number by going up to the line then over to the vertical axis. Of course you should point out that the average would be $500,000 if you faced this situation repeatedly, but it is important for the boss to be aware of the entire range of outcomes as displayed on the cumulative graph.

People often give the boss the mean when "a number" is demanded, but this can be very misleading. For example, if you hijack an airliner, ask for $1 billion, and have one chance in 1,000 of getting away with it, then on average you'll make $1 million. However, this figure alone hardly expresses the uncertainty of the situation. The mean, mode, median, variance, and standard deviation together provide a more complete picture of the situation.

The Distribution Gives the Complete Picture

Actually neither the variance nor standard deviation are very intuitive. Fortunately, the boss need not understand them to benefit from the complete picture provided by the cumulative distribution. Later, however, we will see that the standard error, which is related to the standard deviation, plays a central role in determining the accuracy of the simulation results.

Consider a parallel in which learning the value of some uncertain number is analogous to apprehending a criminal. The mean and standard deviation are similar to the height and weight of the suspect: They are definitely useful information if it's all you've got. The graphs and percentiles resulting from a simulation, on the other hand, are analogous to mug shots and DNA samples of the suspect and provide a complete identification.

Averages of Uncertain Numbers: Diversification and the Central Limit Theorem

As uncertain numbers are averaged together, uncertainty is reduced. This is known as *diversification* and is an important manifestation of the Central Limit Theorem.

It is naive, of course, to think that profit is determined by spinning a spinner and multiplying by a million dollars. Suppose, instead, that profit displays the uncertainty of *two* spins averaged together and then multiplied by a million dollars.

EXERCISE 2.2

Test Your Intuition on Random Variables Again

Before proceeding, again test your intuition by answering the same questions about this more complicated scenario.

a. If you faced this same situation repeatedly. What would profit be on average?

b. What is the likelihood of getting laid off?

c. What should you tell the boss when he demands "a number" for profit?

d. Starting with the following diagram, create a bar graph that shows the percentage of times profit is likely to fall between 0 and .2, .2 and .4, and so on.

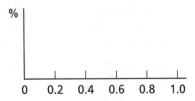

Actually we'll answer question 2.2c right away. In most situations involving uncertain numbers, you should train your boss to start asking, "What's the distribution?" instead of "What's the number?"

Now simulate the average of two spins:

1. Return to the workbook containing the cell modeling profit and replace =RAND() with =(RAND()+RAND())/2 or =AVERAGE(RAND(),RAND()). Be sure to get the parentheses right.

2. Specify the settings exactly as in the single spinner example.

3. Generate simulation statistics, histogram, and cumulative distribution, as in the single spinner example.

The Central Limit Theorem

The simulation yields an average profit of .5 million. So the answer to question 2a remains unchanged from the case of the single spin.

Output Name	Profit in Millions
Average	0.50107
Std Dev	0.21256
Std Err	0.00951
Max	0.96908
Min	0.01883

The histogram goes *up* in the middle with two spins. If you drew anything that went up in the middle for question 2d, give yourself full credit. We will discuss the actual shape a bit more later. But first, why did it go up in the middle, and, more important, so what?

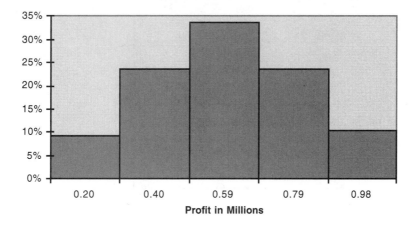

■ **FUNDAMENTALS 2-7** ■ ■ ■ ■ ■ ■ ■ ■ ■ ■ ■ ■ ■

Diversification and Variance Reduction

When random variables are averaged together, the distribution of the average goes up in the middle and down on the ends, becoming more centralized. This centralizing of the distribution is one of the important manifestations of *diversification.*

The width or narrowness of a distribution defines the range of uncertainty of the random variable. The wider the distribution, the greater the variance, standard deviation, and uncertainty; the narrower the distribution, the smaller the variance, standard deviation, and uncertainty.

The answer to the question "so what?" is provided immediately by the histogram. The bars must total 100%, so the fact that the graph got taller in the center means that it must have shrunk on the ends. Therefore the chance of getting laid off has been reduced. This is one of the principle manifestations of *diversification* and is at the heart of the Central Limit Theorem.

Evaluating the Results

The likelihood that the average of the two spins is less than .2 is read from the cumulative graph. This confirms that the probability of getting laid off has dropped sharply from the case of the single spin. In fact, it has dropped from 20% to about 8%.

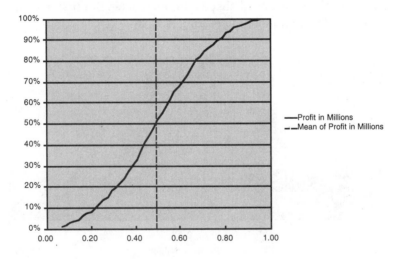

Why Did the Histogram Go Up in the Middle? Consider what happens when you roll a die: You can get any number between 1 and 6 with equal probabilities of 1/6. The histogram looks like the following figure:

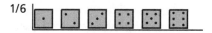

When you roll two dice, you can get any number between 2 and 12, but still with equal probability? If you think so, you'd better stay out of Las Vegas! There is only one way to get a 2 or 12, but six ways to get a 7 and intermediate numbers of ways to get the values in between.

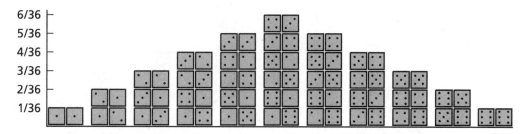

Now back to the average of two spinners: Imagine that the spinner moved in increments of 1/100th. Then the only way for the average of two spins to equal zero is for both spins to be zero. On the other hand, for two spins to average 0.5, you could spin 0 and 1, .01 and .99, .02 and .98, and so on. This change in the shape of the distribution as random variables are added together or averaged, is at the heart of the most important result in probability theory: the Central Limit Theorem.

■ **FUNDAMENTALS 2-8** ■ ■ ■ ■ ■ ■ ■ ■ ■ ■ ■ ■ ■

The Central Limit Theorem

Simulation can be used to visualize the effect of averaging random variables. The figure below, created by running thousands of trials and using the Common Graph option for all outputs, compares the distributions of RAND() and the averages of 2 RAND()s, 3 RAND()s, and 12 RAND()s.

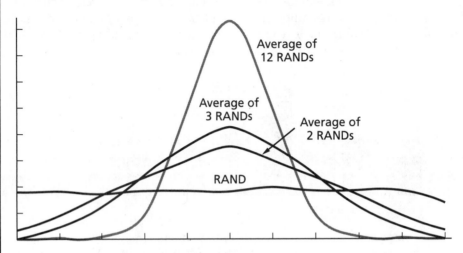

By the time 12 RAND()s have been averaged the resulting distribution is virtually indistinguishable from the famous *normal* distribution or ***bell-shaped curve***. The precise manner in which this occurs is the subject of the ***Central Limit Theorem,*** which states that if enough independent samples of almost any distribution (not just RAND()'s) are averaged together, that the resulting distribution is normal.

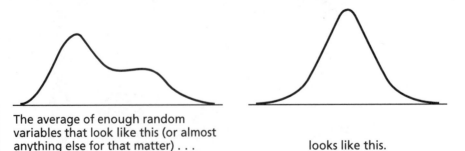

The average of enough random variables that look like this (or almost anything else for that matter) . . .

looks like this.

EXERCISE 2.3

The Distribution of the Maximum of Two Uniform Random Variables

What is the shape of the distribution of the maximum of two independent uniform random variables? *Hint:* Simulate this using the RAND() and the MAX() functions.

EXERCISE 2.4

Simulating Dice

a. Create a cell in the worksheet that simulates the roll of a single die. *Hint:* Use the RAND() and the INT() functions. When creating the histogram of a discrete random variable, it is best to use a large number of bins such as 100.

b. Simulate the roll of two dice and compare the histogram to that of the single die. What do you observe?

EXERCISE 2.5

Creating Histograms Using =FREQUENCY

The Excel function =FREQUENCY(data_array, bins_array) returns the count of numbers in **data_array** that lie in each of a set of intervals specified in **bins_array**. This is known as a frequency distribution, the graph of which is a histogram. The FREQUENCY function is an array formula, which makes it a little tricky to use, but it is very powerful. Refer to the Excel help system to learn how to enter array formulas, then create a histogram of =RAND() as follows.

a. Type =RAND() into a cell A1 in a blank worksheet and copy it down to A50. This will be the data array. In cells B1:B5 type the numbers .2, .4, .6, .8, and 1. This will be the bin array. Select cells C1:C5 to hold the frequency array. Next click the function wizard and select Statistical from the left menu and FREQUENCY from the right menu. Fill in the data_array and bins_array, then click **F̲inish**. Even though you clicked **F̲inish**, you are NOT FINISHED! Your worksheet should now appear as shown in the following figure.

C1		=FREQUENCY(A1:A50,B1:B5)		
	A	**B**	**C**	**D**
1	0.147701	0.2	10	
2	0.781992	0.4		
3	0.153136	0.6		
4	0.160842	0.8		
5	0.843211	1		

b. Be sure cells C1:C5 are selected. If they are not, select them now. Next click in the formula bar to go into edit mode, then press **Shift-Ctrl-Enter (Command-Enter on the Macintosh®)[2]**. The array C1:C5 should be filled in, and {}s should appear around the function in the formula bar. This signifies that you have

---

2. Array formulas are powerful, but require careful application. The complicated set of keystrokes required to use them is analogous to using a baby proof cap on a medicine bottle.

correctly entered the function as an array formula. Press the calculate key a few times and observe frequency count change as you generate random numbers.

c. Graph C1:C5 to produce a histogram. Observe the histogram changes as you press the calculate key a few times. I refer to such a live histogram as a "Blitzogram." Save this file, then go on to the next exercise.

EXERCISE 2. 6 **Creating Simulations From Data Tables**

The Data Table is a very powerful but seldom used spreadsheet concept. Among its many other applications, it can be used to do simple simulations as follows.

a. Starting with the worksheet developed in the last exercise, place the cursor in column A and insert a column with the **Insert Column** command. Next erase all the RAND() formulas (now in column B) except the one in the first row. Now select cells A1:B50 and invoke the **Data Table** command. Then place the cursor in the Column Input Cell field of the dialog box, click on any cell in the worksheet and press enter. Cells B2:B50 should fill up with new trials of the RAND() formula in cell B1. Press the calculate key a few times, and observe the histogram.

b. Next, replace the formula in cell B1 with =(RAND()+RAND())/2 and observe the change in the histogram. Save the worksheet and go on to the next exercise.

c. Your current histogram can handle any random number between 0 and 1. Modify the bin range so that the numbers in column B could take any values.

EXERCISE 2.7 **Using the Histogram Command from the Data Analysis Tools**

Another way to create histograms is with the Data Analysis Tools. Invoke the **Tools Data Analysis** command, then select Histogram from the menu. Specify the same data and bin arrays as used in Exercise 2.5, and experiment with the various options on the dialog box.

Important Classes of Uncertain Numbers: Idealized Distributions

In reality, every uncertain number has its own distribution. However, the theory of probability has discovered important classes of idealized distributions that approximate the behavior of many real world random variables. Given the Central Limit Theorem, it is not surprising that a lot of random variables are approximately normally distributed. Other important idealized distributions include the following:

■ The *Binomial* distribution models a process like a sequence of coin flips in which you are concerned with the total number of heads. For example,

■ FUNDAMENTALS 2-9 ■ ■ ■ ■ ■ ■ ■ ■ ■ ■ ■ ■

The Normal Distribution

The *Normal distribution* is an idealization of the result of averaging a large number of identical, independent random variables.

All Normal distributions look basically the same. They differ from each other in only two respects: where they are centered and how wide they are. They are centered at their *mean* or average, often referred to as μ. Their width is measured by the *standard deviation*, σ, the square root of the variance.

You may think of σ as one-sixth of the distance that spans 99% of all occurrences of the random variable. That is, 99% of the time, a normal random variable will be within 3σ above or below its mean. Also, 95% and 68% of the distribution lies between plus and minus 2σ and 1σ around the mean, respectively.

These percentages only hold for the normal distribution. If you run a simulation, however, you can determine such percentiles from the statistics screen and cumulative graph for any type of distribution.

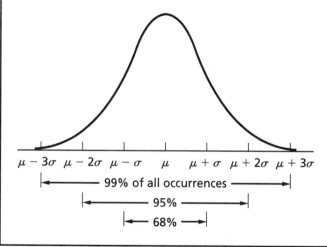

suppose your firm has produced a batch of 50 circuit boards, each of which has a 2% chance of being defective. The total number of defective boards in the batch can be modeled with a binomial distribution.

■ The *Poisson* distribution models a process such as the number of phone calls arriving per minute at a call center, or the monthly number of orders for a product or service.

■ The *Exponential* distribution models the time between phone calls or orders of a product or service.

SIM.xla provides formulas for generating random variables from several idealized distributions, as described in the technical reference. The following example involves a normal random variable.

Comparing Investment Examples

The percentage return on certain financial investments are modeled by normal random variables. As discussed, normal distributions can be fully specified by their means and standard deviations, and a wealth of on-line financial data is available to help you estimate these. In this example, we will explore the effect of splitting an investment budget between two similar but independent funds.

Suppose that you are managing the financial portfolio of a large municipality and must allocate all your investment between a domestic and foreign mutual fund. Imagine that the returns of the two funds are very similar, but independent. That is, the likelihood of either one going up or down is not affected by what the other one does. Analysis indicates that the percentage return of each is normally distributed with a mean of 10% and a standard deviation of 10%. That is, the return from each fund is shaped like the following picture. This means you should expect to earn 10 cents for each dollar invested. There is also a chance of losing money, however, in which case the municipality will default on the salaries of teachers and fire fighters.

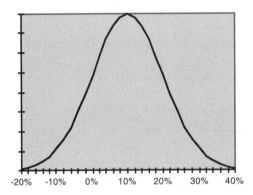

We can find the probability of losing money with either of these funds as follows: Use the following Excel formula for the normal distribution to calculate the probability of making 0 or less (that is, losing money) from an investment with a mean and standard deviation of 10%.

=NORMDIST(0, 0.1, 0.1, TRUE)

The first argument indicates that you are calculating the probability of 0 dollars or less. The next two arguments are the mean and standard deviation respectively. The last argument of this function is TRUE indicating the cumulative form of the distribution. This calculates to about a 16% chance of losing money.

Although this Excel formula allowed us to analyze a single investment, additional knowledge of probability theory would be required to determine the likelihood of losing money with an investment split between both funds. However, it is easy to simulate the returns on the following three strategies:

1. Invest all in the domestic fund.

2. Invest all in the foreign fund.

3. Split investment between both funds.

EXERCISE 2.8

Test Your Intuition about Investments

Perhaps you are ready to answer the following questions:

a. How do the average returns of the three investments compare?

b. What is the relative likelihood of losing money for each of the three investments?

STEPS: SIMULATING THE RETURNS

Model the return of the domestic fund, the foreign fund, and a split investment by following these steps:

Make sure that SIM.xla is loaded, then open a blank workbook. Place the cursor in the cell where you want the return of the domestic fund, then click on the function icon. The Function Wizard dialog box, shown below, opens.

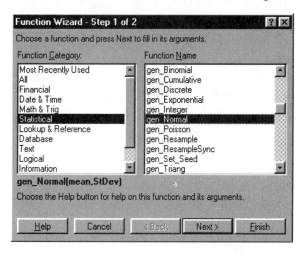

2

Select *Statistical* from the left menu and *gen_Normal* from the right menu and click **Next**, which opens the following dialog box:

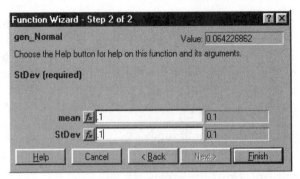

3

Type .1 for both the mean and standard deviation and click **Finish.** Press the calculate key a few times to be sure the cell is properly generating random numbers. *Note:* SIM.xla's random number generator functions all start with "gen_". Before opening an Excel workbook that uses these functions, you must first open SIM.xla. Do not confuse these functions with the built-in distribution functions in Excel such as the NORMDIST function discussed earlier. This function does not return random numbers at all, but is an on-line table of the normal distribution useful in statistical calculations.

4

Copy the domestic fund formula to the cell for foreign return because the foreign fund has the same distribution of returns as the domestic fund. Again press the calculate key a few times. You should see the two numbers vary independently.

Note: Although the domestic and foreign returns have the same distribution, you must *not* place **gen_Normal**(.1, .1) in a single cell which is then referred to by both funds. This would result in the two funds moving in lock step, which would be extremely unrealistic and invalidate the results of the simulation.

5

If we were to split the investment equally between the domestic and foreign funds, the return would be the average of the two returns. So create a new cell with this result, (A3 + B3)/2, as shown in the following figure:

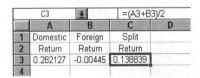

6

In this example we will monitor more than one output cell. The setup screen should appear as shown in the following figure. Run 500 trials.

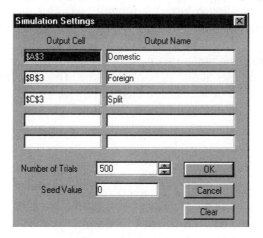

Evaluating Simulation Output

The Statistics. The simulation statistics display both the average returns of each strategy along with other useful statistics.

The average return of all three investments is the same: around 10%. However, the standard deviation of the split investment is significantly lower than the other two (about 7% compared with 10%). Over the hundreds of trials, the pure investments ranged from about 45% maximum to about –25% minimum. The split investment ranged from about 35% maximum to –12% minimum.

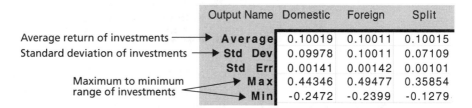

	Output Name	Domestic	Foreign	Split
Average return of investments ⟶	Average	0.10019	0.10011	0.10015
Standard deviation of investments ⟶	Std Dev	0.09978	0.10011	0.07109
	Std Err	0.00141	0.00142	0.00101
Maximum to minimum ⟶	Max	0.44346	0.49477	0.35854
range of investments ⟶	Min	-0.2472	-0.2399	-0.1279

Clearly the outcomes of the pure investments are more uncertain than is that of the split. This is a double-edged sword; in this example, the only way to reduce the downside risk of a big loss is to forego the opportunity of a large gain.

The Percentiles. The percentiles contain the same information as the cumulative graphs but in numeric form. For example, the 25th percentile of the domestic fund (in the first column) is roughly .03. This means that we would expect the domestic fund to have a return of 3% or less with a chance of 25%.

The table shows that the two pure investments (columns 1 and 2) made essentially no money or less about 15% of the time. The split investment, on the other hand, made 0 or less with a chance of 5%. This is three times less likely to lose money than either of the other two.

Percentiles			
5%	-0.0627	-0.0636	-0.0141
10%	-0.0296	-0.0262	0.01003
15%	-0.0044	-0.0015	0.02788
20%	0.01451	0.01815	0.04113
25%	0.03103	0.03297	0.05253
30%	0.0468	0.04813	0.06265
35%	0.06204	0.06158	0.07131
40%	0.07475	0.074	0.0805
45%	0.08766	0.08722	0.08949
50%	0.09962	0.09903	0.09963

At the other end of the spectrum, the pure investments returned about 22% or more 10% (100%–90%) of the time, whereas the split made more than 22% less than 5% of the time.

90%	0.22732	0.22681	0.19033
95%	0.26345	0.26645	0.21752
100%	0.44346	0.49477	0.35854

The Histogram. Because we are interested in the comparative anatomy of these different investments, check the boxes for the variables you want to show on the common graph as shown below.

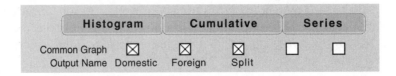

A histogram with three sets of bars is hard to read, so the common histogram uses three lines that have been smoothed by the Excel graph routine.

Because of the smoothing, the numerical results of the smoothed histograms are not dependable, and they should be used for qualitative comparisons only. For quantitative results, use either the percentiles or the common cumulative graph as described later.

The domestic and foreign investments have nearly the same shape whereas the split clearly shows how diversification leads to a more centralized distribution.

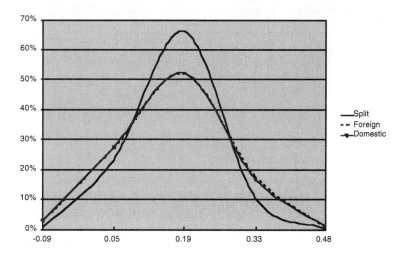

Note: For discrete outcomes you will get a more accurate common histogram by double-clicking the lines of the graph and deselecting the smooth box.

The Common Cumulative Graph. This again shows a single average of 10% for all three investments, nearly identical distributions for the domestic and foreign outcomes, and the clearly narrower distribution of the Split investment. The probabilities of making a given amount or less in each case can be read by going to the desired amount on the horizontal axis, then up to the appropriate curve and over to the vertical axis.

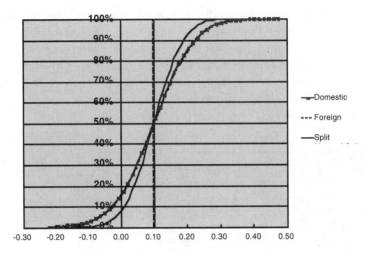

All graphs are generated within Excel and can be edited using the chart wizard as we did earlier.

Uncertain Numbers and Bad Outcomes: Risk Management

Risk management involves the systematic study of the various uncertainties facing an organization for the purpose of identifying both undesirable outcomes and managerial steps that could reduce the likelihood of their occurrence. Simulation can play a central role in this activity.

Risk Attitude: Risk Is in the Eye of the Beholder

Risk can be defined as *the likelihood that something bad will happen given the uncertainty you face.* Unlike uncertainty, however, which is an objective feature of the universe, risk is in the eye of the beholder. It depends on what the beholder is afraid of. This is known as risk attitude. When extremely risk averse individuals get out of bed in the morning, they might be concerned about choking on their oatmeal. Thrill seekers getting out of bed on the same morning, however, might be more concerned about the risk that the cloud cover will postpone their sky diving lessons.

Value at Risk: Managing Risk in the Investment Example

Case 1: Downside Risk. In the previous example, there would be serious consequences if the investment lost money. If this is the risk that concerns you, it would be sound risk management to split the investment rather than invest purely in either the domestic or foreign fund. This reduces the likelihood of losing money from 15% to 5%, keeping the average return at 10%.

Case 2: Upside Risk. Imagine that you are investing privately, have plenty of money in the bank, and few obligations to others. You are not worried about losing money, but will be upset if you don't make at least 16% on your investment. With this risk attitude, you would choose either the pure domestic or foreign fund because each presents only a 70% risk of not making at least 16% compared with 80% for the split investment as read from the percentile table of the simulation.

Value at Risk. A recent method for measuring downside risk that is gaining in popularity is known as *Value at Risk* or *VAR*. Suppose that the amount to be invested in the previous example were $100,000. Then looking back at the percentiles we see that 5% of the time with the domestic fund we would have lost 6.2% or more. Thus, the value at risk at the 5% level for the domestic fund is $6,200. By comparison, the value at risk at the 5% level for the split fund is only about $1,400.

Conclusion

In this chapter we introduced the concept of Monte Carlo simulation in the context of a tutorial involving uncertain profit. We then used this powerful technique to explore some properties of uncertain numbers, or random variables as they are known. In the next chapter we will investigate more complex models involving uncertainty.

3

The Buildings of Uncertainty: Functions of Random Variables

If a man will begin with certainties, he shall end in doubts, but if he will be content to begin with doubts, he shall end in certainties.

FRANCIS BACON, ENGLISH PHILOSOPHER

Every day millions of managers input uncertain numbers into elaborate spreadsheet models.

■ Marketing directors input uncertain levels of customer satisfaction into models to predict profitability.

■ Logistics managers input uncertain demands into models that specify inventory levels.

■ Investors input uncertain security prices into investment models.

■ Personnel directors input uncertain workload requirements into models to estimate labor cost.

The uncertain outputs of worksheet models with uncertain inputs are known technically as functions of random variables. It is tempting to plug "best guesses" as inputs into such models, in the hope that what comes out are the "best guesses" for the outputs. According to Francis Bacon (and confirmed by probability theory), it is doubtful that this hope is realized. Monte Carlo simulation, on the other hand, begins with doubts. That is, instead of plugging in a single "best guess," it keeps the full range of uncertain inputs alive, providing results that are ultimately more certain.

OVERVIEW

Introduction

We discuss more complex spreadsheet models involving uncertain inputs.

Tutorial: Estimating Inventory Costs Given Uncertain Demand

We examine an inventory model with uncertain demand and investigate the implications of using "best guesses" or point estimates as inputs. Two general techniques for estimating input distributions are introduced: resampling past data and generating triangular random variables.

The Buildings of Uncertainty

If uncertain numbers (random variables) are the building blocks of uncertainty then worksheet models with uncertain inputs are buildings. Technically these are known as functions of random variables. This section describes some important business examples and simple ways to analyze them with Monte Carlo simulation. Also discussed are uncertain numbers that are related to each other, known as dependent random variables.

Introduction

In the last chapter we addressed very simple models containing at most one formula beyond the random inputs. Furthermore, we assumed that the random variable inputs were from known idealized distributions: uniform in the spinner examples and normal in the investment example.

In real world situations, the worksheet models are far more complex, and, worse, unless you are a statistician, you will have difficulty in specifying idealized distributions for the input cells. Even if you *are* a statistician and know how to use some distribution with an exotic sounding name, you might have difficulty justifying your assumption to the boss. This is the stage at which people often throw up their hands and pull "a number" out of thin air.

Tutorial: Estimating Inventory Costs Given Uncertain Demand

In this tutorial, we use an example that shows how even a simulation based on informal assumptions can provide valuable insights. Be sure SIM.xla is loaded before proceeding.

An Inventory Problem

A pharmaceutical supply firm inventories cases of a perishable drug for which demand is uncertain, as represented by 36 months of historical data. The average demand has been 5 cases per month, so this is the number the firm currently stocks.

The cost of maintaining the inventory has two components:

■ If at the end of the month the demand has been less than the number stocked, the excess cases will have expired and must be destroyed at a loss of $50 per unit.

■ If the demand is greater than the number stocked, the additional units must be air freighted at additional cost. The air freight rate fluctuates depending on the capacity of the carrier. Although good records have not been kept, the shipping clerk indicates that it is most likely $150 per unit. However, he admits it can range from a low of $100 to a high of $300.

This situation is modeled in INVNTORY.xls, which you should open now. The formulas are displayed below (cells C5, C6, and C8). Note in the following figure that some of the cells have been named for clarity.

	A	B	C	D	E	F	G	H	I
1	Demand		Amt Stocked						
2	5		5						
3									
4	Costs	Per Unit	Total						
5	Expiration Cost	$50.00	=IF(Amt_Stocked>Demand,(Amt_Stocked-Demand)*Exp_Cost,0)						
6	Air Freight	$150.00	=IF(Amt_Stocked<Demand,(Demand-Amt_Stocked)*F_Cost,0)						
7									
8	Overall Cost		=C5+C6						

The sheet also contains 36 months of historical demand data starting in cell B14. Note the average demand of 5 calculated in cell C14.

C14		=AVERAGE(B14:B49
A	**B**	**C**
12 Historical Data		
13 Month	Demand	Average
14 1	10	5
15 2	6	
16 3	10	
17 4	8	
18 5	7	
19 :	:	

Try plugging some of the numbers from the demand column into cell A2 to see how the total cost is affected.

This time the boss says, "What is inventory cost going to be next month? I know it might vary, so just give me the average, and be quick about it." It is common in situations like this to plug in the average of the uncertain inputs, then read the corresponding "average" outputs from the model. This is known as using *point estimates* because you have used single points (5 and 150 in this case) as "best guesses" to represent the entire ranges of demand and freight cost. Plug in 5 and 150 for demand and freight cost, respectively. You should see an overall cost of 0.

Therefore, you might want to tell the boss: "As long as you understand that cost will vary, but if it's just the average cost you want, then 0 is my best guess." Or, then again, you might want to confirm this with a simulation first.

EXERCISE 3.1

Test Your Intuition about Point Estimates

a. What are the advantages of using point estimates in this case?

b. What are the disadvantages?

Simulating the Cost

The Uncertainties

The relationships between the inputs and overall cost have already been modeled in INVNTORY.xls. What remains is to model the random nature of the input cells: Demand and Air Freight. Unlike the previous example, we have no basis on which to assume some idealized distribution such as uniform or normal.

We will use a separate approach for each input cell: *resampling historical data* to model random demand and generating *triangular random variables* to model freight cost.

STEPS: ## RESAMPLING HISTORICAL DATA

This simple but powerful approach to modeling uncertainty works as follows. Imagine 36 ping pong balls, each with one of the 36 historical demands painted on it. Place these in the type of rotating basket used for lottery drawings. To model demand, simply rotate the basket, draw out a ball, read the number and replace the ball in the basket. Repeat this for as many trials as you like. You will find that doing this with SIM.xla is a lot easier than painting numbers on ping pong balls and using a rotating basket.

Unlike the methods of classical statistics, which require you to begin with the assumption of an idealized distribution, resampling lets you pull yourself up as if by your own bootstraps. In fact it is the basis for a powerful new perspective on statistical analysis known as *bootstrapping* (Efron and Tibshirani, 1993, and Simon, 1974).

To resample historical data, use the *gen_Resample* function as follows:

With the cursor in the Demand cell, A2, click on the function icon. The Function Wizard dialog box opens.

1

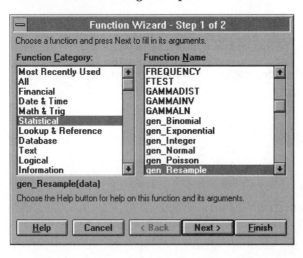

2

Select **Statistical** from the left menu and **gen_Resample** from the right menu. Click **Next**. The following dialog box opens.

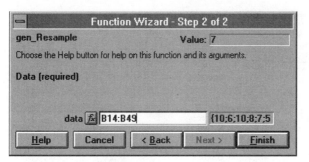

3

Select the cells containing the 36 historical data points, and click **Finish**. This places the gen_Resample formula in cell A2.

4

Press **Home** to get to the top of the sheet, then press the calculate key a few times to be sure the cell is functioning properly.

STEPS: **GENERATING TRIANGULAR DISTRIBUTION**

With air freight costs, all we have is the recollection of the shipping clerk and no time to research the subject. Few things in life have a truly triangular distribution. Nonetheless, it provides a quick and dirty way to specify high, low, and most likely values as indicated by opinion.

Note: The most likely value of the distribution, also known as the *mode*, is not the average in this case because the distribution is not symmetric around its average, as shown in the following figure.

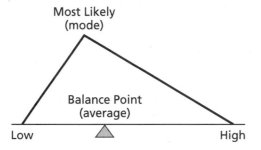

To generate triangular random variables, use the function ***gen_Triang*** and follow these steps:

1

With the cursor in the Air Freight cell, B6, click on the function icon. The Function Wizard dialog box opens.

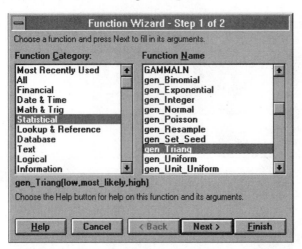

2

Select **Statistical** from the left menu and **gen_Triang** from the right menu, then click **Next**. The following dialog box opens:

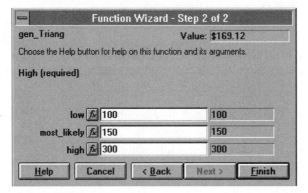

3

Fill in the **low, most_likely,** and **high** values and click **Finish**. This places the gen_Triang formula in cell B6.

4

Press the calculate key a few times to be sure the cell is functioning properly. Once the random input formulas have been specified, save INVNTORY.xls so you do not have to repeat these steps for future experiments. When you re-open the model at a later time, be sure that SIM.xla is opened first.

The boss wanted the answer right away, so we should start with a short run of 100 trials to get a quick feeling for what is going on.

5

After selecting **Run Simulation** from the **Simulate** menu, specify C8, Overall Cost, as the output cell in the following dialog box, then click **OK** to run the simulation.

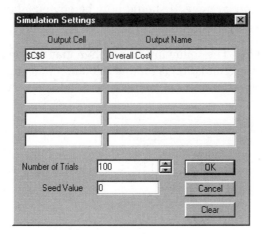

Simulation Results

Statistics. You will recall that plugging in point estimates of 5 for demand and 150 for air freight yielded an overall cost of 0. How does this compare with the average of overall cost on the simulation statistics screen? Remember, because the results are based on random numbers you might not get exactly the same result twice.

The Histogram. Your histogram should look similar to the following figure:

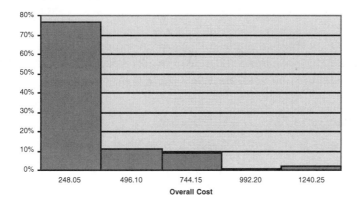

Recall that the average is the point at which it would balance if the histogram were made of blocks sitting on a board. Clearly, it would not balance all the way to the left at 0. A cost penalty is incurred regardless of whether demand is above or below average. It should now be obvious that cost will often be greater than 0 and never less than 0.

The Cumulative Graph. The following cumulative graph shows that the average for this run of the simulation is around $200 and that about 30% of the time cost is over this. 10% of the time it is over $600, a far cry from 0!

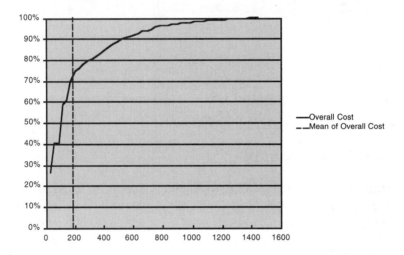

Average Inputs Don't Always Yield Average Outputs. This leads us to one of the most important lessons of this book: *Average inputs don't always yield average outputs.*[1] With this in mind we will answer question 3.1a: What are the advantages of using point estimates in this case? Answer: *NONE!*

In the previous example we gained an important insight by running a simulation for which we did not even have accurate input distributions. Like horseshoes and hand grenades, being close counts with simulation too.

EXERCISE 3.2 **Increasing the Bins of a Histogram**

Run the simulation with 1000 iterations and create a histogram with 50 bins. What is the probability that cost will actually be 0?

---

1. The only time average inputs yield average outputs is when the model is *linear.* And even those few people who know what linear means can't easily tell if a worksheet has this property.

The Buildings of Uncertainty

Even if you are in the small minority who knew that plugging in "best guess" inputs was worthless in the inventory example, you probably work with people for whom this is a time honored tradition. This should be enough motivation to explore in more detail what happens when the building blocks of uncertainty (random variables) are combined into more complex models with uncertain inputs. The resulting buildings of uncertainty, known technically as functions of random variables, display a number of non-intuitive features that can be understood through Monte Carlo simulation.

In this section, we examine the following topics:

■ **Worksheet models based on uncertain numbers: Functions of random variables.** Worksheet models usually have a number of uncertain input cells. Typically "best guesses" are plugged into these cells, leading to answers that are just plain wrong. Monte Carlo simulation can provide a clear picture of the effects of uncertainty, such as hidden costs and unnecessary risks.

■ **Experimenting under uncertainty: Parameterized simulation.** Repeated simulation experiments can determine managerial steps that can both improve average performance and reduce risk.

■ **Uncertain numbers that are related to each other: Statistical dependence.** A company might be uncertain about its future need for cash and future ability to borrow. These uncertainties are related to each other, in that when a company has the most pressing need for cash, it will also find it the most difficult to borrow. The relationships between these uncertainties must be correctly understood and simulated for accurate planning.

■ **How many trials are enough? Convergence.** Simulation might never give the same answer twice. The longer a simulation is run, the more dependable the results. How many trials are needed?

■ **Sensitivity analysis: The big picture.** Simulation can yield insight into the relationships between various aspects of a complex model. This can provide a big picture of what is going on.

Worksheet Models Based on Uncertain Numbers: Functions of Random Variables

We will start by formalizing the notion of a function of random variables. (See Fundamentals Box 3-1.)

■ **FUNDAMENTALS 3-1** ■ ■ ■ ■ ■ ■ ■ ■ ■ ■ ■ ■

A Function of Random Variables

An output that depends on random variable inputs is known as a ***function of random variables***. Thus, any cell in a worksheet that depends directly or indirectly on any other cells that contain uncertain numbers is a function of random variables.

■ **FUNDAMENTALS 3-2** ■ ■ ■ ■ ■ ■ ■ ■ ■ ■ ■ ■

Linear Model

In a ***linear model***, the random inputs can be multiplied by constants and added together. Virtually nothing else, including IF, MAX, and MIN formulas, look up tables, and many other formulas present in most worksheet models, are allowed in a linear model.

In the inventory example, the random variables were demand and air freight rate. The function of these random variables that we wanted to know was the overall cost. We found through simulation that plugging in "best guesses" or point estimates of demand and air freight did *NOT* result in the "best guess" for overall cost.

There is a special class of models, however, known as linear models, for which average inputs do yield average outputs (see Fundamentals Box 3-2).

For instance, suppose that a company has two divisions: A and B. A simple model for the company's total profit *is* linear:

Total Profit = Division A's Profit + Division B's Profit,

Thus,

Expected Total Profit = Division A's Expected Profit + Division B's Expected Profit

In general, however, it is difficult to determine if a large worksheet is linear. It is always safe to assume it is not linear and run a simulation to determine the distribution of the outputs.

We state formally the danger of using point estimates in Fundamentals Boxes 3-2 and 3-3.

■ FUNDAMENTALS 3-3 ■ ■ ■ ■ ■ ■ ■ ■ ■ ■ ■ ■

The Average of a Function of Random Variables

In general, plugging average values of uncertain inputs into a function of random variables **does not** result in the average value of the function. For the special case of *linear* functions, average inputs **do** result in average outputs. In probability or statistics books you might see this written as

$$F(E(x)) \neq E(F(x))$$

unless F is linear, where x is the uncertain number, F is the function, and E is the expected or average value.

A Sobering Example. Point estimates of average inputs are used erroneously in many contexts. This problem can be compared to the fate of a drunk, wandering back and forth on a busy highway. The random *input* is the drunk's position; the *output* is the drunk's fate.

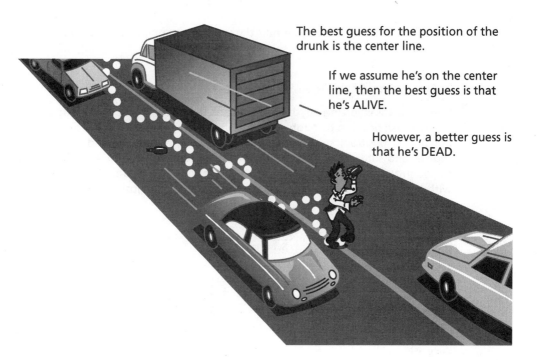

The best guess for the position of the drunk is the center line.

If we assume he's on the center line, then the best guess is that he's ALIVE.

However, a better guess is that he's DEAD.

Some Business Examples. There are numerous examples in business where the use of point estimates leads to erroneous results. A few are described in the following exercises, which are designed to help you identify such situations on your own while you improve your skills with SIM.xla.

EXERCISE 3.3

Estimating Project Duration

The printing of a sales brochure has been split between two printing firms, each of which estimates that their half of the job will take 20 hours. Past experience indicates that the estimates from both firms are accurate on average. However, actual completion time has been normally distributed around the estimates with a standard deviation equal to 15% of the estimated time.

a. What is the expected amount of time to complete the entire job? ***Hint:*** Use the MAX function.

b. What are the chances that the entire job will be completed in 20 hours or less?

c. What is the expected time to complete half the job? ***Hint:*** Use the MIN function.

d. What are the chances that half the job will be completed in 20 hours or less?

EXERCISE 3.4

A Pro Forma Cash Flow Statement

Business plans involving anything from bank loans to venture capital often forecast net cash position through a pro forma cash flow statement. Starting with an initial cash position, subsequent positions are calculated by adding expected sources and subtracting expected cash outlay for each month. PROFORMA.xls, shown in the following figure, models the rosy picture of a business that starts with $250,000 and turns it into more than $1.5 million in just 12 months.

C6	↧		=B6+C4-C5		
	A	**B**	**C**	**D**	**E**	**F**
1		Pro Forma Cash Flow Statement				
2			$000's			
3		Jan	Feb	Mar	Apr	May
4	Cash in	$500	$500	$500	$500	$500
5	Cash Out	$400	$400	$400	$400	$400
6	Net Cash	$350	$450	$550	$650	$750
7						
8	Initial	$250				
9	Cash					

Needless to say, the actual sources and outlays of cash are not always forecast with great accuracy. Suppose that all the projected sources and outlays (but not initial cash) in PROFORMA.xls are normally distributed around their estimated values with standard deviations equal to 25% of the estimated value.

a. What is the minimum net cash position we should expect any time during the 12 months?

b. What are the chances that the minimum will actually be negative, which implies bankruptcy?

EXERCISE **3.5** **Estimating Production Quantity**

A firm manufactures television coaxial cable from four components that it orders from outside suppliers. A single wire forms the center conductor, a woven wire mesh forms the outer conductor, and two types of plastic are used for the inner and outer insulation. Orders have been placed for each component in quantities required for 5000 feet. On average, each supplier has delivered the ordered amount with a uniform variation ranging between plus or minus 100 feet.

a. How much cable should the manufacturer expect to be able to produce?

b. What are the chances it will be less than 5,000 feet?

Hint: Model the amount delivered by each supplier with *gen_Uniform*.

EXERCISE **3.6** **Estimating Overtime Expenses**

A health care facility is planning its personnel budget for the coming year. One nurse with a salary of $1,000 per week is required for every 5 patients. The average patient census is 300, as shown in the file CENSUS.xls, which contains 52 weeks of census data. Therefore, it is estimated that 60 nurses will be needed at an average cost of $60,000 per week. This translates to an estimated annual budget of $3,120,000 for nurse salaries.

On those weeks when the census is below the average of 300, the nurses must be paid full salary anyway. On those weeks when the census is exceeded, $500 in overtime expense is incurred per patient in excess of 300. For example, if the census were 310, an additional $5,000 would be incurred that week.

a. Create a histogram of the census data.

b. What is the average weekly nursing cost?

c. What is the chance that on any given week actual expenses will be less than or equal to that budgeted? *Hint:* Create an output cell that equals 1 if expense is less than or equal to the budget. Such a formula is known as an *indicator*. The average of the indicator is just the likelihood that the budget was met for the week.

d. Given your answer to part c, what is the chance that the overall nursing budget will be met for the year?

EXERCISE
3.7 **Create One of Your Own**

Develop a worksheet based on your own experience of a situation in which averages of uncertain numbers have been inappropriately plugged into a model.

Experimenting Under Uncertainty: Parameterized Simulation

People facing uncertainty have generally achieved one of the following levels of enlightenment:

- *Level 0: Dumb.* When the boss asks what the output of some model will be, this person throws up his or her hands and says, "I don't know because I don't know what the inputs will be."

- *Level Minus 1: Dumber.* One step down from dumb, these people plug best guesses into the model and confidently proclaim that they have the best guess for the output.

- *Level 1: Smart.* A big step up from dumb, these people run a simulation to find the output's range of uncertainty. In the process, they are forced to learn something about the nature of the uncertain inputs of their model, which makes them smarter still.

- *Level 2: Proactive.* Even at level 1, you are simply reporting what is likely to happen. Reaching level two requires a commitment to action given the uncertainty observed at level 1.

Parameterized simulation involves repeating a simulation several times while systematically adjusting some number in the model. Such a number is known as a *parameter*. This is a proactive approach to dealing with uncertainty.

Seeking the Optimal Stocking Level

In the inventory example, an obvious question to ask is this: "Who says we should stock 5?" And, an obvious way to answer this question is to run the simulation several times while experimenting with different quantities stocked. The penalty for understocking is between $100 to $300 per unit, whereas the penalty for overstocking is only $50 per unit. Therefore, increasing the amount stocked above 5 makes intuitive sense. SIM.xla allows as many as five such experiments to be run, so we will try stocking 4, 5, 6, 7, and 8. It is important to keep the original number of 5 stocked so we can compare the results with the status quo. The number being changed each time—in this instance, the number of cases stocked—is known as a parameter.

Seeding the Random Numbers

There is a problem, however. Because of the random nature of simulation, we can expect to get different answers with every run, even with the same number stocked. So, how can we tell if one stocking level is really better than another?

This is analogous to the problem faced by the coach of a minor league baseball team who must choose one of several potential recruits to join the team. To test the players' relative batting abilities, he could put each recruit up against a separate pitcher. But then the coach wouldn't know if the differences in their performance were because of the pitcher or batter. It would be better to test each player against the same pitcher. But the best test of all would be provided by a computerized, laser guided pitching machine programmed to pitch exactly the same sequence of fast balls, slow balls, curves, and so on to each recruit.

This facility is provided in SIM.xla through the *seed* on the settings screen. Think of the random number generator as a ball machine that sends out a sequence of 2^{31} (2,147,483,648) different pitches before repeating. The various potential stocking levels represent the potential recruits. The seed indicates where in the sequence of pitches the ball machine will start for each recruit. This allows you to repeat the experiments. With a seed of zero you do not know where in the sequence the machine will start, and the results will not be repeatable.

STEPS: RUNNING A PARAMETERIZED SIMULATION OF **INVNTORY**.XLS

We will run a parameterized simulation by using the following steps. The uncertain inputs are the same as in the earlier examples, and no changes are required. This time, however, we will test five different quantities to stock (4, 5, 6, 7, and 8).

1 Retrieve INVNTORY.xls as saved from the previous example.

2 Enter 4, 5, 6, 7, and 8 in any contiguous range in the worksheet. Cells D2:D6 are used in the example shown below.

B	C	D
	Amt Stocked	
	5	4
		5
Per Unit	Total	6
$50.00	$100.00	7
$223.14	$0.00	8

Now specify the settings for running five separate simulations of 50 trials, one for each parameter value, by following these steps:

3

Select **Parameterized Sim** from the **Simulation** menu. The following dialog box opens:

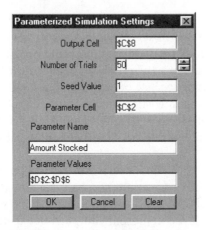

4

Specify C8, Overall Cost, as the output cell.

5

Set the number of trials to 50. This will be enough to allow us to see the effect of different stocking levels. For decisions of economic consequence, however, a larger number of trials is recommended (see the discussion of Standard Error later).

6

Specify a nonzero seed. The number 1 was chosen here, but any positive integer will do.

7

Next specify C2, Amt Stocked, as the parameter cell.

The parameter name is optional but useful in interpreting the simulation output.

8

Finally, specify D2:D6 as the range containing the parameter values, then click **OK**.

Simulation Output

The simulation output indicates that stocking 7 results in the minimum average cost—about 15% lower than stocking 5! *Note:* Your results will depend on the seed used and the number of iterations run.

Amount Stocked	4	5	6	7	8
Average	261.78	204.72	183.56	170.82	184.11
Std Dev	329.6	254.93	176.74	129.03	106.57
Std Err	46.612	36.052	24.995	18.248	15.071
Max	1240.2	1033.5	826.79	620.09	413.39
Min	0	0	0	0	0

This is good news, but the parameterized graph provides additional insight. Click the **Parameterized Graph** button to view the graph.

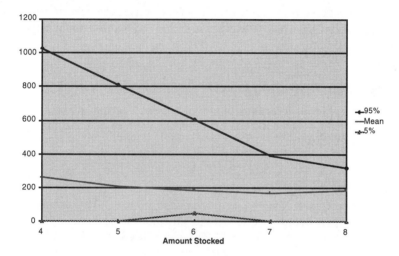

The center line of the graph shows clearly that the mean overall cost is minimized around 6 or 7 units stocked. But, more important, the top and bottom lines show the range of the results. That is, 90% of all overall costs were between the top line (the 95th percentile) and bottom line (the 5th percentile). Notice how dramatically this band of uncertainty narrows as the amount stocked goes from 4 to 7. For managing risk, this reduction in uncertainty can be even more important than the 25% reduction in average cost.

We only ran 50 trials here to get a qualitative feeling. In a real life situation, with results as dramatic as these (which took about 5 seconds to run on a 120 MHz computer), it would make sense to follow this with a run of a few minutes to get more accurate results.

Go back to the Statistics sheet and view the 95th percentile.

90%	672.1	504.07	336.05	250	300
95%	1026	813.02	603.54	394.07	319.59
100%	1240.2	1033.5	826.79	620.09	413.39

Five percent (100% – 95%) of the time we should expect to incur an overall cost greater than or equal to the numbers shown on this line. This is the *value at risk* or *VAR* at the 5% level and is reduced by over 50% as the number stocked goes from 5 to 8. Notice that beyond 6 units stocked there is a trade-off between expected cost and value at risk. Management might reasonably choose to stock between 6 and 8, depending on the relative importance they place on reduction of average cost or reduction of the risk of very high cost. However, stocking 5 does not make sense under any condition.

EXERCISE 3.8 The Optimal Staffing Level

Return to the nursing example and determine the staffing level that minimizes expected cost. Is there a trade off between average cost and the risk of an occasional large cost?

EXERCISE 3.9 Competitive Bidding

Consider a Health Maintenance Organization (HMO) that is bidding for a contract to supply health care services to a medium-sized company for the following year. The management of the HMO believes it will cost $100,000 to provide the required health care services. Two competitive firms are also known to be bidding for this contract. Of course, management does not know with certainty what the competitors will bid, but managers have estimated high, low, and most likely bids for each competitor as follows:

Bid Estimates	Competitor A	Competitor B
High	$135,000	$140,000
Most Likely	$110,000	$115,000
Low	$100,000	$105,000

If the HMO bids too high, one of the competitors is likely to win the contract. If it bids too low, the contract will not be sufficiently profitable even if the HMO does win it. Management wants to determine the amount to bid to maximize the expected profit. This situation is modeled in BID.xls, shown in the following figure:

	A	B	C	D	E
1					
2		Cost of Service Contract ($000's)		Competitive Bids	
3		$100		A	B
4				$110.00	$115.00
5		Bid To Provide Service		Profit	
6		$105		$5	

=IF(B6 < MIN(D4:E4),BID − COST,0)

Management is considering the following bids: $100,000, $105,000, $110,000, $115,000, and $120,000.

a. Use parameterized simulation to determine which of these maximizes the expected profit. *Hint:* Use **gen_Triang** to simulate your competitors' bids.

b. Suppose management was also uncertain about the cost of fulfilling the contract. The costs are estimated to be normally distributed with a mean of $100,000 and a standard deviation of $20,000. How would this influence the amount management would want to bid?

Stock Options: Turning Uncertainty to Advantage

The field of financial engineering has developed numerous techniques for managing and actually exploiting uncertainty. Suppose for example you had reason to believe that because of a possible merger, a particular stock might increase dramatically in value over the next few weeks. On the other hand, if the merger fell through, the stock could also go down dramatically. If you purchase the stock, you have the potential to either make or lose a lot of money. Suppose that you cannot tolerate the risk of such a large loss. Then you can purchase what is known as a *Call Option* on the stock. This provides you with the right but not the obligation to buy the stock at a given price at a future date. This way, if the stock value increases, you can profit by buying it at a low price. If the stock value decreases, you are only out the cost of the option. Although there are many types of options, the most basic options are described here. For a clear explanation of options, see Hull (1991) or Luenberger (1997).

Basic options include the following:

■ The *American Call Option* provides the right but not the obligation to *purchase* a particular stock at a particular price (the strike price), on or before a particular date (the expiration date).

■ The *European Call Option* differs from the American Call in that it can be exercised *only* on the expiration date.

■ The *American Put Option* provides the right but not the obligation to *sell* the stock to someone for the strike price on or before a particular date.

■ The *European Put Option* differs from the American Put in that it can be exercised *only* on the expiration date.

To gain insight into how options behave, open the file OPTION.xls. Make sure SIM.xla is loaded first. This is a simplified model of a 12-week European Call option with a strike price of $21 for a stock that is selling for $20 today.

Note: Cell B10 might contain *#NAME?,* which means that the random number generation formula has not yet been recognized by the worksheet. Edit the formula by clicking in the formula bar (shown in the following figure) then clicking on the check mark. The *gen_Normal* function should now work in cell B10, then it can be copied from B10 through B20. Save the file now, and you won't have to bother with this again.

=B9*EXP(gen_Normal(WK_Rate-(WK_Sigma^2)/2,WK_Sigma))

Stock price movement is often modeled as a *random walk*, that is a set of random steps where the mean of each step is based on the last step. In this model, the current price of $20 is entered in cell A6 and repeated in B9. The price in each subsequent period is determined by multiplying the price in the previous period by a random growth rate. If this growth rate is greater than 1, the stock price goes up. If it is less than 1, the price goes down.

You don't have to understand the precise nature of this random process to gain insight into the qualitative behavior of call options. For those interested, however, the distribution of growth factors is expressed as the number *e* raised to a normally distributed random variable. Because the log of such a variable is normal, it is known as a *lognormal random variable*. See Hull (1991) or Luenberger (1997) for more details.

The value of the option at the expiration date (12 weeks out) is determined as follows: If the stock price in week 12 (P_{12}) is higher than the strike price S, the option is said to be *in the money*. Then you can buy it at S and immediately sell it on the market for P_{12}, pocketing the difference, P_{12}–S. If P_{12} is less than or equal to S, there is no point in exercising the option, and it is worth zero. This is expressed as the maximum of P_{12}–S and 0 in cell H6.

However, the value of the option today must reflect the fact that a dollar in 12 weeks is not worth as much as a dollar today. This is known as the *net present value (NPV)* of the amount in cell H6. Suppose $1 one year from now were worth 5% less than $1 today; that is, the annual rate is 5%. The net present value of $1 in t years for annual rate r can be shown to be e^{-rt}. This has been calculated for the 12 weeks of the option in cell I6.

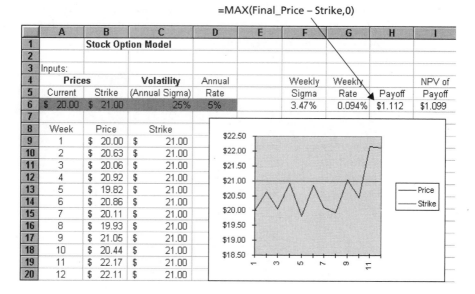

=MAX(Final_Price – Strike,0)

	A	B	C	D	E	F	G	H	I
1		Stock Option Model							
2									
3	Inputs:								
4		Prices		Volatility	Annual		Weekly	Weekly		NPV of
5		Current	Strike	(Annual Sigma)	Rate		Sigma	Rate	Payoff	Payoff
6	$ 20.00	$ 21.00	25%	5%		3.47%	0.094%	$1.112	$1.099
7									
8	Week	Price	Strike						
9	1	$ 20.00	$ 21.00						
10	2	$ 20.63	$ 21.00						
11	3	$ 20.06	$ 21.00						
12	4	$ 20.92	$ 21.00						
13	5	$ 19.82	$ 21.00						
14	6	$ 20.86	$ 21.00						
15	7	$ 20.11	$ 21.00						
16	8	$ 19.93	$ 21.00						
17	9	$ 21.05	$ 21.00						
18	10	$ 20.44	$ 21.00						
19	11	$ 22.17	$ 21.00						
20	12	$ 22.11	$ 21.00						

Press the calculate key a few times and observe the graph of the stock price over time and the value of cells H6 and I6.

How Are Options Priced?

Options trade for roughly their expected net present value. That is the average value of cell I6.

EXERCISE 3.10 **Option Pricing**

a. Run a simulation with 100 trials to estimate the expected NPV of the option.

b. What percent of the time is it in the money? *Hint:* Create an indicator output cell, as discussed in the last section, that equals 1 if the option ends up in the money and zero otherwise. The average value of the indicator is just the percentage of the time the option expires in the money.

The Increase of Option Prices with Uncertainty: Implied Volatility

Another use of parameterized simulation is to estimate the effect of changes in the uncertainty of the inputs. In this case, we will see what effect the stock's *volatility,* a measure of the uncertainty of its future price contained in cell C6, has on the value of the option. Try replacing the volatility with 0 and then 50%. For each value, press the calculate key a few times to see how the volatility effects the graph's behavior.

Next, run a parameterized simulation of cell I6 with values for Sigma equal to .10, .15, .20, .25, and .30. The associated graph should appear as shown in the following figure.

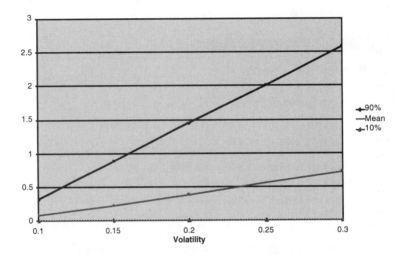

The vertical axis represents the expected NPV of the option, which should be equal to its price. The center line of the graph indicates that the value of the option increases with the volatility of the underlying stock. It is often useful for investors to know this volatility. Assuming that the market in options is efficient, we can look up the price of an option in the newspaper and use an equivalent of the previous graph to determine the *implied volatility* of the stock. In this case, for example, if the price of the option were $0.50, it would imply that the stock's volatility was approximately 25%.

Uncertainty Over Time

It is instructive to observe how the uncertainty of a stock's price increases as you try to predict further and further into the future. We will use the series graph to demonstrate this as follows. As output cells, select the stock price at time 1, 3, 5, 7, and 9 weeks. Then run 500 iterations. When the simulation is complete, select all outputs for inclusion in common graphs and click the **Series graph** button. The series graph (shown in the following figure) has the same form as the parameterized graph, but ranges over the five output cells. The 5th and 95th percentile curves clearly show that the uncertainty in price increases over time, but at a decreasing rate. In theory, the shape of these percentiles should follow the curve of a square root function.

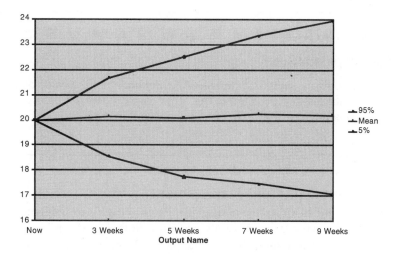

Uncertain Numbers That Are Related to Each Other: Statistical Dependence

The concept of statistical dependence can be explained in terms of the person who brings a bomb whenever he or she flies because the chance of two bombs on a plane is negligible. The fallacy here is that the chance of some other nut bringing a bomb might not be influenced by bringing your own.

Statistical dependence can be subtle and non-intuitive. For example, if you do manage to get your bomb on board the plane, that implies that security is lax. So you have actually *increased* the chance of another bomb on board!

Ignoring the effects of statistical independence or dependence can have serious consequences, and it is important to take these concepts into account when building simulation models.

Resampling Multivariate Data

In INVNTORY.xls we used *gen_Resample* to generate random inputs from a single column of past data. The next example involves two columns of statistically dependent data. In this situation, when we select a number at random from the first column, we must pick the adjacent one in the second column to preserve the statistical dependence. Instead of using *gen_Resample*, this time we will use *gen_ResampleSync* to keep the columns synchronized.

■ **FUNDAMENTALS 3-4** ■ ■ ■ ■ ■ ■ ■ ■ ■ ■ ■ ■ ■

Statistical Dependence

Two random variables are said to be *statistically independent* if the value of one is of no relevance in determining the value of the other. Two random variables are said to be *statistically dependent* if the value of one is relevant in determining the value of the other.

An Example of Yield Management

On commercial aircraft crossing the Pacific, high ground temperature at take off and strong head winds en route both significantly diminish the payload. High temperatures reduce payload because hot air is less dense than cold air and thus there is both less to hold up the wings and less to feed the engines. Strong head winds make the trip take longer, so more fuel must be carried instead of paying passengers. Tables accounting for runway length, temperature, and head winds are used to determine the payload shortly before takeoff. Unfortunately, an airline can't wait until shortly before takeoff to sell tickets for the flight. Therefore, a problem arises in deciding how many seats to sell given the uncertainties of the weather.

In the hypothetical example that follows, seats on a large aircraft can be sold for $2,000 each. If the number sold exceeds the payload, however, there are severe penalties for overbooking as follows: For the first 10 seats overbooked, it is usually possible to re-book the passengers on other airlines. By the time all the paperwork is done, however, this costs an additional $1,000 beyond the lost revenues. If more than 10 seats have been overbooked, things are much worse. In general, it is not possible to find alternate flights for more than 10 people. Not only are there now hotel and other expenses, but the airline also has a group of angry customers on its hands. Management has assessed the cost of both direct expense and goodwill at $10,000 per overbooked passenger beyond 10 passengers.

PAYLOAD.xls models this situation.

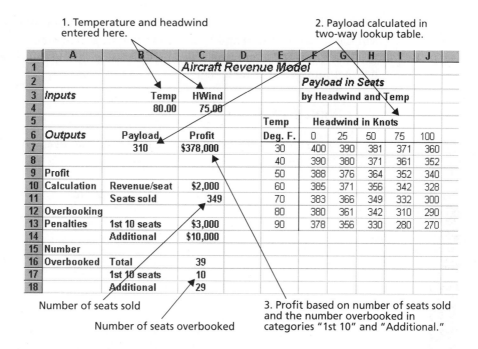

The formula in cell B7 calculates the payload for given values of temperature (B4) and head wind (C4). This requires looking up the temperature and head wind in the table. The formula is

=VLOOKUP(B4,$E$7:$J$13,LOOKUP(C4,$F$6:$J$6,$P$2:$T$2))

Hypothetical weather data for the air route in question is contained in the Weather Data sheet as shown in the following figure. The average temperature and head wind are calculated at the top of each column.

	B	C	D
1		Temp	H-Wind
2	Averages	70.5095	53.9822
3			
4		62.71	41.22
5		76.24	58.29
6		75.25	66.6

Experiment with the model by plugging various values for temperature and head wind into cells B4 and C4 of the payload sheet and observing the changes in payload and profit.

We will compare four approaches in estimating the profit. First, we will use a point estimate based on the average temperature and head wind. (By now, you should be suspicious of this approach.) Then, we will model temperature and head wind as independent random inputs. Next, we will model temperature and head wind including their statistical correlation. Finally, we will perform a parameterized simulation to determine the optimal number of seats to sell.

STEPS: ## USING A POINT ESTIMATE

To use a point estimate, link the average temperature and head wind to cells B4 and C4 as follows:

1 With the cursor in cell B4 of the Payload sheet, press the " = " key to start a formula.

2 Click on the **Weather Data** tab.

3 Click on cell C2 (average temperature) and press **Enter**.

4 Cell B4 of the Payload sheet now contains the formula " = 'Weather Data'!C2", which yields the average temperature. Copy this to cell C4 for the average head wind.

The results show that the payload under average temperature and wind conditions is 349. If 349 seats are sold and these average conditions occur, then revenue will be $698,000.

STEPS: ## SIMULATING TEMPERATURE AND HEAD WIND AS INDEPENDENT RANDOM INPUTS

1 We will replace the average temperature and head wind with random samples from the data. Click on the **Weather Data** tab.

2 Replace the *Average* formulas in cells C2 and D2 with *gen_Resample* formulas using the temperature and head wind data as input. *Note:* To paste in a new function from the function wizard, you must first delete the existing formula. The *gen_Resample* function has the effect of drawing a temperature and head wind at random from past data independently. Thus any relationship between temperature and head wind will be lost.

3 Select *Payload* and *Profit* as output cells and run a few hundred trials.

The results should be close to those shown below. Note that the average payload is higher than 349 (the payload under average weather conditions), but the average profit is lower than $698,000. The minimum profit in this run was only $78,000. Also, profit will be nearly $680,000, or greater, 85% of the time.

Output Name	Payload	Profit
Average	355.48	665388
Std Dev	19.1373	91038.7
Std Err	0.85585	4071.37
Max	390	698000
Min	280	78000
Percentiles		
5%	310	378000
10%	330	578000
15%	342	677000

STEPS: **SIMULATING TEMPERATURE AND HEAD WIND AS DEPENDENT RANDOM INPUTS**

Is there a relationship between temperature and head wind for the data in question? An XY (scatter) plot of the columns on the weather data sheet can be easily created with the Excel Chart Wizard. The following figure shows a strong relationship in which high temperatures tend to go hand in hand with strong head winds. As will be discussed later, this displays a *positive correlation* between the variables.

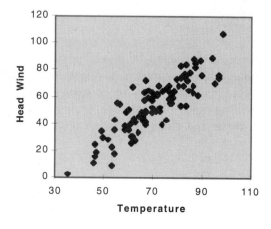

Now simulate the effects of the positive correlation between temperature and head wind by following these steps:

1

Replace both the *gen_Resample* formulas in the **Weather Data** sheet with the *gen_ResampleSync* formula, which is also found in the statistical category of the Function Wizard. This pulls a temperature and a head wind at random from past data in tandem. Thus, the hand-in-hand relationship between these two inputs will be preserved.

2

Again select Payload and Profit as output cells and run a few hundred trials.

The average payload should not have changed too much from the previous run. Average profit on the other hand has dropped by about $30,000, more than 5%. Also, at least one trial actually had negative profit.

Now profit will be only about $380,000 or greater 85% of the time. Or equivalently, 15% of the time, profit will be less than about $380,000, much lower than before. Note that all three percentiles shown for payload and profit are the same, because the cumulative distribution is very flat in this region.

Output Name	Payload	Profit
Average	351.198	627502
Std Dev	26.4537	161214
Std Err	1.18305	7209.72
Max	400	698000
Min	270	-22000
Percentiles		
5%	310	378000
10%	310	378000
15%	310	378000

Why is profit so dramatically affected by taking positive correlation into account? Now, when one thing goes wrong, say high temperature, the other thing (high head wind) is more likely to go wrong. Had these two effects been negatively correlated, that is, high temperatures implied low head winds, and vice versa, the effect on profit would have been just the opposite.

EXERCISE
3.11 **Determining the Optimal Number of Seats to Sell**

Run a parameterized simulation to compare the results of selling 320, 330, 340, 350, and 360 seats.

a. How is average profit affected by number of seats sold?

b. How is the 15% value at risk affected?

The Language of Statistical Dependence

We were able to model the dependence between head wind and temperature in the previous example by resampling past data. In general, however, data might not be available for resampling, and you might have to explicitly describe the statistical dependence between random variables.

The simplest sort of statistical dependence involves an approximately straight line relation between two or more random variables. Consider the variables x and y whose scatterplot is shown in the following figure. As you can see, a high value of x increases the chance of a higher value of y and vice versa.

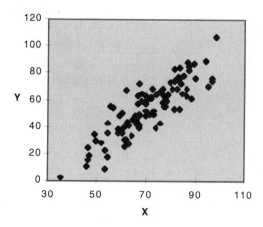

The formula in Fundamentals Box 3-5 does not provide much intuition. However, a geometrical interpretation of covariance might help. Imagine a rectangle with one corner at the point $\bar{x}$, $\bar{y}$ and another at some point x_i, y_i. Its area (width times height) is $(x_i - \bar{x})(y_i - \bar{y})$ as shown in the left part of the following figure.

■ **FUNDAMENTALS 3-5** ■ ■ ■ ■ ■ ■ ■ ■ ■ ■ ■ ■ ■

Covariance

The degree to which x and y go up and down together is quantified by a calculation known as the ***covariance*** or σ_{xy}. This is defined as

$$\sigma_{xy} = \frac{1}{n} \sum_{i=1}^{n} (x_i - \bar{x})(y_i - \bar{y})$$

where n is the number of data points and $\bar{x}$ and $\bar{y}$ denote the average values of x and y respectively. The covariance of two arrays of historical data in Excel can be found using the COVAR(Array1,Array2) formula.

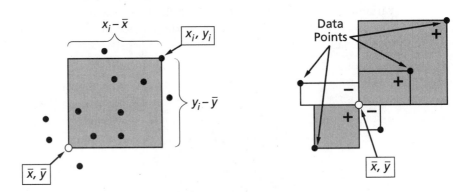

But $(x_i - \bar{x})(y_i - \bar{y})$ is just the term in the definition of the covariance. With this in mind, the covariance can be seen to be the average area of all rectangles starting at point $\bar{x}$, $\bar{y}$ and ending on a data point. Of course, depending on the signs of $(x_i - \bar{x})$ and $(y_i - \bar{y})$, the areas will be either positive or negative and can cancel out as shown in the right side of the previous figure. Thus, if the data points lie roughly on a line running between southwest and northeast, the covariance is positive. On the other hand, if they lie roughly on a line running between northwest and southeast, the covariance is negative.

Although nonzero covariance always implies statistical dependence, zero covariance does not always imply statistical independence. For example, the following scatterplot displays an example of random variables that are clearly dependent but have nearly zero covariance:

■ FUNDAMENTALS 3-6 ■ ■ ■ ■ ■ ■ ■ ■ ■ ■ ■ ■ ■

Correlation

The **correlation, R,** is a measure of the power of x in predicting values of y. It is defined as

$$R = \frac{\sigma_{xy}}{\sigma_x \sigma_y}$$

where σ_{xy} is the covariance, and σ_x and σ_y are the standard deviations of x and y respectively. The correlation can take on any value between -1 and $+1$. $R = +1$ means that y can be perfectly predicted when x is known and increases when x increases. $R = 0$ means that y does not change in a predictable linear manner with x. $R = -1$ means that y can be perfectly predicted when x is known, but decreases when x increases.

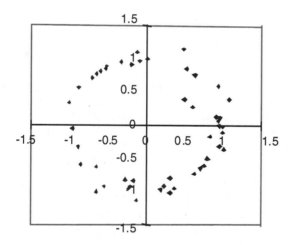

EXERCISE 3.12 **The Correlation of the Hypothetical Weather Data**

Use the CORREL function within Excel to find the correlation between temperature and head wind on the weather data sheet of PAYLOAD.xls.

The Connection with Linear Regression

A linear regression on the previous data involves fitting a straight line to the points as shown in the following figure.

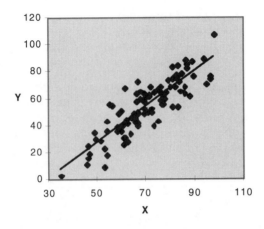

That is, y is expressed as $ax + b$. The numbers a and b themselves can be expressed as the covariance σ_{xy}, as shown in the following equations:

$$\text{The slope of the line:} \quad a = \frac{\sigma_{xy}}{\sigma_x^2}$$

$$\text{The y-intercept:} \quad b = \bar{y} - a\bar{x}$$

The predictive power of a regression is usually expressed by a value known as R^2, which is the square of the correlation defined in Fundamentals Box 3-6.

Reviewing Portfolios of Related Investments

The concept of related random variables is at the heart of the theory of investment portfolios and risk management. In an earlier example we compared pure investments in a domestic and foreign fund with a diversified investment split between both funds. Each fund by itself had an expected return of 10% and a standard deviation of 10%. When the investment was split between these two statistically independent funds, the expected return remained the same, but the degree of uncertainty as measured by the standard deviation dropped to roughly 7%. This was a result of straight diversification.

We will now explore what happens when statistically dependent funds are combined. The main result can be stated as described in Fundamentals Box 3-7.

Two new funds will be added to the earlier example.

■ FUNDAMENTALS 3-7 ■ ■ ■ ■ ■ ■ ■ ■ ■ ■ ■ ■ ■

Correlated Investments

When *positively* correlated funds are combined, the effects of diversification are **re-duced**. When *negatively* correlated funds are combined, the effects of diversification are **increased**.

The International Fund. The returns of this fund, like the domestic and foreign funds are normally distributed with a mean of 10% and standard deviation of 10%. However, this fund is *not* independent of the foreign fund. The companies represented by the international and foreign fund are quite similar in nature. Therefore, if one of these funds does well, the other is also likely to do well. Similarly, if one drops in value, the other is likely to drop as well. Thus, there is a positive covariance between these two funds. Suppose it is estimated to be .5%.

The Hedge Fund. The hedge fund, like the other funds, has returns that are normally distributed with a mean of 10% and standard deviation of 10%. However, this fund is *not* independent of the domestic fund. Historically, the investments composing the hedge fund have tended to move in the opposite direction from the domestic fund. Thus, when the domestic goes up, the hedge tends to go down, and vice versa. Therefore, there is a negative covariance between these two funds. Suppose it is estimated to be −.5%.

The file FUNDS.xls contains the means of each fund along with the covariance matrix relating all four funds.

	A	B	C	D	E	F	G	H	I	J
1		FUNDS.XLS								
2										
3										
4		**Funds**	**Returns**	**Means**			**Covariance Matrix**			
5							Domestic	Hedge	Foreign	International
6		Domestic	12.20%	10%		Domestic	0.010			
7		Hedge	-1.96%	10%		Hedge	-0.005	0.010		
8		Foreign	28.95%	10%		Foreign	0.000	0.000	0.010	
9		International	20.29%	10%		International	0.000	0.000	0.005	0.010

When using this model, keep the following in mind:

■ The covariance, σ_{xy}, of x and y always equals σ_{yx}, so you only have to fill out the diagonal and lower half of the matrix.

■ The diagonal values of .010 are the variances of the funds. Remember that the standard deviations are the square roots of these numbers, or .1.

■ The multivariate normal random variables are generated through a method known as Cholesky Factorization. It is not necessary to understand the details of this process to use the simulation. See Bratley, Fox, and Schrage (1987) and Law and Kelton (1991) for a more thorough explanation of this topic.

Note: Cell M3 might contain *#NAME?*, which means that the random number generation formula has not yet been recognized by the worksheet. Edit the formula by clicking in the formula bar (shown in the following figure), then clicking on the checkmark. The *gen_Normal* function should now work in cell M3, then it can be copied in N3 through P3. Save the file now, and you won't have to bother with this again.

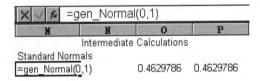

Experimenting with Different Portfolios

Simulating the Individual Funds. Start by running a simulation with one output cell for each of the funds. Run a few hundred trials, and you should find that the distributions of the four funds are virtually indistinguishable. This can be seen clearly by using the common graph option.

Comparing Portfolios. Next we will create three portfolios: Domestic and hedge, domestic and foreign, and foreign and international. Place formulas in FUNDS.xls to compute the returns of each pair of funds. For example, the formula for the domestic and hedge portfolio would be .5 * C6 + .5 * C7 because we are now splitting our investment between these two funds. These cells, which you should label D + H, D + F, and F + I, will be your next simulation's output cells. The results should appear as shown in the following figure:

Output Name	D+H	D+F	F+I
Average	0.0996	0.0998	0.1009
Std Dev	0.0496	0.0702	0.0874
Std Err	0.0011	0.0016	0.0020
Max	0.2567	0.3198	0.4320
Min	-0.0588	-0.1700	-0.2067
Percentiles			
5%	0.0173	-0.0184	-0.0432
10%	0.0348	0.0106	-0.0086
15%	0.0491	0.0265	0.0126
20%	0.0589	0.0409	0.0302
25%	0.0673	0.0523	0.0425
30%	0.0742	0.0623	0.0562
35%	0.0803	0.0736	0.0692
40%	0.0874	0.0831	0.0790
45%	0.0934	0.0916	0.0893
50%	0.0996	0.1008	0.1017

Simulation Statistics. The simulation statistics show that although all three portfolios have the same return on average, the value at risk is lowest for the portfolio comprising negatively correlated domestic and hedge funds, highest for the positively correlated foreign and international funds, and in between for the uncorrelated domestic and foreign funds.

■ The average returns are the same.

■ Standard deviation reflects degree of uncertainty. Remember, because the returns are normal, 95% of them will lie between plus and minus two standard deviations of the average.

■ Percentiles allow you to calculate the value at risk. For example, if $100,000 were invested, then 10% of the time the D + H portfolio will make less than $3,480, D + F will make less than $1,060, and F + I will lose more than $860!

The Common Histogram. The following histogram clearly shows the relative difference in the shapes of the distributions of the three investments. However, the numbers on horizontal axis are not accurate when the common histogram is used with a small number of bins, as in this case. The common histogram should be used for qualitative results only. For numerical results, use the common cumulative graph.

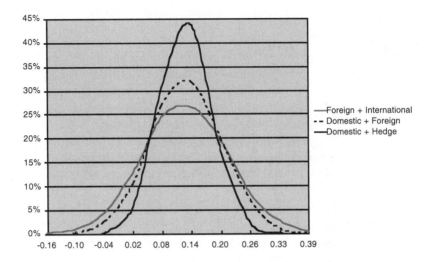

The Common Cumulative Graph. By looking at the previous common histogram, you should be able to tell which line corresponds to each of the portfolios even though they are not labeled in the following graph:

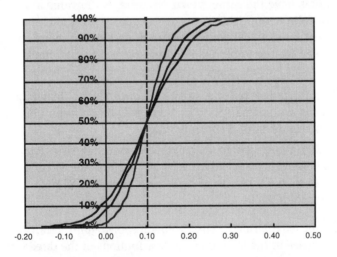

The General Problem of Simulating Correlated Random Variables

As we have seen, *gen_ResampleSync* can generate correlated random variables from past data regardless of their distribution.

In general, if you know the means, variances, and covariances of a set of normal random variables, they can be generated in a manner similar to the funds example earlier. The file MVNORMAL.xls can be used to generate as many as 30 such random variables, known as multivariate normal random variables. The file uses *gen_Normal* and is self documented.

Both the @RISK and Crystal Ball programs offer further facilities that allow you to generate correlated random variables from arbitrary distributions using a method known as *rank order correlation*.

How Many Trials Are Enough? Convergence

If you go back to INVNTORY.xls and repeat the simulation several times for 50 trials with a seed of 0, you will get several different estimates for the average cost. This lack of consistency is because of the inherent randomness of Monte Carlo simulation. Run 50 trials of the INVNTORY model. Click on the **View Trials** button of the **Statistics** sheet, then select the **Trials** tab of the results workbook. Finally, click on the **Rate of Convergence** button to generate the convergence graph shown in the following figure. *Warning:* This process can take a long time if you have run a large number of trials.

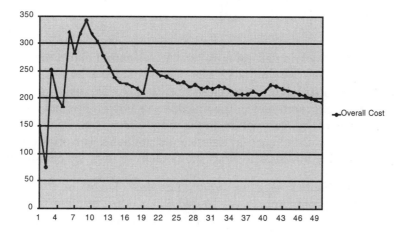

This graph displays the cumulative average of the 50 trials. Note that in this case, after two trials the average overall cost was less than 100. The cost of the third trial must have been a whopper to drag the average up to more than 250. The simulation is said to have *converged* when this graph becomes flat. This has not yet occurred by 50 trials in this example.

Although the convergence graph provides insight into this process, in practice it can take too much time to generate for a large number of trials. Fortunately, there is another way to estimate the accuracy of the simulation using a number known as the *standard error*.

The Standard Error. As we have noted, the average of 50 trials of overall cost is a random variable in its own right. How is this average distributed? According to the Central Limit Theorem, it must be approximately normal. The standard error estimates the standard deviation of the distribution of the average of 50 trials of overall cost. Thus, we can be 95% confident that the true average is 223 ± 2x40 (see the following table). The greater the number of trials performed, the smaller the standard error will be, but there are diminishing returns. The standard error is, in fact, the standard deviation divided by the square root of t where t is the number of trials. Thus, to get twice the accuracy requires four times as many trials. To get three times the accuracy requires nine times as many trials, and so on.

Output Name	Overall Cost
Average	223.048
Std Dev	284.655
Std Err	40.2562
Max	1306.97
Min	0

Standard error ⟶ Std Err

Note: The standard deviation of 284.655, displayed above the Standard error, refers to the distribution of overall cost (not the average of 50 trials). Because the distribution of overall cost is distinctly not normal (see the histogram of overall cost in the inventory example), it is ***not*** true that 95% of the time overall cost will lie in the range 223 ± 2x285. The standard deviation is not a useful concept for such distributions. The probability of overall cost taking on various values should be read from the cumulative graph.

What Is Your Computer Doing Tonight? There are currently about 100,000,000 computers in the United States. Most of these are idle at least ten hours per day for a total of at least 1 billion wasted computer hours. From the perspective of someone in 1970, when a computer hour cost roughly $1,000, we are squandering the Gross National Product every 24 hours measured in computer power, so feel free to run thousands of trials!

Sensitivity Analysis: The Big Picture

In exploring the effects of uncertainty, it is important to understand the manner in which one uncertainty affects other uncertainties.

Steps: **Exploring Demand versus Overall Cost**

We will explore the relationship between demand and overall cost in the inventory example worked previously.

1

Return to the simulation of INVNTORY.xls. If you have left Excel, you must first open SIM.xla, followed by INVNTORY.xls. If you did not save your earlier changes, you must re-specify the random inputs for demand and freight cost. For purposes of this experiment, stock 5 units of inventory even though we now know this is not optimal.

2

This time specify *Demand* as the first output and *Overall Cost* as the second output. Run 50 trials.

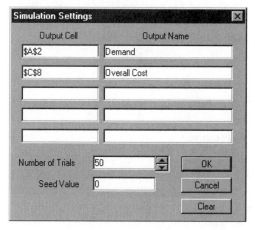

3

When the simulation is complete, click on the **View Trials** button on the **Statistics** sheet. The trials should appear as shown below:

	A	B
1	Demand	Overall Cos
2	3	100
3	2	150
4	2	150
5	5	0
6	7	244.4414
7	7	434.5016
8	7	368.9925
9	5	0
10	5	0
11	6	146.977
12	4	50
13	3	100
14	3	100

4

Select the entire range of trials (A2:B51) and create an XY scatterplot (refer to the Excel Help system for details).

The resulting graph shows how overall cost (on the vertical axis) varies with demand (on the horizontal axis). It is clear that cost only equals 0 when demand is exactly 5, and that cost increases for both higher and lower values of demand. The vertical lines above demand = 6 and 8 reflect the various rates of air freight incurred at those demands during the 50 trials.

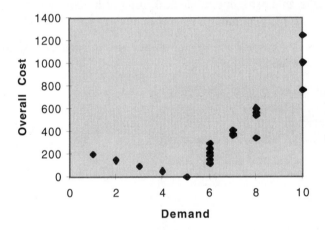

Once you have seen this graph, it is difficult to hold on to the illusion that average overall cost is zero. This picture also helps explain the concept of *linear model*. Had the model been linear, all the points on the scatter plot would have been clustered about a single straight line. In this case, they are clustered about a "V" shaped region.

Conclusion

Uncertain numbers are common in every aspect of business. Traditionally, analytical solutions to most such problems were so difficult that managers plugged in "best guesses" for the inputs and hoped for reasonable outputs. As we have seen, this often leads to errors. Today's micro computers allow Monte Carlo simulation to be applied to many of these problems in the managerial vernacular of the spreadsheet, so that even the boss can understand the results.

4

Uncertainties That Evolve Over Time

For tribal man space was the uncontrollable mystery.
For technological man it is time that occupies the same role.

MARSHALL MCLUHAN, CANADIAN COMMUNICATIONS THEORIST

As we have seen, Monte Carlo simulation investigates the possible outcomes of a single event by generating numerous possible inputs at random and recording the distribution of outputs. This idea can be extended to systems that evolve over time subject to a continual barrage of uncertain inputs.

- Municipal planners must estimate the disruption to traffic flow caused by toll booths or construction projects.

- Engineers must predict the performance of telecommunications networks given uncertain levels of equipment failure and message traffic.

- The Federal Aviation Agency must implement air traffic control systems that prevent excessive congestion and lengthy holding patterns given uncertain aircraft arrival.

- Marketing managers must estimate the manner in which their market share will evolve over time.

Discrete-event simulation and Markov chains are two approaches to modeling systems that evolve over time.

OVERVIEW

Introduction

This section contains a short introduction to discrete-event simulation and instructions for installing and running QUEUE.xla and Q_NET.xla, which model simple queues and queuing networks in Excel.

Simulation Through Time: Discrete-Event Simulation

This section introduces the concept of discrete-event simulation. First, the spread of a forest fire is modeled as a fixed-time-increment simulation. Then queues (waiting lines) and queuing networks are modeled as event incremented simulations. Examples include cars waiting at a toll booth, customers waiting for service at a bank, and air traffic control.

Markov Chains

Certain evolving systems can be modeled effectively as Markov chains, which are also discussed in this chapter and implemented in MARKOV.xls.

Introduction

Systems That Evolve Over Time

Many systems involve the interactions of discrete random events such as cars arriving at a toll booth or customers showing up at a bank. These systems evolve over time, with traffic jams or lines at the tellers arising and then dissipating. Although large-scale discrete-event simulation is beyond the capability of spreadsheets, a spreadsheet is sufficient to illuminate some important aspects of this technique. Simple queues and interconnected queuing networks can be simulated with QUEUE.xla and Q_NET.xla, add-ins for modeling simple queues and small queuing networks, respectively. Markov chains are a powerful way to model evolving populations. These can be populations of customers moving between products, patients moving between states of health, or equipment moving between various states of repair or disrepair. MARKOV.xls is a scalable worksheet used to model several examples.

QUEUE.xla and Q_NET.xla

QUEUE.xla is used with QUEUE.xls to model a simple queue. Q_NET.xla is used with Q_NET.xls to model a queuing network. *QUEUE.xla and Q_NET.xla should not both be loaded at the same time.* Both QUEUE.xla and Q_NET.xla require Excel 5.0 or higher.

Running QUEUE.xla and Q_NET.xla.   Launch Excel and open QUEUE.xla and QUEUE.xls or Q_NET.xla and Q_NET.xls from the File menu. QUEUE.xls and Q_NET.xls can be modified and saved under any desired file name. *Important:* Make sure your worksheet's calculation mode is set to automatic under **Tools Options** before running these add-ins.

Auto Load Option.   If you want QUEUE.xla or Q_NET.xla to load every time you launch Excel

1. Select **Add-ins** from the **Tools** menu in Excel.

2. Select QUEUE.xla or Q_NET.xla from the list of add-ins and click **OK**. You can later go back and deselect either of them from the Add-in menu to prevent Excel from loading them automatically. Do not load them both at once as they will not run correctly.

Simulation Through Time: Discrete-Event Simulation

It is quite simple to predict the behavior of a single automobile arriving at a traffic light on an empty road, but very difficult to predict the overall traffic flow in a large city at rush hour. By creating a computer model of a large number of cars sharing the same roads, however, we can learn about the dynamics of the larger system. Simulation such as this involves a sequence of discrete random events through time and is known as **discrete-event simulation**. See Law and Kelton (1991) for a thorough treatment of this subject.

Although spreadsheets were not designed for discrete-event simulation, a technique we refer to as the *paste special method* can be used to model a wide variety of situations. Imagine a workbook with two sheets, one called **NOW** and the other called **NEXT TIME**. The **NOW** sheet contains a model of the world at the current time and contains numbers only, no formulas. The **NEXT TIME** sheet contains only formulas, describing how the current state of the world will change by the next time increment. The following example shows a fixed increment simulation of a clock that ticks to a new minute between **NOW** and **NEXT TIME**. Note that the time in **NEXT TIME** is the time in **NOW** plus 1.

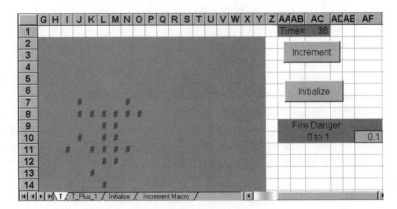

The iterative step to make this clock tick is to copy the contents of **NEXT TIME**, and paste the values only (not formulas) into **NOW** using the **Edit Paste Special Values** command. At this point, **NEXT TIME** will display the state of the world at the following next time, or 3 in this case.

A Fixed Time Incremented Simulation of a Forest Fire

The file FIRE.xls contains a fixed-time-increment simulation of a forest fire based on the general approach just described. This file uses a macro to automate the **Paste Special** step. *Important:* Make sure your worksheet's calculation mode is set to automatic under **Tools Options** before attempting to run this model.

The forest is modeled as a grid of squares, one-quarter mile per side. Each square can either contain fire (1), or contain no fire (0). The sheet has been formatted so that 0's appear as blanks and 1's appear as number signs (#). The fire spreads according to two rules:

1. If a square contains fire now, then it will contain fire next time.

2. If a square does not contain fire now, then the probability that it will contain fire next time is proportional to both the number of neighboring squares containing fire and the overall fire danger.

Retrieve FIRE.xls, shown in the following figure.

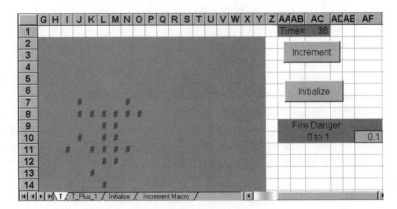

■ **FUNDAMENTALS 4-1** ■ ■ ■ ■ ■ ■ ■ ■ ■ ■ ■ ■

How Time Is Advanced in Discrete-Event Simulation

Time is generally advanced or *incremented* in one of the following two ways in discrete-event simulation:

- ■ *Fixed-Time Increments.* Time in the simulation advances minute by minute, hour by hour, or by some other fixed increment. Various events either occur or do not occur within each time increment, based on both the system's current state and random variables.

- ■ *Event-Incremented Time.* Time in the simulation advances to the next event of interest. The next event and its time of occurrence are based on both the system's current state and random variables. In practice, most discrete-event simulations are of this type.

There are four sheets in FIRE.xls. **T** displays the state of the forest at the current time and contains only numbers. The fire danger is entered in cell AF10 of this sheet. **T_Plus_1** displays the state of the forest one hour from now and contains formulas that impose the rules of fire spread. For example, the formula that defines the state of cell D3 in sheet **T_Plus_1** is

$$\text{=IF(T!D3=1,1,IF(Danger*SUM(T!C2:E4)/8>RAND(),1,0))}$$

The **Initialize** sheet contains the initial state of the forest. **Increment Macro** contains the Visual Basic code used to initialize and increment the simulation.

EXERCISE 4.1

Explaining the Formula for the Spread of Fire

a. Explain how the formula in **T_Plus_1** models the fire spreading rules.

b. How would you model a wind blowing from the west that made it more likely for the fire to spread to the east?

Now experiment with the model:

c. Click **Initialize**.

d. Type 1 into squares where fire has started.

e. Click **Increment** to simulate fire spread. The higher the fire danger, the faster the spread.

This same basic approach could be extended to model the following:

- The movement of some new popular product into a market
- The spread of a disease through a population
- The progress of a military engagement

Queuing Models

A process often modeled with discrete-event simulation is a queue of people, jobs, or machines waiting for some sort of service. Consider for example, the arrivals of cars at an automated toll booth on a highway. The number of such arrivals can often be modeled by a *Poisson* distribution as discussed later. Suppose in this case that historical data indicates that the number of cars arriving per minute is Poisson distributed with a mean of 3.67 and the maximum number of cars that can be serviced per minute is also Poisson distributed with a mean of 5.

Because the average number that can be served is higher than the average number of arrivals, we would not expect a tremendous traffic jam. But this doesn't mean there might not occasionally be some cars waiting in line. How many should we expect to be waiting, and how long might they wait on average? We will discuss this from a theoretical perspective, then run a time incremented simulation.

3.67 cars arrive every minute on average. Equivalently, the average time between cars is 0.273 minutes.

Up to 5 cars may be serviced per minute on average. Equivalently, the average time to service a car is 0.2 minutes.

There is extensive theory on the subject of queues, such as that provided by Hillier and Lieberman (1990). Here we cover only the most fundamental aspects of the theory (see Fundamentals Box 4-2).

EXERCISE 4.2 **The Average Number of Cars Waiting at a Toll Booth**

How many cars will be in line at the toll booth on average according to theory?

■ **FUNDAMENTALS 4-2** ■ ■ ■ ■ ■ ■ ■ ■ ■ ■ ■ ■ ■

M/M/1 Queues

- Simple queues like the one at the toll booth in which both arrival rate and maximum service rate are Poisson distributed are known as M/M/1 queues. Mathematicians have developed a good theoretical understanding of the behavior of these simple queues. The arrival and service rates of a queue are often denoted by λ (lambda) and μ (mu), respectively. The ratio λ/μ is known as the *utilization factor,* ρ (rho). In the current example, $\rho = 3.67/5 = 0.73$.

- The theoretical *average length* of an M/M/1 queue is given by this formula:

$$L_q = \rho^2/(1 - \rho).$$

  If the arrival rate exceeds the service rate, we would expect big trouble at the toll booth. But notice that according to the formula, the average queue length becomes infinite even if the arrival rate just equals the service rate, that is, $\rho = 1$.

- The *average waiting time* someone spends in line is given by this formula:

$$W_q = L_q/\lambda.$$

Classifying Queues

Queues come in all shapes and sizes. They are typically classified according to three properties:

- The distribution of arrivals
- The distribution of service times
- The number of parallel servers

The toll booth example is known as an M/M/1 queue because both the interarrival times and service times are exponentially distributed (see the following discussion of exponential distribution). This in turn implies that the amount of time you would expect to wait for a car to arrive at the toll booth is independent of how long you have waited without seeing a car. Such a process is known as memoryless or Markovian. That explains the two M's, one for the arrivals and one for the service times. The 1 indicates that there is a single server (the toll booth in this example). So, for example, a queue with distribution A of arrivals and distribution B of service times with N servers would be an A/B/N queue. The theory of queues covers many special cases beyond the M/M/1 queue. In complex circumstances, a queue with distribution A of arrivals and distribution B of service times with N servers would be an A/B/N queue. The theory of queues covers many special cases beyond the M/M/1 queue. In complex circumstances, however, the theory gets overwhelmed and discrete-event simulation can provide the best indication of how such a system will behave.

Fixed- versus Event-Incremented Time

As discussed earlier, a fixed-time-increment simulation models the *number* of events occurring *within a given time* increment. This is a *discrete* random variable (that is, 0, 1, 2, and so on), often Poisson distributed, as in the toll booth example. For a more thorough discussion of the Poisson distribution, see Law and Kelton (1991), or any book on probability or statistics.

An event-incremented simulation, on the other hand, models the *time between* events. This is a *continuous* random variable that is *exponentially* distributed if the number of events per time period is Poisson distributed. The relationship between Poisson and exponential distributions is described in Fundamentals Box 4-3.

Therefore a fixed-increment simulation of the toll booth would model the number of cars arriving per minute as a Poisson random variable with $\lambda = 3.67$. An event-incremented simulation of the toll booth models car interarrival time as an exponential random variable with $\alpha = 1/3.67 = .273$ minutes.

It is useful to compare the graphs of these two distributions. A Poisson distribution with an average arrival rate of 3.67 is shown on the left in the following figure. The corresponding exponential distribution with an average interarrival time of $1/3.67 = 0.272$ is on the right.

Poisson distribution average arrivals/minute, $\lambda = 3.67$

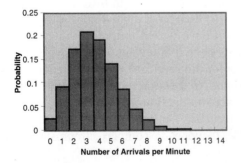

Exponential distribution, average time between arrivals in minutes, $\alpha = 0.272$

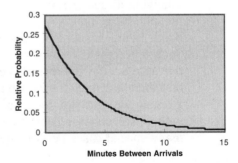

■ **FUNDAMENTALS 4-3** ■ ■ ■ ■ ■ ■ ■ ■ ■ ■ ■ ■

Relation Between Poisson and Exponential Distributions

If the number of events occurring in a fixed increment of time is a *Poisson* random variable with a mean of λ per time period, then the amount of time occurring between events is an *Exponential* random variable with a mean of $1/\lambda$ time units, and vice versa. $1/\lambda$ is often referred to as α (alpha) in this context.

STEPS: **SIMULATING AN EVENT INCREMENTED QUEUE**

To run an event incremented simulation of a queue, we will use QUEUE.xls. This file does not require SIM.xla but does require that we open QUEUE.xla. Proceed as follows:

1 Open QUEUE.xla. QUEUE.xla contains the programs that run the simulation using the paste special method introduced earlier. It adds a **Queue** menu to Excel when loaded.

2 Open QUEUE.xls. QUEUE.xls, shown below, contains the model of the queue. This file can be modified and saved under other file names.

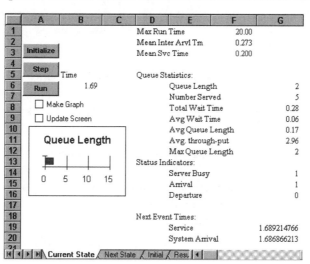

3 Specify parameters. Enter total time to simulate, mean interarrival time, and mean service time in cells F1:F3.

4

Initialize counters. Click on the **Initialize** button or choose **Initialize** from the **Queue** menu to set all counters to the initial state stored on the **Initial** tab of the workbook.

5

Single step the simulation. Click on the **Step** button, use the **Single Step** command, or press **Alt-S** to move the simulation to the next event.

6

Run the simulation. To run the simulation for a specified simulated time, enter the desired stopping time in cell F1, click the **Make Graph** and **Update Screen** boxes, then click on the **Run** button or choose **Run Simulation** from the **Queue** menu. Statistics for the run will appear on the **Current State** tab. A graph of the queue length over time will appear on the **Results** tab as shown below.

Queue Length over Time

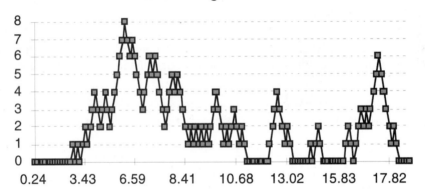

The graph will vary a great deal from run to run. Also, since we started the queue length at zero (not its average), it will generally take several events for the queue to reach more representative behavior. This is known as the *startup* or *transient effect*.

7

Quick run the simulation. **Quick Run** runs faster, but does not produce the graph. This is the model used by the **Run** button when the **Make Graph** box is not checked. Removing the check from the **Update Screen** box will also greatly enhance runtime. To halt the simulation while it is running, hold down the **Ctrl** and **Break** keys simultaneously.

8

Quit. This removes QUEUE.xla from memory and **Queue** from Excel's menu bar.

EXERCISE
4.3 **Simulating a Queue**

a.   Run a simulation of one hour of simulated time with a graph of the queue length.

b.   Reinitialize and perform this experiment for various lengths of time. Compare this simulated average with the theoretical average calculated in Exercise 4.2. You might find that it takes a very long time before the average queue length converges to its theoretical value.

Queuing Networks

It is rare that a queue exists in isolation as in the toll booth example. More often a process consists of a number of queues connected in some way. Such situations are known as queuing networks and can be modeled with Q_NET.xls.

Parallel Queues.   As an example, suppose the automated toll booth begins to have mechanical problems running at a service rate of 5 cars per minute. It is determined that the maximum rate at which it can consistently provide service is only half the original rate, or 2.5 cars per minute.

In an effort to provide the same level of service, the highway department contemplates putting in two toll lanes. Each lane will have a booth with a maximum service rate of 2.5 cars per minute, or average service time of 0.4 minutes. Assume that incoming cars choose a lane at random with equal probability. This situation is pictured below.

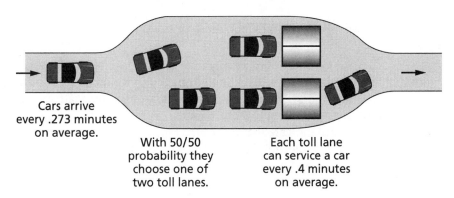

Cars arrive every .273 minutes on average.

With 50/50 probability they choose one of two toll lanes.

Each toll lane can service a car every .4 minutes on average.

Because each toll booth receives, on average, one-half the traffic of the single toll booth and can service one-half the number of cars per minute, we might expect the performance of this system to be similar to the single toll booth.

Q_NET.xls and Q_NET.xla. Q_NET.xls (with Q_NET.xla) works in the same general manner as QUEUE.xls (with QUEUE.xla), with a *current, next,* and *initial* sheet. Instead of a single column of queue statistics, however, there is one column for each of the two stations in the network.

A transition matrix controls the flow between the stations. In the example shown, a system arrival (Station 0) has a probability of 1/2 of going to station 1 or 2. Anything leaving station 1 or 2 has a 100% chance of going to the exit (station 3). New stations can be added or deleted as desired. The **Run** button is on the **Current** sheet, as in QUEUE.xls. The results sheet displays a graph of average throughput of the system over time.

Open Q_NET.xls and Q_NET.xla, shown in the following figure. The worksheet models a general queuing network. Its original configuration represents two parallel queues.

The **Transition Matrix** sheet of Q_NET.xls displays the average system inter-arrival time in cell H17 and average service times for the two queues in cells I17 and J17. This sheet also has a transition matrix that defines the flow of traffic through the network. For example, the values of 0.5 in cells I10 and J10 indicate that a car arriving at the system has a 50% probability of entering either toll lane. The value of 1.0 in cell K11 indicates that a car leaving toll booth 1 has a 100% chance of exiting the system. ***Note:*** The rows of this matrix must sum to 1. Probability check sum formulas appear in column M.

The commands for Q_NET are the same as those for QUEUE except for commands to add or delete stations from the network. Also, the graph produced by Q_NET is that of the average throughput of the system as a whole (the number served/total elapsed time), rather than the length of a single queue.

When adding or deleting stations you must edit both the transition matrix and expected arrival and service times. The rows of probabilities in the transition matrix must sum to 1, but other than that there are no restrictions. In fact, the probabilities in the matrix can be calculated as formulas that depend on the current state of the system. In this way, quite general queuing networks can be simulated.

EXERCISE 4.4

Simulating Parallel Queues

a. Run a simulation of 20 minutes without asking for the graph. Compare the results with Exercise 4.3. In particular, what are the average queue lengths and waiting times?

b. What is the theoretical value of ρ for each of the two parallel queues?

c. Based on this value of ρ, what is the theoretical average queue length at each of the toll booths?

d. What is the expected waiting time?

e. What would happen to overall system performance if N toll booths, each with 1/Nth of the original service rate, had been placed in parallel?

f. Repeat Exercise 4.2 and Exercise 4.3 for the case of two parallel toll booths, each of which can serve cars at the original time of .2 minutes.

If you successfully completed the last exercises, you should have discovered that the average performance of a single, high-service-rate queue is far superior to two parallel queues chosen at random by customers, where each queue has one-half of the original service rate. In reality, it is unlikely that customers would choose the queues at random. Instead, they would choose the shorter of the two queues.

EXERCISE 4.5

A More Realistic Simulation of Parallel Queues

Again model the double toll booth situation in which the cars' expected inter-arrival time is 0.273 minutes and each toll booth has an expected service time of .4 minutes. This time, however, the cars will choose the shorter of the two queues. Compare the results with those from Exercise 4.3. *Hint:* The probabilities in the transition matrix must now be formulas based on the current states of the queues. Make sure that the rows always sum to 1.

Serial Queues

Queues commonly feed into each other. The next exercise provides an example of a system of serial queues.

EXERCISE
4.6

Modeling an Assembly Line

In assembly, a component commonly runs through a sequence of machines, each of which performs a required step in the production process. In the system shown in the following figure, unfinished components enter station 1 at an average of 9 per minute. Stations 1 through 3 each can process the components at an average of 10 per minute whereupon manufacturing is completed.

a. Model this situation with Q_NET and run a 60-minute simulation with a graph of system throughput. You will need to add a third station, then fill in the transition matrix to correspond to the system shown in the following figure. Don't forget that the rows must sum to 1.

b. Suppose that station 3 also performs quality inspection. Suppose further that 10% of the products passing station 3 must be returned to station 1, and 10% to station 2. Model this situation and run a 60-minute simulation.

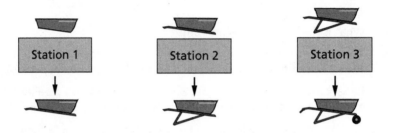

Multiple Queues, Multiple Servers

Another type of queuing system common in banks and airline ticket counters consists of more than one server, each with its own queue as shown in the following figure. This is similar to the two toll booths.

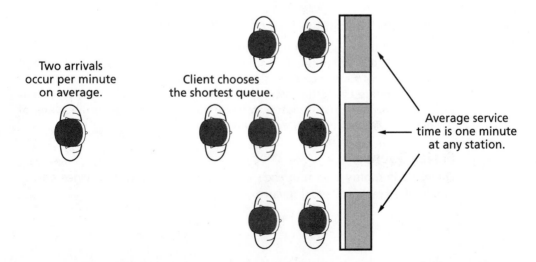

Two arrivals occur per minute on average.

Client chooses the shortest queue.

Average service time is one minute at any station.

Single Queue, Multiple Servers

A single queue can feed more than one server, as shown in the following figure.

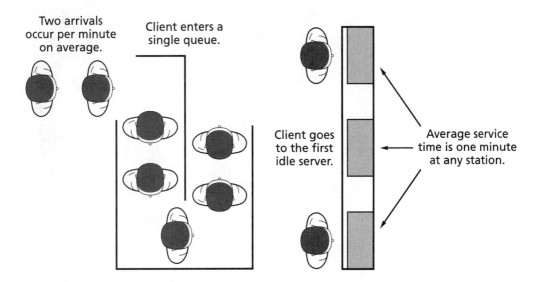

Two arrivals occur per minute on average.

Client enters a single queue.

Client goes to the first idle server.

Average service time is one minute at any station.

EXERCISE 4.7

Service at a Bank

Consider a bank in which two clients arrive per minute on average. Three tellers perform service, which lasts an average of one minute.

Model this bank's service using each of the two previous queuing systems. Compare the total waiting time from each case. ***Hint:*** For the single queue case, create a new station that corresponds to leaving the queue and walking to the available teller. The service time for this station should be zero, because as soon as someone leaves the queue, it is possible for the next person to leave if another teller is free. For the multiple queue case, assume that people will choose the shortest of the lines.

It is interesting to note that most banks and ticket counters used to use the multiple queue, multiple server approach. Now they mostly use single queues and multiple servers.

EXERCISE 4.8

Air Traffic Control

Consider an example in air traffic control in which planes arrive at an airport control zone and either land or enter a holding pattern as follows:

Runway

Landing Pattern

(a) Planes enter the system with exponential interarrival times, 1 1/4 minutes apart on average.

(b) If the landing pattern is full, the planes enter a holding pattern. They are cleared to the landing pattern on a first-come-first-serve basis. Once cleared, the time required for a plane to reach the landing pattern is uniformly distributed between zero and two minutes.

(c) Planes are allowed to enter the landing pattern no less than one minute apart. Once in the landing pattern they all fly at precisely the same speed, eliminating any uncertainty in the remaining time spent in the system.

Simulate this situation using Q_NET. **_Hint:_** Model the landing pattern as a station with a fixed service time of 1 minute. Model the transition between the holding pattern and the landing pattern as a station with a service time uniformly distributed between 0 and 2 minutes. You will need to modify the next service time formula for those stations. The transition matrix will require formulas that depend on the current state of the system.

Markov Chains

Certain evolving systems can be modeled in a particularly elegant manner. Consider a population of individuals, each of which can change state as time progresses. For example, the individuals might represent consumers, whose states correspond to the brand of detergent they are currently using. Or they might correspond to machines whose states represent various levels of operating efficiency. Time is modeled in fixed increments. In going from time T to time T + 1, the individuals transition between states with certain probabilities. Such a system is known as a Markov chain. For a more complete discussion of Markov chains, see Luenberger (1979).

An Example: Market Share

Markov chains have been used to model the dynamics of competitive markets. Consider, for example, a population of software developers, where the state of a given developer is defined by the programming language in which he or she is currently developing code. Here, Markov chains can be used to predict the market share of the various languages over time.

New generations of programming languages commonly replace older ones. Generally, the newer languages are better in most respects than their predecessors. But often the older languages remain superior for certain tasks.

Suppose that in a particular application area, virtually all developers are currently using language A when two new competing languages, B and C, are introduced. Language B has similar syntax to A, but is more powerful. Language C is more powerful still and shares some properties with B, but is a complete departure from A. Suppose the probability that a developer using language A will stay with A over the next three months is 65%. The probabilities that the developer will move to either B or C during this period are 30% and 5%, respectively. Of developers who move to B, 75% stay with this environment, 10% return to A, and 15% move on to C. Of those who use C, 90% stay with this language and 10% move to B.

Before continuing, try to guess what the market shares of these three programming languages will look like over time.

■ FUNDAMENTALS 4-4 ■ ■ ■ ■ ■ ■ ■ ■ ■ ■ ■ ■

Markov Chains

Markov chains model evolving systems such as populations of individuals, each of which can move from state to state. The probability that an individual moves from one state to another is known as the *transition probability* between those states. If the transition probabilities do not change over time, the Markov chain is said to be *stationary*.

The transition probabilities for software developers moving between programming languages can be displayed in an array known as a *transition matrix*, shown in the following table:

To Language	From Language		
	A	B	C
A	65%	10%	0%
B	30%	75%	10%
C	5%	15%	90%

Notice that the columns sum to 100%, implying that all developers will be using one of the three languages.

MARKOV.xls

Open MARKOV.xls, shown in the following figure:

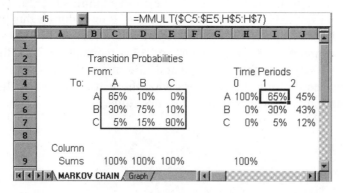

Notice that the transition probabilities are in the upper left corner and that the formulas in row 9 are used to check that the columns sum to 100%. Column H contains the percentage of developers across the three languages in the initial time period and must also sum to 100%.

Given the numbers using each language at time 0, what are the numbers at time 1? The percentage using language A at time 1 is the sum of those who stayed with A from time 0, plus those who moved to A from B, plus those who moved to A from C. This is

$$65\%*A(0)+10\%*B(0)+0\%*C(0).$$

Similarly, the percentage using B is

$$30\%*A(0)+75\%*B(0)+10\%*C(0)$$

and the percentage using C is

$$5\%*A(0)+15\%*B(0)+90\%*C(0).$$

A convenient way to calculate this is with the MMULT formula as shown in the formula bar in the screen shot of MARKOV.xls. See the Excel help system for a full explanation of MMULT. As implemented here, MMULT is equivalent to a SUMPRODUCT formula in which the first range is a row and the second range is a column. With careful use of absolute $ references, a single instance of this formula has been copied down and across to calculate the percentage of programmers in each state for 36 periods.

Notice that by two time periods after introduction, language B has captured 43% of the market, and A has dropped to 45% from its initial 100%. Language C, on the other hand, has only managed to capture 12% of the market. If we were myopically tracking this market activity, it would be tempting to predict that B was the big winner and that C was a loser. However, the Markov model clearly shows otherwise. To get an idea of the dynamics of this situation, click on the **Graph** tab to view the changes in market share for each of the three languages over time. You should see the following figure.

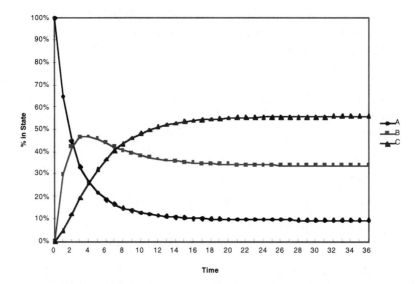

Notice that language C eventually ends up with 56% of the market, followed by B with 34%, and A with only 10%. These market shares are known as the *equilibrium* percentages or equilibrium distribution of the Markov chain.

A Remarkable Property of Markov Chains

As a thought experiment, imagine that at time 0, language B had the entire market instead of A. Model this by setting A(0) (cell H5) to 0 and B(0) (cell H6) to 100%. The results are graphed in the following figure.

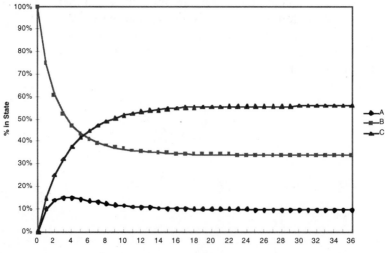

■ **FUNDAMENTALS 4-5** ■ ■ ■ ■ ■ ■ ■ ■ ■ ■ ■ ■

Markov Chain Equilibrium

- A Markov chain is said to be *irreducible* if it is possible to eventually move between any two states.

- This will be the case unless there is a set of states from which it is not possible to escape. Such a set is known as an *absorbing* class of states.

- If a Markov chain is irreducible, then its long-term or *equilibrium* behavior does not depend on the initial percentages across states.

The market displays a very different dynamic for the first 10 periods, but the shares later settle down to exactly the same equilibrium as before. Try any initial market share for this transition matrix (remember column H must sum to 100%), and the market share will always reach the same equilibrium!

This remarkable property implies that it might be more important to understand the transition between states than to understand the current distribution of the population across states.

EXERCISE 4.9 Solving for Markov Chain Equilibria

Enter the transition matrix below and place all programmers in state A at time 0.

To Language	From Language		
	A	**B**	**C**
A	99%	10%	0%
B	1%	75%	1%
C	0%	15%	99%

Although theoretically there should be an equilibrium, you will see that it has not been reached by the 36th period. Use the Excel Solver to change the values of A(0), B(0), and C(0) until they equal A(1), B(1), and C(1) respectively. The resulting percentages do not change from period to period, so they are in equilibrium. Don't forget that your percentages at time 0 must be non-negative and must sum to 100%. See Chapter 7 on optimization to learn more about the solver.

STEPS: **MODELING MACHINE REPLACEMENT**

Imagine a manufacturing environment in which a number of identical machines are used to process material. The quality of the machines deteriorates from month to month as follows. In the first month after replacement, 90% of the machines are still OK, but 10% of them are worn. Of the machines that are OK in a given month, 60% are still OK in the next month, 30% are worn, and 10% fail. Of the worn machines, 60% are still worn by the next month, and 40% fail. Whenever a machine fails, it is replaced by a new one. This situation is reflected in the transition matrix shown below.

To Condition	From Condition			
	New	**OK**	**Worn**	**Fail**
New	0%	0%	0%	100%
OK	90%	60%	0%	0%
Worn	10%	30%	60%	0%
Fail	0%	10%	40%	0%

Proceed as follows to model the machine replacement scenario.

1 Open MARKOV.xls, and save it as MACHINE.xls.

2 We need four states to model this situation, so insert a row and column in the transition matrix. The formulas to the right of the transition matrix will display ##### or #VALUE. This is all right. *Note:* Do not insert the new rows and columns at the first row and column of the current matrix.

3 Fill in the transition matrix and its labels.

4 Specify 100% new machines at time 0.

5 Copy the MMULT formula in cell J5 down to J8 to complete period 1.

6 Copy J5:J8 to the desired number of future periods. The number of time periods should be sufficient to ensure convergence to the equilibrium distributions. For this example, 20 periods will be adequate.

7

Using the Chart Wizard, create a new graph of the percentages over time as shown below.

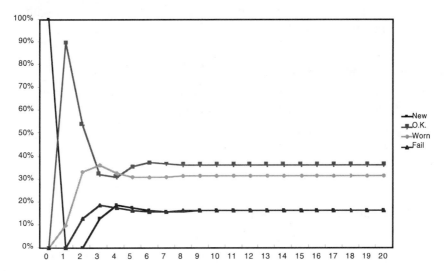

Clearly, equilibrium has been reached well before month 20. In this transition matrix it is possible to eventually move from any state to any other (perhaps first passing through the Fail and New state). Therefore the equilibrium is independent of the initial distribution and is shown in this table.

New	16%
OK	36%
Worn	31%
Fail	16%

Each month, just over 16% of the machines fail and must be replaced with new ones.

Modifying the Transition Matrix to Evaluate Replacement Strategy

Suppose that when a machine fails, it spoils $2,000 worth of materials. Also suppose that a new machine costs $1,000. Then the equilibrium cost per machine per month is

$1000 * \text{Equilibrium \%New Machines} +$
$2000 * \text{Equilibrium \%Failed Machines} = \$484.85$

Set up this formula in the worksheet and experiment with different replacement policies.

EXERCISE 4.10 Machine Replacement

Try to find a better strategy than waiting until the machines fail to replace them. For this alternative strategy determine the following:

a. The new transition matrix

b. The equilibrium distribution

c. The equilibrium cost per machine per month

EXERCISE 4.11 Health Care Screening

In this exercise, we examine the results of two different health management policies: screening or not screening a population for a particular treatable but potentially fatal disease (PFD). Here are the key facts about PFD:

- It is not contagious, but occurs in any member of the population at large with a 10% chance in any year.

- For those who are not screened, there is only a 1% chance that PFD will be detected early and a 9% chance that it will be detected late. For those who are screened, 9% are detected early and 1% late.

- It is much more treatable if detected early than if it is detected late. Of those detected late, only 10% will be cured by the following year and 90% will be deceased. Of those detected early, 90% will be cured by the following year and only 10% will be deceased.

- Those who have been cured of PFD have a 20% chance of getting it again in any year. But because they are regularly screened, it is always detected early.

- It goes without saying that those who die from PFD in a given year will remain deceased the following year.

This is represented by the following transition matrix:

	From Condition					
To Condition	**Unscreened**	**Screened**	**Early Detect**	**Late Detect**	**Cured**	**Deceased**
Unscreened	90%	0%	0%	0%	0%	0%
Screened	0%	90%	0%	0%	0%	0%
Early Detect	1%	9%	0%	0%	20%	0%
Late Detect	9%	1%	0%	0%	0%	0%
Cured	0%	0%	90%	10%	80%	0%
Deceased	0%	0%	10%	90%	0%	100%

Note that because Deceased represents a state from which you cannot leave, the matrix is not irreducible. Thus, the behavior of this system will be somewhat different than those discussed earlier.

a. Without constructing the Markov chain, predict the equilibrium state of this system if you start with 100% of the population unscreened and wait long enough.

b. Create a Markov chain and graph covering 26 years into the future.

c. If you start with 100% of the population in the unscreened state at time 0, what percentage is deceased by period 26?

d. What percentage is deceased by period 26 if the population that has not had PFD is screened every year?

Conclusion

We have seen that complex evolving systems can be modeled using discrete-event simulation. Powerful graphical simulation software exists that can actually show the movement of people, airplanes, or other items while the process is underway. For certain evolving systems, Markov chains can provide a powerful theoretical understanding on long-term behavior.

5

Forecasting

Tomorrow is an old deceiver, and his cheat never grows stale.

SAMUEL JOHNSON, ENGLISH AUTHOR

Modern forecasting falls into two broad categories, causal forecasting and time series analysis.

Causal forecasting predicts how an uncertain quantity is related to other quantities. Causal forecasting could be used by

- A retail outlet to determine the extent to which business is increased through advertising.

- A pharmaceutical lab estimating the influence of dosage on the effectiveness of a new pain killer.

Time series analysis predicts future values of an uncertain quantity based on past values of the same quantity. Time series analysis might be used by

- A telecommunications firm to predict future demand for service based on several years of past data.

- An integrated circuit manufacturer to estimate next year's sales so it can expand its plant to meet required production.

Regardless of the technique used, forecasts are generally not exact. It is important, therefore, not to ignore the estimates of errors also produced by most types of forecasts.

OVERVIEW

Introduction

This section contains a short introduction to causal forecasting and time series analysis. It also includes instructions for using the regression routines that come with Excel and FORECAST.xla, a time series analysis add-in.

Tutorials: Regression and Time Series Analysis

This section's tutorials cover regression to estimate sales based on advertising level, and time series analysis to predict future business based on past history. The second tutorial shows how forecasting can be tied to Monte Carlo simulation.

The Importance of Errors

Forecasting errors provide valuable insight into the reliability of the results. Errors also allow the forecast to be linked to Monte Carlo simulation. Random and nonrandom errors are discussed.

Regression and Exponential Smoothing

Intuitive explanations of regression and exponential smoothing are provided.

Introduction

Modern forecasting falls into two broad categories. Causal forecasting predicts how an uncertain quantity is related to others quantities. Time series analysis predicts future values of some quantity based on past values of the same quantity. We introduce these topics in this chapter, but for a more extensive presentation, see Gardner (1986, 1992).

Causal Forecasting

The term "causal" implies that these methods determine the extent to which changes in one quantity **cause** changes in another. Generally, all that is learned from causal forecasting, however, is the extent to which the changes in two or more quantities are statistically linked, and linking alone does not imply causality.

For example, it has been known for decades that there is a strong link between smoking and lung cancer. Does this necessarily mean that smoking causes lung cancer? Without additional medical evidence, you could make either of the following arguments:

- *Argument 1:* More smokers get lung cancer than do nonsmokers. Therefore, smoking must be one of the causes of lung cancer.

- *Argument 2:* People prone to getting lung cancer have discomfort in their lungs that can only be alleviated by inhaling nicotine. Thus, although smoking and lung cancer are indeed linked, it is the propensity for getting lung cancer that causes people to smoke in the first place. That is, cancer causes smoking!

This issue was not conclusively settled until recently when medical researchers were finally able to determine the biochemical process whereby smoking does indeed cause cancer.

Regression is the most commonly used form of causal forecasting. In its simplest form regression fits a straight line to the scatter plot of two quantities that are suspected of being related. This line can be used to predict the value of one of the quantities given the value of the other. For example, as shown in the following figure, we might be able to predict monthly sales based on the amount of advertising.

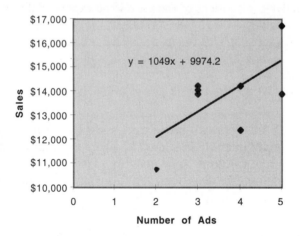

You can get regression results from within Excel using one of three methods. The most thorough of these is contained in the Analysis ToolPak, which will be discussed later.

Time Series Analysis

Time series analysis predicts future values of some quantity based on past values of the same quantity. For example:

Web site hits by day

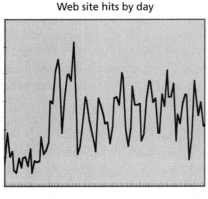

Yen/dollar ratio by week

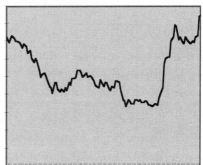

Motorcycle sales by month

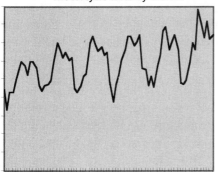

Corporate sales by year

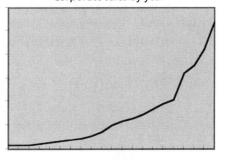

There are many varieties of time series analysis and numerous software packages that provide this capability. Most time series software programs take historical data as input and estimate expected future values as output along with a confidence interval.

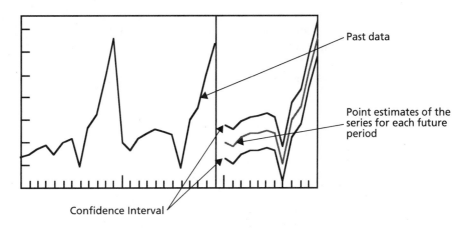

Past data

Point estimates of the series for each future period

Confidence Interval

Management is likely to plug these point estimates of the future into spreadsheet models to predict future business conditions while ignoring the confidence intervals. This can lead to serious errors as average inputs will not necessarily result in average outputs. An analogy exists between the future values of the series and the position of a drunk wandering around on a busy highway, described on page 63. The estimates of the future values of the series correspond to the most likely position of the drunk or the highway's center line. However, we cannot assume that the drunk will remain alive just because his most likely position is the center line where he is safe. Similarly, we cannot assume that plugging in most likely future values of the series will result in the most likely future values of profit, cost, or other measures of business.

Fortunately, there is a convenient solution to this problem. Most forms of time series analysis also produce a set of errors that correspond to the past deviations of the drunk away from the center line. These errors can help estimate the reliability of the forecast, or, better yet, they can be used to run a simulation of the future instead of simply outputting a point estimate. This will be demonstrated in the tutorial.

FORECAST.xla is a time series analysis add-in for Excel 5.0 and higher that performs exponential smoothing on series with or without a trend or seasonality. An option allows you to create a formula that simulates the behavior of the quantity one period into the future. This formula can be used to run a simulation in conjunction with SIM.xla.

Regression in Excel and FORECAST.xla

Regression

You can get regression results from within Excel through three separate methods.

1. *Analysis Tools.* Choose **Data Analysis** from the **Tools** menu. From the Data Analysis dialog box that opens (shown in the following figure), select **Regression**.

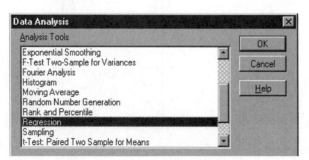

This provides the most detailed output statistics, which in some cases are more than are needed. *Note:* The analysis tool pack must be installed to use this regression routine. Use the Excel **Help** command for details.

2. *Scatterplot.* If there are only two variables, you can create a scatter plot of the data, then click on the data points. Then select **Trend Line** from the **Insert** menu. This is a quick-and-dirty way to determine the significance of any linear trends in data.

3. *Linest and Trend Functions.* The = Linest() and Trend() functions will instantly calculate regression statistics from "live" data.

Running FORECAST.xla. Launch Excel and open FORECAST.xla from the **File Open** command.

Auto Load Option. If you want FORECAST.xla to load every time you launch Excel, follow these steps:

1. Select **Add-ins** from the **Tools** menu in Excel.

2. Select **FORECAST.xla** from the list of add-ins and click **OK**.

3. You can later go back and deselect **FORECAST.xla** from the **Add-in** menu to prevent Excel from loading it automatically.

Tutorials: Regression and Time Series Analysis

The basic steps of both causal and time series forecasting are these:

1. Eyeball the data.

2. Choose and run a forecasting technique.

3. Observe the results and possibly go back to step 2.

We will begin by discussing causal forecasting with regression.

Regression: Estimating Sales Based on Advertising Level

Consider a restaurant in a large city that has experimented with newspaper ads on eight occasions over several years. For each experiment, they have kept track of the number of newspaper ads placed, along with that month's sales. Managers have already concluded that whatever effect an ad has is limited to the month in which it ran. Hypothetical data for this situation is contained in the range **Ads_vs_Sales** in the file SERIES.xls[1], which contains numerous sample data sets for experimentation. The first sheet of SERIES.xla contains an index shown in the following figure, which lists the range names of the various data sets.

	A	B	C	D	E	F	G
1		Range name					
2	Historical Data			Hypothetical Data			
3		AIRCONDITIONERS			Ads_vs_Sales		
4		BEER			TRANS VS PETROL		
5		CALCULATORS			Dish Washers		
6		CHAMPAGNE			Kitchen Ranges		
7		CIGARS			Exercise Equipment		
8		CLOTHING			Bicycles		
9		COMPANY			RAND()		
10		DEMAND			TREND		
11		EMPLOY			CONVEX		
12		FIBERS					
13		FRANCE					
14		FUEL DEMAND					
15		GASOLINE					
16		IBMSALES					

Select the **Ads_vs_Sales** data by pulling down the range name list at the far left of the formula bar as shown. Or, press the F5 key to access the range names.

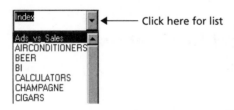

──── Click here for list

Once the **Ads_vs_Sales** series has been selected, copy and paste it into a blank workbook, then close SERIES.xls. See Fundamentals Box 5-1 for definitions of dependent and independent variables.

Eyeball the Data

Statistical techniques are best used with common sense and intuition, and a good way to gain intuition about data is by graphing it. In this example, the dependent variable is sales and the independent variable is number of ads. We can easily imagine other independent variables that might influence sales as well, such as weather, the state of the economy, and so forth.

---

1. I am indebted to Professor Everette S. Gardner Jr. of the University of Houston who provided the historical data for SERIES.xls as well as advice about the time series programs.

▓ FUNDAMENTALS 5-1 ▓ ▓ ▓ ▓ ▓ ▓ ▓ ▓ ▓ ▓ ▓ ▓

Dependent and Independent Variables

The variable you want to predict is known as the *dependent variable*. The variable(s) on which the prediction is based is(are) known as the *independent variable(s)*.

STEPS: **CREATING A SCATTERPLOT**

1 Start by creating an XY scatterplot with Ads on the X axis and Sales on the Y axis (refer to the Excel Help system for details).

2 Because all sales figures are greater than $10,000, it is helpful to scale the vertical axis of the graph to start at $10,000. To do this, first double-click the graph. Then double-click the vertical axis. In the Format Axis dialog box that opens, click the **Scale** tab and type 10000 as the minimum y value as shown in the following dialog box.

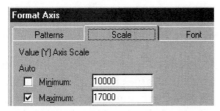

3 The graph should now appear as follows:

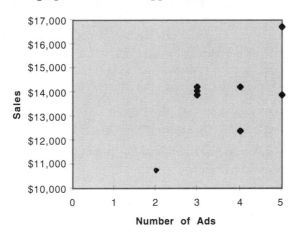

The Inter Ocular Trauma Test. Over the years many statistical tests have been developed for verifying hypotheses: f tests, t tests, and the like. A biostatistician at the Mayo clinic, Joe Berkson, had his own favorite, which he called the *Inter Ocular Trauma Test* (that is, it hits you between the eyes). The IOTT as applied to this situation indicates that sales tend to increase with advertising, but can we be more precise?

Choose and Run a Forecasting Technique

The simplest relationship to describe how one thing goes up or down with something else is a straight line. This assumes that when the independent variable x is increased by one unit, the dependent variable y is expected to increase or decrease by a fixed amount a. This is shown in the following figure.

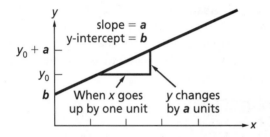

Although few things in life are truly linear, linearity is often a reasonable assumption, especially if the range of x values is small. Assuming a linear relationship exists between sales and advertising level, we now show how linear regression can provide estimates of a and b in the previous figure.

If a straight line relationship seems reasonable visually, then linear regression can be a useful technique. Of course there is still plenty of uncertainty in sales left over, even after we have accounted for the number of ads, so we wouldn't expect a straight line to fit the data perfectly. Nonetheless, linear regression does its best to fit such a line, where "best" is defined as minimizing the sum of squares of the vertical distances by which the line misses the data points.

STEPS: **PERFORMING REGRESSION WITH A SINGLE VARIABLE**

If there is only a single independent variable, a simple way to perform regression in Excel is as follows:

1 Double-click on the scatter plot of sales versus ads created earlier.

2 Single click on any of the data points. The data points should be highlighted with the graph series specification appearing in the formula bar.

3

Invoke the command to add a trend line to the chart: For Excel 97, use **C**hart Add **T**rendline, or, for Excel 5 or 7, use **I**nsert **T**rendline

4

In the Trendline dialog box, select **L**inear, but also note the other types.

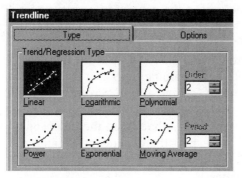

From the **Options** tab, check **Display Equation on Chart**. Then click **OK**.

5

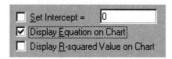

The regression line and equation will appear on the chart as shown below.

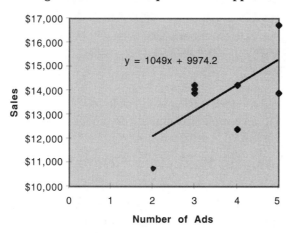

$$y = 1049x + 9974.2$$

Observe the Results of the Regression

The equation indicates that the predicted sales with no ads is $9,974.20 and that the expected increase in sales per ad is $1,049. Thus, if six ads were placed, a reasonable estimate for sales would be $9,974 + 6 * $1,049 or $16,268. Remember that $16,268 is just an estimate of the mean of the distribution of possible sales. We will discuss the distribution further in the section "The Importance of Errors," later in this chapter.

If there were two independent variables, the data would consist of a cloud of dots in three dimensional space, and instead of a line, linear regression would fit a plane to the data. Similar analogies hold for any number of independent variables, but the picture becomes impossible to visualize. This could not have been done within the context of a scatter plot. The regression routines from the analysis tools are required to perform this task, known as *multivariate linear regression.*

A common mathematical relationship that is not linear is the exponential model. This is used to describe quantities that grow at a roughly constant rate, for example, money earning a fixed percent per year in a savings account.

The exponential model assumes that when the independent variable x is increased by one unit, we expect the dependent variable y, to be multiplied by a fixed amount, as shown in the following figure. This model applies to many areas in finance.

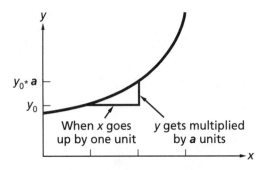

With exponential models, it is convenient to work with the logarithm of the dependent variable because this makes the model linear.

Time Series Analysis: Predicting Future Sales Based on Past History

If you flip a coin repeatedly, it will continually have a 50/50 chance of coming up heads. The number of heads appearing on each toss (either 0 or 1) is known as a stationary random variable. On the other hand, if you draw playing cards from a deck, the chance of getting an ace goes down if you have already drawn three aces and goes up if you have drawn many cards already without drawing an ace. The number of aces appearing on a single draw from a deck (again 0 or 1) is not a stationary random variable.

When you are forecasting future values of a random variable based on past values, it is important to determine whether or not it is stationary.

■ **FUNDAMENTALS 5-2** ■ ■ ■ ■ ■ ■ ■ ■ ■ ■ ■ ■

Stationary Random Variable

A random variable whose statistical properties do not change over time is known as a *stationary* random variable.

Two common causes of nonstationarity are *trend* and *seasonality*. Trend means that in the long run, the average value of the random variable is either rising or falling. Seasonality means that the series has repeating highs and lows in the data caused by seasonal effects.

You should identify these two primary characteristics visually if possible before applying FORECAST.xla.

An Example: Champagne Sales

Eight years of monthly sales data will be used to forecast future sales of champagne. Select the champagne data from SERIES.xls by pulling down the range name list on the formula bar as shown. Or, press the F5 key to access the range names. Once the champagne series has been selected, copy it and paste it into a blank workbook, then close SERIES.xls.

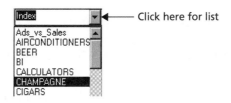 ◀—— Click here for list

Forecasting with FORECAST.xla

STEPS: **EYEBALLING THE DATA**

Make sure that FORECAST.xla is loaded before beginning these steps. To graph the series proceed as follows:

1 Select the champagne data in the workbook just created.

2 Create a line graph (see the Excel Help system for details). We want a line graph this time instead of an XY plot because the X values are equally spaced time intervals

3

You should see the following pattern in which the X axis represents months:

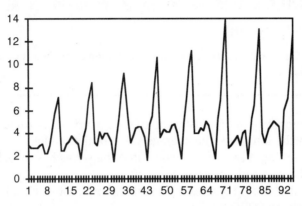

The inter ocular trauma test reveals two things: First, champagne sales are seasonal with a high peak in December and a smaller one in summer. Second, in the long run there appears to be an upward trend in sales.

EXERCISE **Accounting for the Two Peaks in Champagne Sales**

5.1 Given what you know about the consumption of champagne, explain the two peaks that occur in sales each year.

STEPS: CHOOSING AND RUNNING A FORECAST TECHNIQUE

1

Select the champagne sales series that you copied to the new worksheet.

2

Invoke the **Forecast Run Forecast** command. You will see the following dialog box.

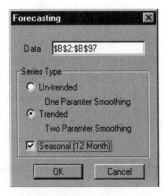

3

Because this series has a *trend* (rising in this case), select **Trended**. Because the series displays 12-month *seasonality*, click **Seasonal**. Then click **OK**. Several sheets are set up for intermediate calculations, then the final results are displayed. An explanation of the calculations behind the forecast will be presented later.

4

Save the results to a file called FCAST.xls for future reference using the **Forecast Save Results** command.

Observe the Results of the Forecast

Columns A, B, C, and D of the results sheet contain the month number, historical data, the warm-up or fitted series, and the future forecast, respectively. The warm up series is fitted to the historical data, then extrapolated into the future to create the forecast. Notice that the forecast column does not have meaning until the first period into the future. For the current example, this is month 97.

Month number	Historical data	Warm-up series	Forecast

	A	B	C	D
94	91	4.633	3.8930256	#N/A
95	92	1.659	1.9687498	#N/A
96	93	5.951	4.9789832	#N/A
97	94	6.981	6.5575442	#N/A
98	95	9.851	9.797299	#N/A
99	96	12.670	12.349683	#N/A
100	97	#N/A	#N/A	4.0471454
101	98	#N/A	#N/A	3.6973346
102	99	#N/A	#N/A	4.3430024
103	100	#N/A	#N/A	4.5046615

Thus, the point estimate for month 97 is 4.047. Later we will examine some of the additional output provided by FORECAST.xla and show how the forecast can be refined by further reducing the errors between the warm-up series and historical data.

A graph of the forecast, shown in the following figure, is also provided.

The fitted series is displayed in blue

The forecast is displayed in green

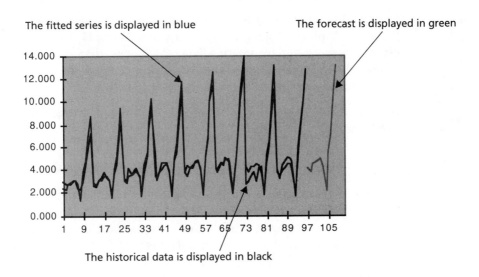

The historical data is displayed in black

STEPS: SIMULATING THE FUTURE BASED ON FORECAST ERRORS

You will find the full distribution of an uncertain number to be more helpful than a point estimate. The distribution of champagne sales in the first future period can be simulated as follows:

1 Make sure that the current forecast of champagne is the active workbook. Then, open SIM.xla if it is not open already.

2 Invoke the **Live Simulation** command from the **Forecast** menu. A simulation based on the errors of the forecast will be created in a separate workbook as shown below. Save this workbook as LIVESIM.xls.

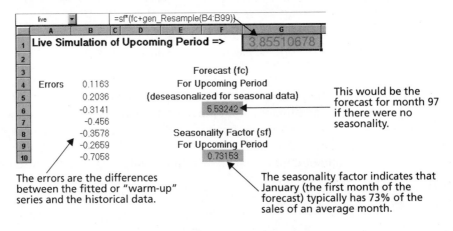

The errors are the differences between the fitted or "warm-up" series and the historical data.

This would be the forecast for month 97 if there were no seasonality.

The seasonality factor indicates that January (the first month of the forecast) typically has 73% of the sales of an average month.

3

The simulated first future period sales, shown in cell G1, is created by adding one of the randomly chosen past errors to the deseasonalized forecast in F6, then multiplying by the seasonality factor in F10. Press the calculate key a few times to make sure it is working. Cell G1 can now be used as input to any model such as INVNTORY.xls, which was presented in Chapter 3.

EXERCISE **5.2**

Linking Forecasting to a Simulation Model

As a major distributor of champagne, you must order champagne for month 97 based on the previous forecast (assume the units of the forecast are thousands of cases). If you do not meet demand, you forego a profit of $50 per case for each missed sale. On the other hand, if you overpurchase, the storage and capital costs are $7.50 per excess case. How many cases should you order (in multiples of 250) to maximize expected profit? *Hint:* Modify INVNTORY.xls to reflect the new costs. Then link the live simulation to the demand cell as follows. Place the cursor in cell A2 of INVNTORY. Type "=". Move to LIVESIM.xls using the Excel **Window** command. Place the cursor in cell G1. Then press **Enter**.

The Importance of Errors

Forecasting is somewhat like throwing darts. You rarely get a bull's eye, but by observing your errors, also known as residuals, you may be able to improve your technique. Fundamentals Box 5-3 describes the differences between random and systematic errors.

EXERCISE **5.3**

Forecasting Freight

The U.S. freight manager for a foreign airline complained that the home office always gave him terrible forecasts: They were "consistently too high." When he complained about the quality of their forecasts, management in the home office challenged him to provide them with a better forecast. How could the freight manager have improved the home office forecasts?

■ FUNDAMENTALS 5-3 ■ ■ ■ ■ ■ ■ ■ ■ ■ ■ ■ ■ ■

Random versus Systematic Errors

When there is no pattern to the errors, as depicted in the left figure below, the errors are known as *random*. If the errors are random, there might be no obvious way to improve the forecast. However, the errors are still a valuable source of information concerning the reliability of the forecast.

If there is a clear pattern to the errors, as depicted in the right figure below, the errors are known as *systematic*. Systematic errors will usually suggest some obvious way to improve the situation.

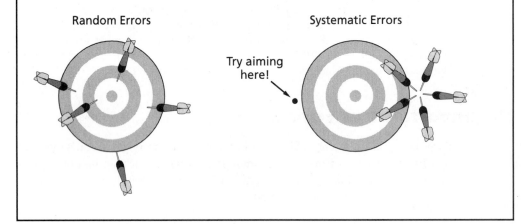

Errors Generated by Regression

The coefficients found by regression ensure that the sum of squares of the errors has been minimized. We will return to the tutorial example where we analyzed the advertising effect on sales to further investigate these errors. This time, however, we will use the regression routines in Excel's Data Analysis Tools to investigate the reliability of the results.

STEPS: **RUNNING REGRESSION FROM THE DATA ANALYSIS TOOLS**

1

Copy the Ads_vs_Sales data in SERIES.xls to a blank workbook.

2

From the worksheet containing your copy of the Ads_vs_Sales data, invoke the **Tools Data Analysis** command, as shown below.

3

Select **Regression** from the **Analysis Tools** menu.

4

Fill in the dialog box as shown below. Then click **OK** to initiate the regression calculation.

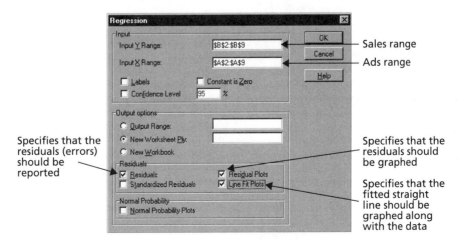

Specifies that the residuals (errors) should be reported

Sales range

Ads range

Specifies that the residuals should be graphed

Specifies that the fitted straight line should be graphed along with the data

Interpret the Results

The regression routine outputs more results than are needed in many situations. We will discuss a few of the more important results.

Residual Plot. It is a good idea to view the residual plot, shown in the left of the following figures, in effort to spot systematic errors. In this case, the errors appear to be random. The three points in a straight line above the X Variable 1 at 3 do not represent systematic errors, but merely indicate that on three occasions, exactly three ads were run.

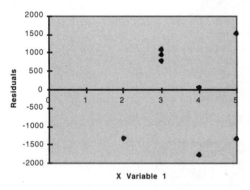

Random Residuals

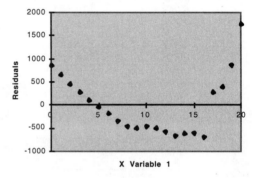

Nonrandom Residuals

Had the errors displayed any obvious systematic (nonrandom) pattern, such as shown in the figure on the right, this would indicate that there was not a linear relationship between sales and ads, and it would not make sense to use the linear regression. Because the errors do appear random, however, the next step is to look at the regression outputs. We will cover only the most fundamental regression outputs. For a complete explanation, see a text on statistics.

Regression Statistics. The regression statistics appear as shown in the following figure and brief descriptions.

Regression Statistics	
Multiple R	0.652413114
R Square	0.425642871
Adjusted R Square	0.329916683
Standard Error	1396.063433
Observations	8

■ *Multiple R:* This is the correlation between the sales and ad data (see the discussion of correlation in Chapter 3).

■ *R Square:* The square of the correlation. The R^2 measures the percentage of the variance of sales explained by the variance in ads.

■ *Adjusted R Square:* The R^2 is usually adjusted to reflect the number of data points. This is often used as a measure of the ultimate predictive power of the regression, with a value of 1 signifying perfect prediction and 0 signifying none.

■ *Standard Error:* An estimate of the standard deviation of the errors.

■ *Observations:* The number of data points.

Coefficients. The coefficients for the linear equation, Y = Slope * X Variable 1 + Intercept, are shown in the following figure, with descriptions following. Had the regression been run on more than one type of ad—say, radio, newspaper and so on—there would have been a corresponding X coefficient for each one.

	Coefficients
Intercept	9974.218447
X Variable 1	1049.028216

■ *Intercept:* The Y intercept, which shows predicted sales with zero ads.

■ *X Variable 1:* Slope, which is the expected increase in sales per ad.

The Reliability of the Regression Results

The following picture is a reminder that for any value of the independent variable, the regression line is just a point estimate for the mean of the dependent variable. We must not forget that the true value of the dependent variable is distributed about this line. The standard error is an estimate of the standard deviation of this distribution for the example of sales versus ads.

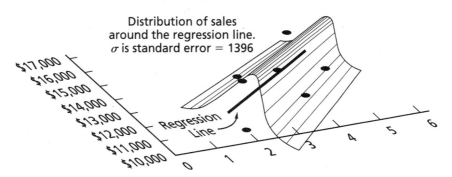

Distribution of sales around the regression line. σ is standard error = 1396

Recall from the tutorial that the estimate of sales with six ads was $16,268. However, we almost certainly would not get exactly this amount if we actually took out six ads. The standard error of 1396 indicates that to be 95% confident, we must accept a range of $2,792 (two standard errors) to either side of this figure—a range between $19,060 and $13,476. This is a far cry from being certain that sales will be $16,268.

Standard errors associated with each coefficient also can provide additional insight. For example, it seems very likely that sales increase with ads, as the expected rate is $1,049 per ad. What is the chance sales might actually decrease with the number of ads? The standard error of the slope (X Variable 1 coefficient) in this case is about 500. For the actual slope to be negative, it would have to be more than two standard errors below the estimate of $1,049. The chance of this is less than 2.5%, so we can be very sure that advertising does indeed increase sales.

EXERCISE 5.4 **A Simulation Based on a Regression**

Suppose we plan to run four ads.

a. Use the slope and intercept to calculate the expected sales given four ads.

b. Load SIM.xla and use gen_Resample with the residuals of the regression to simulate the uncertainty in sales.

c. We can often reasonably assume that the residuals are normally distributed. In a separate cell, simulate the uncertainty in sales using gen_Normal(0,S) where S is the standard error determined by the regression.

d. Run a simulation of both cells and compare the results.

e. What are the advantages of each approach?

Errors Generated by Time Series

No one would ever apply an experimental drug to a human patient without first testing it in a controlled laboratory experiment. The same thing holds for applying forecasts. The controlled experiment in this case, is forecasting the past. By using early periods of past data to predict later periods of past data, we can get a feeling for the method's accuracy. A period called the *forecast period* is set aside at the end of the historical data as a surrogate for the future. The remaining period is known as the *warm-up period*.

STEPS: **PREDICTING THE PAST**

1 Make sure FORECAST.xla is open, then retrieve FCAST.xls (the champagne forecast saved from the tutorial).

2 Click on the tab labeled **Smooth (2P)**. This sheet contains the formulas that calculate the nonseasonal part of the trended forecast using two-parameter exponential smoothing. These formulas will be discussed in more detail in Appendix B. Here we discuss the forecast and warm-up periods.

Indicates that data was de-seasonalized

	I	J	K	L
1			Use Deasoned Data	
2			TRUE	
3				
4				
5		Warm-up	Forecast	Total Data
6	Data Points	96	0	96

Indicates a total of 96 data points

Indicates that we are forecasting none of the past periods

3 To forecast the last three years of data from the first five years, type 36 into cell K6 of the smoothing sheet.

The value in cell J6 now equals 60. This means that the forecast is now based only on the first 60 months of data. To find out how this forecast compared with the next three years of actual sales, look at the Forecast graph on the results sheet, as shown below.

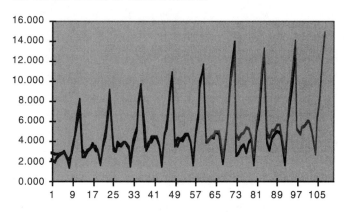

Minimizing the Error

The solver built into Excel can adjust forecasting parameters to come up with a "best fit" to the historical data. Look at the smoothing sheet again.

Mean of the squared errors — MSE

Two parameters that affect the fitting of past data

	I	J	K	L
1			Use Deasoned Data	
2			TRUE	
3				
4				
5		Warm-up	Forecast	Total Data
6	Data Points	96	0	96
7	Data Range	B4:B99		
8	Error Ranges	G4:G99	G100:G99	
9	MSE	0.484	#N/A	
10	Slope	0.021		
11	Y-Intercept	3.781		
12				
13				
14		Alpha	Beta	
15		0.1	0.01	
16				

Sheet1 / Deseason \ Smooth

The parameters alpha and beta, discussed in Appendix B, are set to values that provide reasonable forecasts for most trended time series. The mean squared error (MSE in cell B9) is the average of the square of the difference between the actual data and the fitted series. For any particular series, the mean squared error can generally be reduced further by adjusting Alpha and Beta.

EXERCISE 5.5 — Minimizing Mean Squared Error in Time Series Analysis

Use the built-in solver in Excel to change alpha and beta to minimize the mean squared error (MSE). *Note:* Alpha and Beta must be constrained to be between 0 and 1.

Modeling the Error in Future Months

In the time series tutorial, we generated a live simulation of the first period into the future based on the past errors. Industrial time series analysis packages generally include information about the uncertainty in periods further into the future.

For example, many time series packages provide confidence intervals as shown in the following figure. In this case, we can be 95% confident that the actual series will lie within the range shown in any particular future month. If we assume the errors are normally distributed, then the difference between the expected results and the 95% percent intervals will be 2σ.

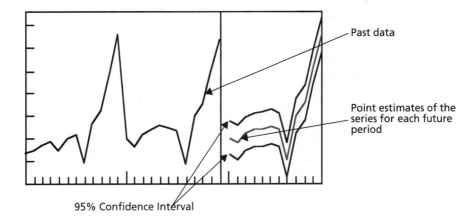

Past data

Point estimates of the series for each future period

95% Confidence Interval

To accurately forecast the future confidence intervals is beyond the scope of this work. The approach used in the next exercise will serve as a useful approximation, however.

EXERCISE **5.6**

Simulating Future Periods of a Time Series Based on Confidence Intervals

The following table contains a forecast and upper and lower 95% confidence intervals for 12 periods. Assuming that the errors are independent and normally distributed, create a simulation for each of the months.

Month	Lower	Forecast	Upper
1	1.25	4.05	6.84
2	0.76	3.70	6.63
3	1.26	4.34	7.43
4	1.27	4.50	7.74
5	1.40	4.80	8.20
6	1.31	4.88	8.45
7	0.48	4.23	7.98
8	-1.83	2.10	6.04
9	1.28	5.42	9.55
10	2.66	7.00	11.34
11	5.84	10.39	14.95
12	8.31	13.09	17.88

Explanation of Regression and Exponential Smoothing

Regression

The basic idea of linear regression is to find a straight line that "best" fits the data. The "best" fit is defined as the line that minimizes the sum of the squares of the differences, or errors e, between the model and the data. The parameters that linear regression can adjust in trying to fit the line to the data are the line's slope a and its y-intercept b. This is shown in the following figure. Note that $\bar{x}$ and $\bar{y}$ refer to the mean of the x and y values respectively.

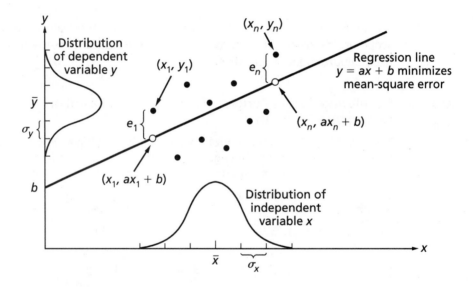

The formulas shown in Fundamentals Box 5-4 refer to the previous figure. They relate the slope and intercept of the regression line to the concepts of covariance and correlation introduced in Chapter 3.

■ **FUNDAMENTALS 5-4** ■ ■ ■ ■ ■ ■ ■ ■ ■ ■ ■ ■ ■ ■

The Formulas of Linear Regression

The slope **a** and y-intercept **b** are found through the following formulas:

$$\text{Covariance} = \sigma_{xy} = \frac{1}{n} \sum_{i=1}^{n} \{x_i - \bar{x}\}\{y_i - \bar{y}\}$$

$$\text{Correlation} = r = \frac{\sigma_{xy}}{\sigma_x \sigma_y}$$

$$\text{Slope of line} = a = \frac{\sigma_{xy}}{\sigma_x^2}$$

$$\text{y-intercept} = b = \bar{y} - a\bar{x}$$

Exponential Smoothing

To explore exponential smoothing, a common form of time series analysis, we will start with the game of basketball. We will forecast the movement of an offensive player running down the court with the ball.

Forecasting the Offensive Player's Position

Our mathematical model of a basketball player makes an important simplifying assumption. The player's motion **down** the court is assumed to be constant, only his position relative to the center line, or **across** the court, is uncertain. The time series consists of the player's off-center distances (OCD) at regular time intervals of 2 seconds. Four time periods of this time series are shown in the following figure, with the position of the player marked by **O**.

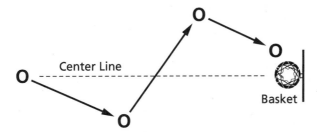

Now consider a defensive player, **D**, who must defend against **O**. At each time interval, **D** tries to forecast **O**'s off-center distance (OCD) at the next time interval. We will examine three simple defensive strategies for **D**, each in the context of to **O**'s path as depicted in the previous figure.

First Defensive Strategy: Avoid the "Fake Out."   To avoid being faked out by his opponent, **D** pays no attention whatsoever to **O**'s current position. According to this strategy, **D** simply repeats his own current OCD.

Suppose, for example, that defense knows that the average position of all players over the game's history has been the court's center line. Then **D** might simply stay on the center-line regardless of what **O** does.

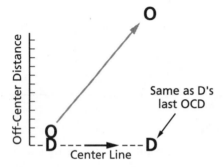

This unadaptive strategy allows **O** a leisurely shot from the side as shown in the following figure.

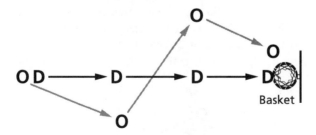

Second Defensive Strategy: Monkey See Monkey Do.   This is the extreme opposite of Avoiding the Fake-Out. **D** tries to do exactly what **O** does. According to this strategy, **D**'s OCD next time will be the same as **O**'s OCD this time, as shown in the following figure.

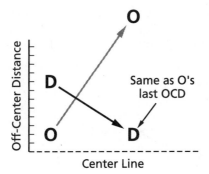

If defense adopts this strategy, **O** can throw **D** off his intended course, or "fake him out," by devious feinting as shown in the following figure.

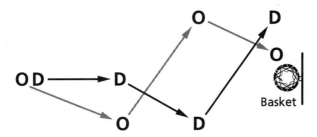

Third Defensive Strategy: Split the Difference. This adaptive approach is a compromise between the previous two. According to this strategy, defense observes the difference between his last prediction of **O**'s OCD, (**D**'s current OCD) and **O**'s current OCD. **D**'s next off-center distance will split this difference halfway.

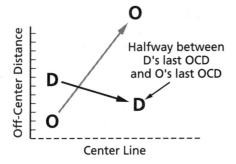

In summary, the first strategy is so tied to past history that it cannot react to current events, and the second strategy takes no account of past history whatever. The third strategy is a compromise between these two extremes.

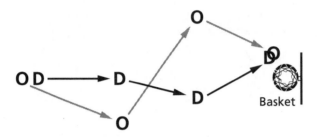

This strategy has two notable characteristics. First, **D**'s current position is based on 50% of his last position, which is based on 50% of his position before that, and so on. Thus **D**'s past history decays exponentially. Secondly, **D**'s trajectory is smoother than **O**'s.

This third strategy is an example of the important family of forecasting techniques known, not surprisingly, as *exponential smoothing* and discussed in detail in the next section. Specifically, this is single parameter exponential smoothing with a parameter of .5. The parameter value .5 refers to the fact that at each step **D** moves half way from his previous guess toward the offense's actual position. Technically speaking, strategies one and two are also extreme cases of exponential smoothing with parameter values that equal 0 and 1, respectively.

One Parameter Exponential Smoothing

Exponential smoothing is a family of moving weighted average techniques that considers all past observations of a time series, putting less and less weight on the early observations. One parameter exponential smoothing, the simplest of this family of techniques, is applicable to time series whose mean is either **constant** or **slowly changing** over time. The three basketball defenses described earlier are special cases of one parameter exponential smoothing. We discuss two parameter exponential smoothing in Appendix B.

The Formulas for One Parameter Exponential Smoothing. Given a time series $Y(t)$, a series of forecasts, $F(t)$, are made that adapt to $Y(t)$ over time. $Y(t)$ and $F(t)$ correspond to the off-center distances at time t of O and D, respectively, in the basketball analogy. As a new observation $Y(t)$ arrives in time period t, a forecast $F(t+1)$ is made for the observation $Y(t+1)$, which will arrive in time $t+1$. These estimates are computed as follows:

1. A value of *F(1)* is chosen. This might be *Y(1)* itself, the average of historical data, or some other reasonable estimate. Even if this first forecast is not very accurate, future estimates will improve because of the adaptive nature of the technique.

2. In each additional time period *t*, *F(t)* = *F(t–1)* + *aE(t–1)*, where *E(t–1)* = *Y(t–1)* - *F(T–1)* is the error of the forecast in the previous period and α, known as the smoothing parameter, is a number between 0 and 1.

Notice that if *F(t–1)* is too low, then *E(t–1)* is positive, and the forecast is raised in the next period. If *F(t–1)* is too high, then *E(t–1)* is negative, and the forecast is lowered in the next period. This behavior has been compared to that of a thermostat that monitors the difference between desired and actual temperature and adjusts an air conditioning system accordingly.

Future Forecasts. If there are *n* time periods of actual data, then the forecast for period *n + 1* is

$$F(n+1) = F(n) + \alpha E(n)$$

But how about periods further in the future? The series *Y(t)* was assumed to have either a constant or slowly changing mean. Hence for all future periods we have

$$F(t) = F(n+1), t > n+1$$

The Effect of Changes in α. The number α is the adjustment that controls how fast or slow the weighting of past observations diminishes.

A value of 0 puts all the weight on past history and corresponds to the Avoid the "Fake Out" strategy. A value of α = 1 puts all the weight on the current observation and corresponds to the Monkey See Monkey Do strategy. A value of α = 0.5 corresponds to the Split the Difference strategy. In the basketball analogy, as α ranges from 0 to 1, D's next off-center distance changes continuously between D's current OCD and O's current OCD. In practice, typical values of α in time series analysis are not as large as the 0.5 of the basketball example.

For time series with trends, a two parameter version of exponential smoothing is used. FORECAST.xla can perform either one or two parameter smoothing, with or without seasonality. The formulas for two parameter smoothing and seasonality are discussed in Appendix B.

Note that linear regression can also be used to forecast trends. However, exponential smoothing places more weight on recent data and is therefore more adaptive than regression, which places equal weight on all past data points.

6

Decision Trees

Simple it's not, I'm afraid you will find,
for a mind-maker-upper to make up his mind.

We must often decide between a few alternative actions in the face of uncertainty. For example:

- A pharmaceutical manufacturer must decide whether or not to pursue an experimental drug that might or might not be effective and, even if effective, might not be approved for use.

- A petroleum exploration firm must decide either to drill for oil on a particular site or abandon the site without knowing how expensive it will be to drill or whether oil is present.

- A toy manufacturer must decide between a large or small production run of a new toy, without being certain about either production costs or the price that the toy will ultimately sell for.

- A legal team must decide whether or not to settle a case out of court, given the uncertainty of a trial outcome.

- Military strategists, uncertain about the capabilities of potential adversaries, must decide in advance between two or three responses to hostile action.

Decision trees can sharpen and formalize the decision-making process in situations such as these. They can both aid us in making up our minds and bring into focus future events that should change our minds.

OVERVIEW

Introduction

This section introduces the use of decision trees in making yes/no decisions in the face of uncertainty. Also presented are instructions for installing and running TREE.xla, a decision tree add-in for Excel.

Tutorial: Building a Decision Tree

Use of decision trees is introduced through the example of a pharmaceutical manufacturer deciding whether or not to pursue an experimental drug whose effectiveness, as well as approval for use, are in question.

Decision Analysis: Basic Concepts

Through examples, this section presents basic decision analytic concepts: utility, probability, expected value, decision trees, sensitivity analysis, value of information, and state variables.

Introduction

An Example: Ice Cream and Parking Tickets

Suppose, while driving home from an errand, you pass an ice cream parlor and suddenly develop the urge for a cone. You must decide whether to pull over and buy an ice cream cone for $1, or go straight home where a sink full of dirty dishes is waiting for you. This decision can be represented by the following diagram:

The choice between eating ice cream and doing dishes generally does not require advanced analysis, but now you notice that the only place to park your car is an illegal spot on the end of the block. The uncertainty of getting a $20 parking ticket has just transported you to the realm of decision analysis. We will start by quantifying the various aspect of this problem using what are known as *state variables*. State variables quantify the possible states of the world we can find ourselves in. In this example, only two state variables are of any consequence:

1. The number of ice cream cones we get (either 0 or 1)
2. The number of parking tickets we get (either 0 or 1)

Notice that we get to specify the number of cones we get, but that the number of tickets is uncertain.

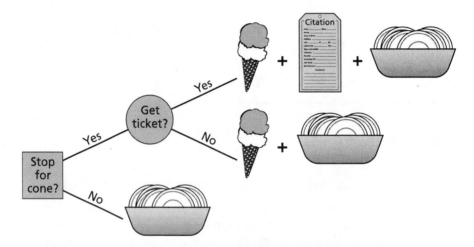

The figure displaying this situation looks like a tree on its side, hence the term *decision tree*. Decision trees are a tool for sharpening and formalizing the decision-making process. They can both aid us in making up our minds and help us focus on future events that might change our minds. As with most analytical techniques, the insight derived from using the tool is an important part of the process.

EXERCISE 6.1 **Umbrella Problem**

Suppose you have traveled to London and have forgotten your umbrella. The probability that it will rain is 40%. If you get caught in the rain, you will do $75 worth of damage to your suit. The cost of an umbrella is $25.

a. What are the state variables for this problem?

b. Draw the decision tree.

EXERCISE
6.2

Fastest Route

Suppose that you need to travel from your job to your home located 60 miles away. You can travel by four-lane expressway or surface road, which you estimate will take 60 minutes or 90 minutes, respectively. However, you think that three of the expressway's four lanes might be closed because of road work, in which case travel by expressway would take 120 minutes. Draw a diagram that represents this decision situation.

a. What are the state variables for this problem?

b. Draw the decision tree.

Good Decisions versus Good Outcomes

In all decision making, it is important to appreciate that good decisions can lead to bad outcomes and vice versa. For example, you can carefully look both ways before crossing the street, then get killed by a plane that crashes into the intersection. On the other hand, you can cross the street blindfolded and survive unscathed. Yet, before the fact, no one would dispute that looking both ways is a better decision than using a blindfold. Thus, with decision analysis, there are no guarantees. The process is analogous to carefully studying the traffic pattern on the street and then deciding how to cross.

TREE.xla

TREE.xla is an add-in for Excel 5.0 and higher. It is easy to install and learn and works in either Windows or Macintosh environments.

Running TREE.xla. Launch Excel and load TREE.xla from the **File Open** command.

Auto Load Option. If you want TREE.xla to load every time you launch Excel, follow these steps:

1. Select **Add-ins** from the **Tools** menu in Excel.

2. Select TREE.xla from the list of add-ins and click **OK**.

3. You can later go back and deselect TREE.xla from the **Add-in** menu to prevent Excel from loading it automatically.

Tutorial: Building a Decision Tree

Experimental Drug Development

The development of a new drug poses many risks. The following simplified example focuses on two primary risks: Will the drug be effective, and, if so, will it be approved for use in humans?

Imagine that you work for a pharmaceutical company that has been investigating cures for *Some Horrible Disease* (SHD). If a cure could be developed, it would be a boon to humankind and yield a profit of $200 million. Initial research indicates a 25% chance that a particular compound X will be effective against SHD. However, it will require an additional $10 million in research and development to know for sure. Furthermore, even if the resulting compound is proven effective, another $10 million in testing will be required to get it approved for use in humans. It is estimated that there is a 40% chance that the testing will reveal serious side effects and approval will be denied.

As SHD's project director, you are concerned with two primary issues. First, should you pursue the commercial development of compound X? Second, if you do pursue development, what value should you place on the project when comparing it with competing projects?

Building a Decision Tree with TREE.xla

The basic steps of building a decision tree are the following:

1. Starting the tree and specifying state variables if needed.
2. Adding decision and uncertainty forks.
3. Entering utility values at the leaves of the tree.
4. Performing sensitivity analysis.

Make sure that TREE.xla is loaded. Then proceed with the following tutorial.

Note: If you make a mistake in adding a decision or uncertainty fork, you can remove it with the **Remove Subtree** command. See Appendix C, "Software Command Reference," for details.

STEPS: STARTING THE TREE

1

Select **New Tree** from the **Tree** menu to open the dialog box shown below.

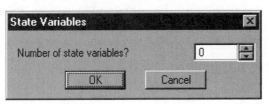

2

Click **OK** to proceed, as this simple example will not require the explicit use of state variables.

A new workbook is created that contains the root of the tree as shown in the figure below. Note that there are hidden columns in this worksheet that can be viewed with the **Show Variables** command (discussed in Appendix C, "Software Command Reference").

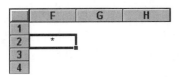

STEPS: ADDING DECISION AND UNCERTAINTY FORKS

1

Add a two-branch Decision Fork by invoking **Tree**, **Add Decision Fork**, **2 Branches**. The sheet should now look like this:

F2	▼		=MAX(J2:J3)
F	**G**	**H**	**J**
1			
2	0	Alternative	*
3		Alternative	*
4			

Note that the formula in cell F2 is simply the maximum of cells J2 and J3. This cell is formatted as bold blue, denoting that this is a decision fork.

Type the two alternatives, "Develop" and "Abandon," as shown.

2

	F	**G**	**H**	**J**
1				
2	0	Develop		*
3		Abandon		*
4				

3

To see how the decision fork works, imagine that there were no risks in developing the drug. Then the value of developing the drug would be $200 million, and the value of abandoning would be $0. Type these values (in millions) into the corresponding cells containing asterisks, then place the cursor in cell F2.

	F2	▼		=MAX(J2:J3)
	F	**G**	**H**	**J**
1				
2	**200**	Develop	==>	200
3		Abandon		0
4				

As you can see, given the choice of the values in cells J2 and J3, the decision fork took the maximum, 200. Also, notice that an arrow points along that branch of the best decision.

4

Of course you cannot be sure of getting that $200 million if you proceed with development, so we will add an uncertainty fork at cell J2. Normally, this would have been done without first typing a number into the cell containing the asterisk. With the cursor in cell J2, invoke **Tree**, **Add Uncertainty Fork**, **2 Branches**. The sheet should appear as shown below.

	J2	▼		=SUMPRODUCT(L2:L3,N2:N3)		
	F	**G**	**H**	**J**	**K**	**L**	**N**
1							
2	0	Develop	==>	*0*	Outcome 1	Prob.	*
3					Outcome 2	1	*
4							
5		Abandon	==>	0			
6							

Note that cell J2 now contains a SUMPRODUCT formula that will be discussed in detail later. This cell is formatted as italicized red, denoting that it is an uncertainty fork.

5

Type the two outcomes, "Effective" and "Ineffective," in cells K2 and K3, and the probability that the compound is effective, .25, in cell L2.

	L3	▼		=1-SUM(L2:L2)		
	F	**G**	**H**	**J**	**K**	**L**	**N**
1							
2	0	Develop	==>	0	Effective	0.25	*
3					Ineffective	0.75	*
4							
5		Abandon	==>	0			
6							

Note that cell L3 contains 1 minus the probability in cell L2, or .75.

Next, add the uncertainty of approval. With the cursor in cell N2, invoke **Tree, Add Uncertainty Fork, 2 Branches.** Then type the outcomes in cells O2 and O3 and the probability of approval, .6, in cell P2.

	F	G	H	J	K	L	N	O	P	R
1										
2	0	Develop	==>	0	Effective	0.25	0	Approved	0.6	*
3								Not Approved	0.4	*
4										
5					Ineffective	0.75	*			
6										
7		Abandon	==>	0						
8										

STEPS: **ENTERING UTILITY VALUES AT THE LEAVES OF THE TREE**

1

Each end node or leaf of the tree corresponds to a different state of the world. And in this case, each state of the world has an associated monetary value. Fill these into the leaves of the tree as follows.

Cell	State of the World	Value
J7	The project was abandoned. Nothing is ventured, lost or gained.	0
N5	The initial $10 million is invested but the compound proves ineffective.	-10
R3	The compound is effective after the first $10 million investment, but the drug does not get approved after the additional $10 million in testing.	-20
R2	The compound is effective and the drug is approved. Company receives $200 million in net profit	200

Evaluating the Decision Tree

Once the leaves have been filled in, the tree evaluates automatically and should appear as shown in the following figure.

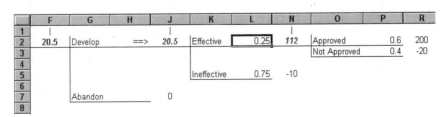

	F	G	H	J	K	L	N	O	P	R
1										
2	20.5	Develop	==>	20.5	Effective	0.25	112	Approved	0.6	200
3								Not Approved	0.4	-20
4										
5					Ineffective	0.75	-10			
6										
7		Abandon		0						
8										

Node N2 contains the expected value given that the compound is effective, calculated as follows:

Probability that drug is approved given that it is effective (.6)	x	Value if approved (200)	+	Probability that drug is not approved given that it is effective (.4)	x	Value if drug not approved given effective (−20)

This is calculated as = SUMPRODUCT (P2:P3,R2:R3) and results in an expected value of *112*.

Node J2 contains the expected value given that the drug is developed, calculated as follows:

Probability that compound is effective given development (.25)	x	Expected value if effective (112)	+	Probability that drug is ineffective given development (.75)	x	Value if drug is ineffective given development (-10)

This is calculated as = SUMPRODUCT (L2:L5,N2:N5) and results in an expected value of *20.5*.

Node F2 contains the expected value of the entire project, calculated as follows:

Maximum of	Expected value given development (20.5)	and	Expected value given no development (0)

This is calculated as = MAX(J2:J7) and results in an expected value of *20.5*.

Notice that the arrow indicates that the best choice is to develop the drug, but—far from $200 million—the expected value is only $20.5 million. If you must choose between this and some other potential cure for SHD, you should compare their relative expected values and risks.

Performing Sensitivity Analysis

In practice, it is seldom possible to know the inputs to a decision tree with great accuracy. However, by performing sensitivity analysis on the uncertain inputs, we can increase our confidence in the decision suggested by the tree. Furthermore, the decision tree can help you see future events that should make you change your mind. Sensitivity analysis can be quite involved or very simple as demonstrated in the following exercise.

EXERCISE **The Probability of Effectiveness**

6.3 The probability that the experimental compound will be effective is not easy to determine and opinions vary widely from person to person. Suppose the opinions that count in this case are the chief SHD researcher (35%), chairman of the board (15%), and you (25%). Return to the model and experiment with the probability that the drug is effective, located in cell L2, to determine how small a value still leads to the choice to develop the drug. Does this finding make it easier to sell the project?

Decision Analysis: Basic Concepts

Now that decision trees have been discussed, we return to the example involving ice cream and parking tickets. Such everyday questions can reveal a lot about the way we make more important decisions. The basic concepts are the following:

- *Utility.* The concept of utility helps us compare things that are as different as apples and oranges, or as ice cream and parking tickets.

- *Probability.* We must analyze what we mean by the chance or probability of uncertain events before we can make a reasonable decision. In this example, the uncertain event of concern is whether or not we get a parking ticket.

- *Expected Value.* Expected value defines what would happen "on average" if we were to imagine repeating the situation numerous times.

- *Decision Trees.* Decision trees are a tool for sharpening and formalizing the decision-making process. They are constructed from forks representing decision alternatives and uncertain outcomes.

- *Sensitivity Analysis.* Often the inputs to a decision tree are not known with certainty. Sensitivity analysis can increase your confidence in the decision making process by revealing input ranges over which particular decisions are optimal.

- *Value of Information.* One benefit of decision analysis is that it can quantify the value of obtaining additional information, even if that information is not completely dependable.

- *State Variables.* State variables are a convenient way of describing the various states of the world in which decision makers can find themselves. State variables allow you to develop complex utility functions that depend on numerous inputs.

- *Mustering the Courage of Your Convictions.* Just because you or your organization have determined a rational course of action in the light of uncertainty does not mean it will be expedient to carry it out.

For a more thorough discussion on these topics, see any Winston, Christian, and Broadie (1997) or any other textbook on decision analysis.

Utility

Recall the dilemma raised in the introduction, which led to the following figure. This example allows us to think about things we can relate to on a day-to-day basis. Yet even here it is not so easy to compare outcomes involving ice cream, dirty dishes, and parking tickets. One approach is to ask, for each outcome, what amount of cash would be of equal value to you.

For example, would you rather have one dollar than the ice cream? Probably not. The ice cream costs a dollar, and we assume that you are more than willing to pay that for it. How about two or three dollars? Of course, it depends on your personal tastes and even on the time of day, but suppose at this moment you would be indifferent to receiving either $5 in cash or the ice cream. Then one would say that your *utility* for a single ice cream cone at this moment is $5, and your *net utility* is $4 because the cone cost $1. Note that utility is not the equivalent of money. It is unlikely that you would be indifferent to receiving $500 in cash or 100 ice cream cones.

Also, two people's utility for the same thing need not be the same. For example, if you are allergic to milk, you have very low utility for ice cream under any conditions. Furthermore, this is just your utility for one cone.

The parking ticket would appear to have a utility of –$20, but this is not necessarily the case. Suppose you have many unpaid tickets and fear the consequences of another one. You might find that you would be as upset getting another ticket as you would be paying $30. Thus, the ticket would have a utility to you of –$30.

As for the dishes, you will have to do them sooner or later anyway. Therefore, for the decision at hand, it doesn't matter what utility you place on doing them. For convenience, we will use a utility of $0.

It is not necessary that money be used to evaluate the various items. The important thing is to place *relative* values on them. So for example, we could have measured everything in terms of free ice creams (FICs). In this case, paying $1 for ice cream would be worth 4/5 of a FIC, a ticket would be worth –6 FICs, and dishes would still be zero. The full theory of utility also accounts for such factors as your willingness to take risks in decision making. As a reminder, the net utilities we will use for this example are shown in the following figure.

Item			
Net Utility	$4	–$30	$0

EXERCISE 6.4 Utility for Ice Cream

What are your own utilities for each of the possible outcomes in the ice cream problem?

EXERCISE 6.5 Utility for the Umbrella

What are your utilities for each of the possible outcomes in the umbrella problem?

EXERCISE 6.6 Utility for Fastest Route

What are your utilities for each of the possible outcomes in the Fastest Route problem? Remember that because TREE.xla maximizes utility, you will want something that decreases with increasing time wasted on the road.

■ FUNDAMENTALS 6-1 ■ ■ ■ ■ ■ ■ ■ ■ ■ ■ ■ ■ ■

Probability

- Consider an uncertain **event** that can have multiple **outcomes**. For example, the event of rolling a die might have the outcomes 1,2,3,4,5, or 6. The *probability* of an outcome means the likelihood that the outcome will occur.

- The probability of any particular outcome is between 0 and 1. For example, the probability that the number 3 will occur when you roll a die is 1/6.

- The complete set of outcomes along with their associated probabilities is known as the *distribution* or *histogram* of outcomes as discussed in Chapter 2, *The Building Blocks of Uncertainty.*

- The sum of the probabilities of **all** outcomes is 1. That is, the chance that you will roll **some** number on the die is a 1.

- The probability that an outcome **will not occur** is 1 minus the probability that it does occur. Thus, the probability of not rolling a 3 is 1 − 1/6 = 5/6.

- If two outcomes are **mutually exclusive**, then the probability that **either** will occur is the **sum** of their probabilities. The probability of rolling a 3 or a 4 is 2/6 or 1/3.

- If two outcomes are **independent**, then the probability that they **both** occur is the **product** of their probabilities. The probability of rolling a 3 on the first of two dice, and a 4 on the second, is 1/6 times 1/6 or 1/36.

Probability

We cannot make a sensible decision concerning the ice cream problem without assessing the likelihood or probability of getting a ticket. What do we really mean by probability? Although a full definition of probability is beyond the scope of this work, an intuitive explanation is provided in Fundamentals Box 6-1. Fundamentals Box 6-2 provides an alternative subjective definition.

Imagine that you had stopped at this same place for ice cream one thousand times in the past and got 100 tickets. Then you would assess the probability of a ticket as being 10%. The greater the number of times you have stopped in the past, the more accurate the estimate. The probability of no ticket is 100% − 10% = 90%.

But let's get real! You've never even been in this part of town before, let alone parked here 1,000 times. As in most situations involving uncertainty, you must estimate the probability of getting a ticket based on your personal beliefs.

■ **FUNDAMENTALS 6-2** ■ ■ ■ ■ ■ ■ ■ ■ ■ ■ ■ ■

Subjective Definition of Probability

The probability of an event is an estimate based on your personal beliefs.

To assess your estimate of the probability of event A, imagine two games of chance. In the first game, you win $100 if event A occurs. In the second game, you win $100 if you get YES on the probability wheel (discussed in the text). Now adjust the probability on the wheel by clicking the arrows until you are indifferent as to which game you play. The number on the wheel is your subjective probability that A will occur.

The probability wheel is a device that helps people assess the probability of a given outcome based on their personal beliefs. A decision analyst named Carl Spetzler developed this concept in the mid 1960s while helping oil executives assess uncertain investments. Although originally constructed of clear plastic and colored paper, we will use a software version accessible by loading SPINNER.xls and selecting **Probability Wheel** from the Settings screen.

Click the **Spin** button a few times and you should see that the outcome is **YES** about 50% of the time. Next, adjust the probability to 25% by clicking the down arrow and repeat the experiment. Now you should get **YES** about 25% of the time.

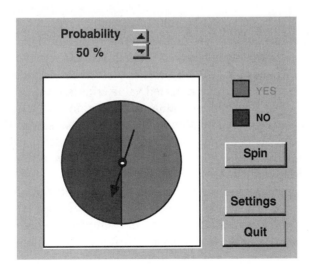

As an example of subjective probability, suppose that event A is "you get a ticket," and suppose you are indifferent to playing the two games when the wheel is set to 10%. This means you believe there is a 10% probability of getting a ticket.

This doesn't mean you are right. This just means that this is what you think. But what you think is what is important when you are the decision maker.

EXERCISE 6.7

Course Grade

If you are using this book in a graded course, you will receive an A, B, C, D, or F. What is the probability that you will receive an A?

EXERCISE 6.8

Thumb Tacks

A classroom exercise used to demonstrate the concept of personal probability involves tossing a thumb tack in the air. It will either land head up or point up (which we will call tails). Unlike a coin which is symmetric, and therefore has equal probably of heads or tails, the tack is quite asymmetric.

a. Use the probability wheel to assess your probability that a tossed thumb tack will come up heads without experimenting with a real thumb tack.

b. Perform an experiment with a real thumb tack to improve your estimate of the probability.

Expected Value

Decision analysts use several criteria for making decisions under uncertainty. A common one is known as *expected value*. If you can specify utilities for all the outcomes in your problem and can also estimate the probabilities of the uncertain outcomes, then the expected value criterion can be used. Intuitively, you can view the expected value of a situation as the average outcome if you could repeat the situation many times. As we saw in Chapter 2, even situations that can't be repeated can often be modeled using Monte Carlo simulation. In this case, the expected value would be estimated by the average on the Simulation Statistics screen.

Once you have assessed the utilities and probabilities of all uncertain outcomes, you can calculate the expected value of a situation. The expected value is calculated by summing the utility of each possible outcome multiplied by the probability of that outcome's occurrence. Fundamentals Box 6-3 shows the formulas used for expected value.

■ **FUNDAMENTALS 6-3** ■ ■ ■ ■ ■ ■ ■ ■ ■ ■ ■ ■ ■

Expected Value

Expected Value =   (Probability of outcome 1)(Utility of outcome 1)

+   (Probability of outcome 2)(Utility of outcome 2)

:   :

:   :

+   (Probability of outcome k)(Utility of outcome k)

or more compactly $EV = \sum_{i=1}^{k} P_i U_i$

where P_i and U_i are the ith probability and utility, respectively, with a total of k outcomes.

EXERCISE

6.9 Expected Values

a.   Suppose you are betting on a coin and will win $1 if you throw heads and lose $1 if you throw tails. What is the expected value?

b.   What is the expected value of each of the options in the umbrella problem?

c.   What is the expected utility of each of the two routes in the fastest route problem of Exercise 6.2? Use .2 as the probability that three lanes of the expressway are closed. Use the negative of time of travel as a measure of utility. For example, the utility for traveling 60 minutes by expressway is –60, and so on.

Decision Forks

Observe that the diagram on page 158 resembles a tree turned on its side. By adding utilities and probabilities to the figure, we create what is known as a *decision tree* that can be used to determine the alternative that maximizes expected utility.

Decisions are modeled by forks with one branch for each alternative facing the decision maker at a given stage. The utility value of the associated alternative goes into each branch, whereupon the decision node displays the utility of the best alternative.

An analogy may be helpful in gaining insight into the nature of decision forks. Imagine that the fork is made of pipe with a valve on each branch.

■ **FUNDAMENTALS 6-4** ■ ■ ■ ■ ■ ■ ■ ■ ■ ■ ■ ■

Decision Trees

Decision trees, like real trees, are made of forked branches that in turn lead to additional forked branches. The base of each fork is known as a *node*. The base of the first fork is known as the *root*. Branches that do not lead to additional forks are known as *leaves*.

There are two kinds of forks. **Decision forks** represent the alternatives the decision maker will have at various stages. **Uncertainty forks** represent the uncertainties the decision maker will face at various stages.

Water of different temperatures flows into each branch where the temperature represents the utility, that is, the hotter the better. You get to decide how to open the valves. You want hot water, so you open the valve on the hottest branch and close all others. A schematic diagram of a two alternative decision fork is shown in the following figure.

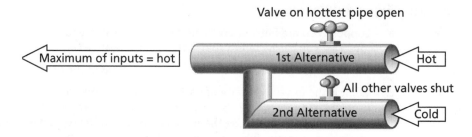

When a decision fork is created using TREE.xla, the node contains a formula of the form MAX(Utilities of all inputs), which in effect automatically opens the valve to the hottest branch.

Uncertainty Forks

Uncertainties are modeled by forks with one branch for each possible outcome of an uncertainty facing the decision maker at a given stage. For each possible outcome, its utility value as well as its probability of occurrence go into a branch. The uncertainty node then displays the expected (or average) utility of all outcomes.

Again using the hot water analogy, the valve of the uncertainty fork corresponding to the outcome that actually occurs will be open, with all others being shut. But you don't know which one will be open in advance, so you don't know what temperature the water coming out will be. You can determine the expected temperature, however, by opening each valve in proportion to the probability of the associated outcomes. A schematic diagram of a two-outcome uncertainty fork is shown below.

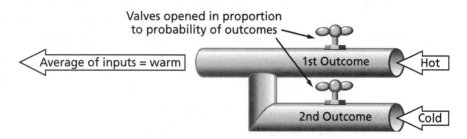

When an uncertainty fork is created using TREE.xla, the node contains a formula of the form SUMPRODUCT(Probabilities of Inputs,Utilities of Inputs), which calculates the expected utility.

The following figure shows the decision tree for the ice cream example. Usually decision nodes are drawn as squares, and uncertainty nodes as circles. Notice that the decision is to stop for ice cream, and that the utility of the root is $1. This means that if you were offered $1 to go straight home and wash the dishes, you would be indifferent.

Decision Fork   **Uncertainty Fork**

Ticket P = 0.1 — Utility = 4 − 30 + 0 = −26

0.1* (−26) + 0.9* 4 = 1

Stop for ice cream

No ticket P = 0.9

Utility = 4 + 0 = 4

Maximum of 0 and 1 = 1

Go home

Utility = 0

EXERCISE **The Ice Cream Example's Decision Tree**

6.10   Use TREE.xla to create the decision trees for the following:

a.   The ice cream example. No state variables are needed, so leave the number set to 0 when you make the new tree. If you have difficulty, go through the tutorial in the last section. Save the workbook as ICECREAM when you are done.

b. The umbrella problem. Save your completed workbook as LONDON.

c. The fastest route problem. Save your completed workbook as FASTEST.

Sensitivity Analysis

Often the inputs to a decision tree are not known with certainty. For example, you usually can't accurately estimate the probability of getting a ticket. Sensitivity analysis can increase our confidence in the decision-making process by revealing input ranges over which certain decisions are optimal.

In the next exercise, we experiment with our estimates of probabilities.

EXERCISE 6.11

Experimenting with Probability Estimates

a. Retrieve the ICECREAM model created earlier and incrementally increase the probability of getting a ticket until you are just indifferent to stopping for the cone or going home. Record the result.

b. Retrieve the LONDON model and adjust the probability of rain until you are indifferent to whether or not you buy the umbrella.

c. Retrieve the FASTEST model and adjust the probability that the three expressway lanes are closed until you are indifferent to taking the expressway or surface street. What is this probability? What is the expected value of the two routes at this probability?

STEPS: **USING A GRAPHICAL APPROACH TO SENSITIVITY ANALYSIS**

It is often useful to determine how the expected utility depends on some particular aspect of the situation. Here we will plot expected utility versus the probability of getting a ticket for the ice cream example by using a data table.

1

Retrieve ICECREAM, move to cell G8 (any empty cell below the tree will do) and enter 0, then .01 in the same column as pictured below.

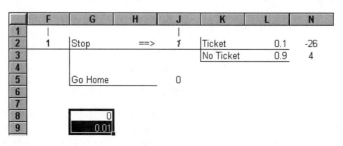

	F	G	H	J	K	L	N
1							
2	1	Stop	==>	1	Ticket	0.1	-26
3					No Ticket	0.9	4
4							
5		Go Home		0			
6							
7							
8			0				
9			0.01				

2 Select the two cells just entered (as shown in Step 1), click on the small black square in the lower right corner, and drag downward until the series reaches .2 as pictured below.

	G	H
7		
8	0	
9	0.01	
10	0.02	
11	0.03	
12	0.04	
13	0.05	
14	0.06	
15	0.07	
16	0.08	
17	0.09	
18	0.1	
19	0.11	
20	0.12	
21	0.13	
22	0.14	
23	0.15	
24	0.16	
25	0.17	
26	0.18	
27	0.19	
28	0.2	

3 In cell H7, enter "=F2" to make "overall utility" drive the table.

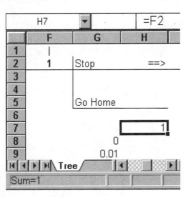

4

Select cells G7 through H28 (don't forget to start in row 7), then invoke the **Data Table** command. The table dialog box shown below will appear. This is a column table for which the "input" is the probability of a ticket (L2).

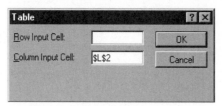

5

With the cursor in the **Column Input Cell** field, select cell L2.

6

Click **OK** and you should see the following table.

	G	H
7		1
8	0	4
9	0.01	3.7
10	0.02	3.4
11	0.03	3.1
12	0.04	2.8

7

To graph this relationship, select cells G8:H28 (this time you are starting in row 8), click on the Chart Wizard icon, and then highlight a range in the worksheet for a graph. This will initiate the Chart Wizard. Select a line graph.

Be sure to specify the 1st column as **Category (X) Axis Labels**.

8

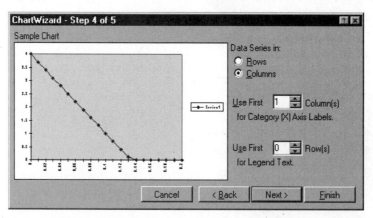

This graph's X axis represents a range of probabilities of getting a ticket, and its Y axis represents the utility of the overall situation. The next exercise involves interpreting this graph.

The Probability of Getting a Ticket, Revisited

a.   Why is the value 4 when the probability of a ticket is 0?

b.   The graph consists of a bent line. Why does it bend, and what do the two straight segments correspond to?

Value of Information

In almost any decision-making situation, it is possible to obtain additional pertinent information at some cost. One benefit of decision analysis is that it can be used to quantify the value of such information.

Returning to the ice cream example, suppose you have a friend on the police force with information on the whereabouts of the ticket patrol. Imagine that you can call your friend from your cellular phone as you arrive at the ice cream parlor. What would this information be worth to you?

The Value of Perfect Information

Let us first assume that your friend knows the ticket patrol's exact location and will relay this to you correctly. This is known as *perfect information*. Now, unlike the uncertain case, you get to learn if you will get a ticket *before* you decide instead of *after*.

One of two things can happen. First, there is 90% chance that you will get the "all clear" from your friend, in which case you will go in and get your $4 worth of utility from the ice cream. Second, there is a 10% chance that you will be warned of the ticket patrol, in which case you will go straight home and get 0 utility from washing the dishes. Thus, the expected utility is 90%*$4 + 10%*$0 = $3.60.

Now suppose your friend implies that a donation to the Policeman's Benevolent Association would be appreciated before he gives you his information.   The maximum amount you should be willing to pay (cost of the call plus the donation) is the difference between the expected utility with perfect information ($3.60) and that without any information ($1.00). So in this case the *value of perfect information* is $2.60.

This analysis can be thought of as simply reversing the order of the decision and uncertainty forks in the original example, as shown in the following diagram.

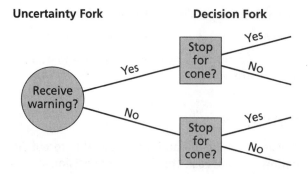

Uncertainty Fork   **Decision Fork**

EXERCISE 6.13 **Friend's Information**

What would the value of your friend's information be if the probability of getting a ticket was 5% instead of 10%?

EXERCISE 6.14 **Expressway Hotline**

To help you decide which route to take, you call the expressway hotline to obtain an accurate report of expressway roadwork. You believe that there is a 5% chance that the report will say there is roadwork in which case you will travel by city road. Otherwise, there is a 95% chance that the report will say there is no roadwork and you will travel by expressway.

a. Modify the FASTEST decision tree that you drew earlier to reflect this new situation.

b. What is the expected value of this situation? Remember that your utility is in terms of the negative of travel time rather than in terms of money.

c. What is the most (again measured in time) that this information is worth?

You proceed to call the hotline. When you call, however, all lines are busy, and a recorded message tells you to expect a 30-minute wait before a representative can answer your line.

d. Should you wait?

The Value of Imperfect Information

Going back to the ice cream example, suppose that your friend's warnings are not completely accurate. That is, the information provided is imperfect. We will still assume an overall 10% probability of the ticket patrol's arrival.

However, now suppose that past experience indicates that your friend gives a warning 20% of the time, but that such warnings are only 30% accurate. In other words, the probability of a ticket is only 30% given that you have received a warning. Thus, the joint probability of being warned *and* actually getting a ticket is 20% * 30% = 6%.

What about the other 80% of the time, when you don't get a warning. Let *p* denote the probability of a ticket, given that you don't get a warning. The overall probability of a ticket is 10% of which we have only accounted for 6%, so we know that 80% * p = 4%. Thus p = 4%/80% = 5%.

This is summarized in the following table:

	Probability of **Ticket** Given Warning = 30%
Probability of **Warning** = 20%	
	Probability of **No Ticket** Given Warning = 70%
	Probability of **Ticket** Given No Warning = 5%
Probability of **No Warning** = 80%	
	Probability of **No Ticket** Given No Warning = 95%

STEPS: **MODELING IMPERFECT INFORMATION**

Most decision trees are made up of repeated subtrees. To calculate the value of imperfect information, we will repeat the original ice cream decision tree once for the Warning case and once for the No Warning case. Proceed as follows:

1 Open the ice cream file that you saved earlier.

2 Create a new tree with the **Tree New** command.

3 Start the tree with a two-branch uncertainty to model the uncertainty of whether or not you receive a warning from your friend. Replace Outcome 1 with "Warning" and Outcome 2 with "No Warning" and enter the probability .2 of receiving a warning.

	F	G	H	J
1				
2	0	Warning	0.2	*
3		No Warning	0.8	*
4				

4

In the next steps, we will graft the original tree onto each branch. Carefully count the rows in the model containing the original tree. There should be four.

5

Add a four-branch decision fork to the current tree in cell J2. This is just a placeholder for the subtree you are about to graft on. *Note:* If the subtree had taken five rows, you would have added a five-branch fork here.

	F	G	H	J	K	L	N
1	|			|			
2	0	Warning	0.2	0	Alternative		*
3					Alternative		*
4					Alternative		*
5					Alternative		*
6							
7		No Warning	0.8	*			
8							

6

Use the **Window** command to move to the ICECREAM workbook, then select the entire tree starting at the root (cells F2:N5). Copy this selection to the clipboard with the **Edit Copy** command.

	F	G	H	J	K	L	N
1	|			|			
2	1	Stop	==>	1	Ticket	0.1	-26
3					No Ticket	0.9	4
4							
5		Go Home		0			
6							

7

Move back to the new tree and paste the subtree first into cell J2, then into cell J7.

	F	G	H	J	K	L	N	O	P	Q	R
1	|			|							
2	1	Warning	0.2	1	Stop	==>	1	Ticket	0.1	0.02	-26
3								No Ticket	0.9	0.18	4
4											
5					Go Home		0				
6											
7		No Warning	0.8	1	Stop	==>	1	Ticket	0.1	0.08	-26
8								No Ticket	0.9	0.72	4
9											
10					Go Home		0				
11											

8

Next, change the probabilities of getting a ticket to reflect the information received in each case. Move the cursor to the probability of getting a ticket given the warning (this should be cell P2) and replace 0.1 with 0.3. Move the cursor to the probability of getting a ticket given no warning (this should be cell P7) and replace 0.1 with 0.05.

	F	G	H	J	K	L	N	O	P	Q	R
1											
2	2	Warning	0.2	0	Stop		-5	Ticket	0.3	0.06	-26
3								No Ticket	0.7	0.14	4
4											
5					Go Home	==>	0				
6											
7		No Warning	0.8	2.5	Stop	==>	2.5	Ticket	0.05	0.04	-26
8								No Ticket	0.95	0.76	4
9											
10					Go Home		0				
11											

The overall expected value of this tree is $2. The difference between this and the original value with no information is $1. This is known as the *value of imperfect information*. Your contribution to the Policeman's Benevolent Association should not be as great as with perfect information.

State Variables

As mentioned in the ice cream example, state variables are a way of quantifying the various states of the world in which decision makers might find themselves. When there are numerous state variables, it is convenient to keep track of them within the tree, as in the following example.

A classic problem addressed by decision analysis is the one faced by a wildcatter deciding whether or not to drill for oil at a particular site. Although the example below is greatly simplified for demonstration purposes, it shows how state variables can increase the power of decision trees by consistently keeping track of the possible states of the world.

Imagine that a wildcatter owns a lease that grants him the rights to any oil discovered at a particular site. This lease can be sold for a guaranteed $150,000. On the other hand, if the wildcatter endures the multiple risks of drilling for oil, much greater rewards might be in store. The first state variable, L, is the amount of money received for the lease. This is $150,000 if the lease is sold, and $0 otherwise.

The first risk is the uncertainty in the actual cost of the drilling operation. There is a 70% chance that the cost will be high ($2,000,000) and a 30% chance that it will be low ($200,000). The state variable (C) is thus $2,000,000 with probability 70% or $200,000 with probability 30%.

There is the even bigger risk involving the quantity (Q) of oil found. There is only a 5% chance of a real gusher (1,000,000 barrels) and a 95% chance of 50,000 barrels. Finally, the price (P) of oil by the time the well comes in is expected to be $20 per barrel with probability 40% and $15 per barrel with probability 60%.

The utility is calculated as Revenue from Selling Lease – Cost of Drilling + (Quantity of Oil × Price of Oil). This can be rewritten as

$$\text{Utility (Lease, Cost, Qty, Price)} = \text{Lease} - \text{Cost} + \text{Qty} \times \text{Price}$$

Thus, in the event that the lease is sold, Lease = $150,000 and Cost, Quantity, and Price are 0. If the well is drilled, then Lease = 0 and Cost, Quantity, and Price are all uncertain, as described. Lease, Cost, Quantity, and Price are known as the problem's *state variables*.

A possible tree for the wildcatter's problem is shown in the following figure. Note that the uncertainties could have been modeled in any order in this situation.

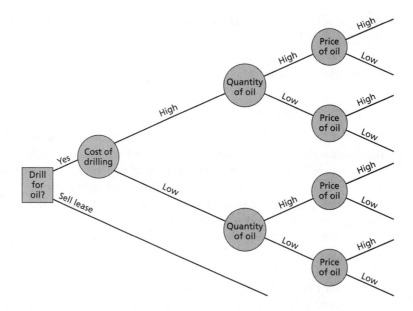

We could solve this problem without state variables, but it would be difficult to keep track of what utility to place at each of the leaves of the tree.

State variables streamline the process by letting you enter values for the lease revenue, cost, quantity, and price as the tree is constructed. When the tree is completed, a single formula for the utility of the top leaf is entered and copied down to the remaining leaves, at which point the tree is evaluated automatically.

STEPS: **USING STATE VARIABLES TO DRILL FOR OIL**

We will now create a new tree and name the state variables for the wildcatter's problem. Proceed as follows:

First, specify the state variables: Invoke the **Tree New** command, specifying four state variables. The root of the tree will be created with places for these four variables.

	B	C	D	E	F	G	H	I	J
1	I			Var 1	Var 2	Var 3	Var 4	JP	
2	*	Root	1					1	*
3									

Type "Lease," "Cost," "Qty," and "Price" into the cells containing Var 1 through Var 4.

	B	C	D	E	F	G	H	I	J
1	I			Lease	Cost	Qty	Price	JP	
2	*	Root	1					1	*
3									

The cell labeled JP is involved in calculating the joint probabilities of the outcomes as described later.

Specify the root decision: Move the cursor to the root (J2) and add a two-branch decision fork. Label the two alternatives: "Drill" and "Sell Lease."

Move the cursor to M3, the value of L if the lease is sold, and enter 150 (all numbers will be in 1,000's in this model). Because the value of the lease will be 0 if you drill, leave cell M2 as it is.

	J	K	L	M	N	O	P	Q	R
1	I			Lease	Cost	Qty	Price	JP	
2	0	Drill		0	0	0	0	1	*
3		Sell Lease		150	0	0	0	1	*
4									

Specify the drilling cost uncertainty: Move the cursor to the "*" in cell R2 (the utility at the end of the Drill branch) and insert a two-outcome uncertainty fork. Name the outcomes "Hi Cost" and "Low Cost" respectively.

Enter a probability of 0.7 in cell T2 for the chance of a high drilling cost. Note that T3 becomes 0.3. Enter 2000 and 200 (remember all numbers are in 1,000's) for the high and low values of cost in cells V2 and V3.

7

Move the cursor to the "*" in cell R5 (the utility at the end of the Sell Lease branch) and insert a one-branch (null) decision fork. This keeps all the leaves of the tree in the same column.

	Q	R	S	T	U	V	W	X	Y	Z
1	JP				Lease	Cost	Qty	Price	JP	
2	1	0	Hi Cost	0.7	0	2000	0	0	0.7	*
3			Lo Cost	0.3	0	200	0	0	0.3	*
4										
5	1	*		==>	150	0	0	0	1	*

8

Specify the quantity uncertainty: Move the cursor to the "*" in cell Z2 (the utility at the end of the High Drilling Cost branch) and add a two-branch uncertainty fork. Name the outcomes "Hi Qty" and "Low Qty," respectively.

9

Enter a probability of 0.05 in cell AB2 for the chance of a high quantity of oil. Enter "1000" and "50" for the high and low values of Qty, the quantity state variable (cells AE2:AE3).

	Z	AA	AB	AC	AD	AE	AF	AG	AH
1				Lease	Cost	Qty	Price	JP	
2	0	Hi Qty	0.05	0	2000	1000	0	0.035	*
3		Lo Qty	0.95	0	2000	50	0	0.665	*
4									
5		*							

10

Move the cursor to the "*" in cell Z5 (the utility at the end of the Low Drilling Cost branch) and add a two-branch uncertainty fork.

11

Because you face exactly the same quantity of uncertainty in either the Hi Cost or Low Cost case, you can simply copy the uncertainty fork in cells AA2:AH3, then use **Edit Paste** to place it over the fork you have just entered in cell Z5. Or, you can simply reenter the same information.

12

Move the cursor to the "*" in cell Z9 and insert a one-branch decision fork. As before, this keeps all the leaves of the tree in the same column. Before continuing, notice that the state variables always inherit the values of their parent branches.

Lease revenue if you sell out   Hi Costs   Lo Costs

	Y	Z	AA	AB	AC	AD	AE	AF	AG	AH
1	JP				Lease	Cost	Qty	Price	JP	
2	0.7	0	Hi Qty	0.05	0	2000	1000	0	0.035	*
3			Lo Qty	0.95	0	2000	50	0	0.665	*
4										
5	0.3	0	Hi Qty	0.05	0	200	1000	0	0.015	*
6			Lo Qty	0.95	0	200	50	0	0.285	*
7										
8										
9	1	*		==>	150	0	0	0	1	*

13

Specify the price uncertainty: Move the cursor to the "*" in cell AH2 (the utility at the end of the Hi Cost, Hi Qty branch) and insert a two-branch uncertainty fork. Name the first and second outcomes "Hi" and "Lo Price," respectively.

14

Enter a probability of 0.4 in cell AJ2 for the chance of a high price of oil. Enter "20" and "15" for the high and low values of Price, the price state variable (cells AN2:AN3).

15

Add two-branch uncertainty forks at cell AH5, then at AH9, and finally at AH12. Copy the uncertainty fork in cells AH2:AP3 to cells AH5, AH9, and AH12. *Note:* We have specified the quantity of oil in thousands of barrels and the price per barrel in dollars. Thus, revenues will be in thousands of dollars, consistent with our cost figures.

16

Move the cursor to the "*" in cell AH17 and insert another one-branch decision fork. There should now be nine "*"s in column AP representing the leaves of the tree.

	AH	AI	AJ	AK	AL	AM	AN	AO	AP
1	I			Lease	Cost	Qty	Price	JP	
2	0	Hi Price	0.4	0	2000	1000	20	0.014	*
3		Lo Price	0.6	0	2000	1000	15	0.021	*
4									
5	0	Hi Price	0.4	0	2000	50	20	0.266	*
6		Lo Price	0.6	0	2000	50	15	0.399	*
7									
8									
9	0	Hi Price	0.4	0	200	1000	20	0.006	*
10		Lo Price	0.6	0	200	1000	15	0.009	*
11									
12	0	Hi Price	0.4	0	200	50	20	0.114	*
13		Lo Price	0.6	0	200	50	15	0.171	*
14									
15									
16									
17	*		==>	150	0	0	0	1	*

17

Specify the utility of the leaves: Carefully inspect cells AH2:AP17 and compare them with the cells in the previous figure to verify that the correct values of the state variables are associated with each leaf of the tree. Recall that the utility as a function of the state variables is Utility = Lease – Cost + Qty * Price. Place this formula in the top leaf by entering " = AK2 – AL2 + AM2 * AN2" in cell AP2. The result should be 18000 as shown below.

AP2	▼		=AK2-AL2+AM2*AN2				
	AJ	AK	AL	AM	AN	AO	AP
1		Lease	Cost	Qty	Price	JP	
2	0.4	0	2000	1000	20	0.014	18000
3	0.6	0	2000	1000	15	0.021	*

18

With the cursor still in cell AP2, invoke the **Tree Copy Utility** command. The utility formula will be copied to each of the remaining leaves of the tree.

19

Inspect the tree: Invoke the **Tree Hide Variables** command to hide the columns containing the state variables and joint probabilities. Use the **View Zoom** command if necessary to get the whole tree to fit on the screen. You will see that the decision is to drill, yielding an expected value of $197,500. Notice the arrow pointing down the Drill branch.

arrow indicating recommended branch

20

We now discuss the joint probabilities. The joint probability columns are labeled JP. Invoke the **Tree Show Variables** command and move the cursor to AO2. The value in this cell indicates that given that you drill, the *joint probability* of simultaneous high values of cost, quantity, and price is 1.4%. Similarly, cell AO3 indicates that the joint probability of a high cost, high quantity, and low price is 2.1%. Cell AO17 indicates that given that you decide to sell the lease instead of drilling, then the probability that you actually do so is 100%.

The joint probabilities of all leaves emanating from the same decision branch should sum to 1. Save your model as WILDCAT.xls.

EXERCISE
6.15

Experimenting with the Probability of a Gusher

At what probability of a gusher would you be indifferent to drilling or selling the lease? Don't forget this probability appears in more than one cell in your model.

EXERCISE
6.16

Toy Manufacturing

A toy manufacturer must decide between a large (100,000 unit) or small (50,000 unit) production run of a new toy. The production costs are uncertain, but it is known that there are economies of scale. For 50,000 units, there is believed to be a 50/50 chance that the cost per unit will be either $5 or $4. For 100,000, there is a 50/50 chance that the cost per unit will be either $4 or $3. The demand for the toy is thought to be elastic—that is, to sell a larger quantity, the firm will have to lower the price. The price at which 50,000 units can be moved is estimated to be $10 or $8, with equal probability. At 100,000 units, this drops to $6 and $5, again with equal likelihood. How many toys should the firm produce to maximize expected profit?

STEPS: USING TWO-WAY SENSITIVITY ANALYSIS

Earlier we investigated the sensitivity of the utility of the ice cream scenario relative to the probability of getting a ticket. We will now perform a more complex sensitivity analysis on the drilling decision. The greatest uncertainties in oil exploration generally involve both the probability of making a high quantity discovery, and the size of the discovery itself. This time, instead of changing a single parameter (probability of a ticket), we will simultaneously vary both the probability of a high quantity and the high quantity itself by means of a two-way data table.

Start with the wildcat model developed earlier, and display the state variables.

1   First, we must make sure that when we change the value of one of the parameters of interest, it changes throughout the tree. In cell AB9, enter the formula " = AB2" for the probability of a high quantity of oil. In cell AE9, enter the formula " = AE2" for the high quantity itself.

2   Create a two-way data table in a blank section of the worksheet as follows. (See your spreadsheet manual for details of the two-way data table if necessary.)

3   Create a column of values in cells AS3:AS18 for the high quantity running down the left side of the table from 2000 to 500 decremented by 100.

4   Then, in cells AT2:BI2, create a row of values for the probability of a high quantity from 0 to .15 incremented by 0.01. Now select columns AT through BI and reduce the column width so the entire row fits on a single screen. *Hint:* Reducing the font size with the **Format Cells** command will allow a tighter fit.

5   Next, in cell AS2, enter the formula " = IF(J2 = R2,"D","."). J2 is the root of the tree, and R2 is the expected utility if the well is drilled. So this formula returns a "D" if the combination of the probability of a high quantity and the quantity itself are sufficient to make drilling the optimal decision. Otherwise it returns ".".

6

Next, select cells AS2:BI18 and invoke the **Data Table** command, selecting AB2, the probability of high quantity, as the Row input and AE2, the quantity itself, as the column input.

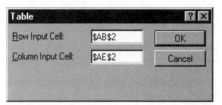

Your table should look like the one below. This shows that as the probability of a gusher drops below .02, no quantity of oil shown is adequate to justify drilling. Similarly, we also see that once the probability of a gusher reaches .1, any amount of oil greater than 500 justifies drilling.

| AS2 | ▼ | | | | =IF(J2=R2,"D",".") | | | | | | | | |

	AS	AT	AU	AV	AW	AX	AY	AZ	BA	BB	BC	BD	BE	BF
1														
2	D	0	0.01	0.02	0.03	0.04	0.05	0.06	0.07	0.08	0.09	0.1	0.11	0.12
3	2000	.	.	.	D	D	D	D	D	D	D	D	D	D
4	1900	.	.	.	D	D	D	D	D	D	D	D	D	D
5	1800	.	.	.	D	D	D	D	D	D	D	D	D	D
6	1700	.	.	.	D	D	D	D	D	D	D	D	D	D
7	1600	.	.	.	D	D	D	D	D	D	D	D	D	D
8	1500	.	.	.	.	D	D	D	D	D	D	D	D	D
9	1400	.	.	.	.	D	D	D	D	D	D	D	D	D
10	1300	.	.	.	.	D	D	D	D	D	D	D	D	D
11	1200	.	.	.	.	D	D	D	D	D	D	D	D	D
12	1100	.	.	.	.	.	D	D	D	D	D	D	D	D
13	1000	.	.	.	.	.	D	D	D	D	D	D	D	D
14	900	.	.	.	.	.	.	D	D	D	D	D	D	D
15	800	.	.	.	.	.	.	D	D	D	D	D	D	D
16	700	.	.	.	.	.	.	.	D	D	D	D	D	D
17	600	.	.	.	.	.	.	.	.	.	D	D	D	D
18	500	.	.	.	.	.	.	.	.	.	.	D	D	D
19														

Mustering the Courage of Your Convictions

Just because you or your organization have determined a rational course of action in the light of uncertainty does not mean it will be expedient to carry it out. In a fascinating book entitled *Weapons and Hope*, Freeman Dyson (1984) relates the following first hand account of such a difficulty.

As an operations research analyst in the British bomber command during World War II, he determined that the allied pilots, anxious about mid-air collisions, were not flying in tight enough formations. This left them vulnerable to attack by enemy fighters. Dyson worked out the optimal formation pattern to minimize expected losses from all causes. This required the pilots to start having five times as many mid-air collisions! Freeman writes, "The Command followed our advice, and the crews reluctantly obeyed. This decision confirmed the crews' belief that their commander in chief, familiarly known as Bert Harris or Butcher Harris, was as callous toward them as he was toward the Germans."

7

Overview of Optimization

For want of a nail, the shoe was lost, For want of a shoe, a horse was lost,
For want of a horse, a rider was lost, For want of a rider, a battle was lost,
For want of a battle, the kingdom was lost, And all for the want of a horseshoe nail!"

MOTHER GOOSE

Human endeavor has always involved activities that compete for scarce resources. Imagine yourself as a medieval king, preparing to battle an adversary. You take inventory of your horses, men, swords, shields, armor, horseshoes, and nails, and head over to the local arms merchant with your war chest. You must coordinate your purchases to maximize the likelihood of a successful military campaign. If you could postpone the conflict for 1,000 years, you would have access to mathematical optimization, which would provide the best allocation of your men, materials, and funds. Further, it would illuminate the true value of scarce resources such as horseshoe nails in the coming conflict.

The following are some modern resource allocation problems:

- A boat manufacturer with limited raw materials must specify production quantities for several types of small craft to maximize profit.

- A municipality must schedule its police force for maximum effectiveness while meeting work rules such as shift length, number of work breaks, and overtime hours.

- Managers of a pension fund want to invest their assets to achieve 8% growth while minimizing risk.

- A steel mill must determine how to ship its product to meet demand at minimum cost.

OVERVIEW

Introduction

This section contains a short introduction to optimization followed by brief descriptions of two widely used spreadsheet optimization packages, the Excel Solver and What's*Best!* All optimization examples in this book have been included in formats to run with both of these packages.

A Tutorial: Maximum Profit

A boat manufacturer with limited raw materials must specify production quantities for several types of small craft to maximize profit.

Basic Examples

Additional linear optimization examples are introduced in product mix, blending, scheduling, transportation, and network flow models.

Introduction

Optimization means determining the best way to accomplish an objective given the limited resources under your control. The field of mathematical optimization has produced several powerful techniques for dealing with a wide class of problems in such areas as manufacturing, transportation, scheduling, and finance. A simple ABC checklist can help you optimize a given situation.

The ABC's of Optimization

A. What can you adjust? That is, what is under your direct managerial control? This includes such things as the number of widgets to manufacture, the number of people to hire for the 9 o'clock shift, or the amount of money to invest in a given security.

B. What do you mean by best? This constitutes the desired objective. Is the best solution the one that maximizes profit, minimizes cost, or maximizes the chance that you keep your job? The answer to this question depends on management's preferences.

You cannot optimize more than one objective at one time. You might hear people say that they want to both maximize profit and minimize cost simultaneously. But these objectives are mutually exclusive—bankruptcy minimizes cost but does nothing for profit, and making a profit requires an investment.

C. What constraints must be obeyed? In taking managerial steps to optimize your objectives, certain things are simply impossible. These are known as constraints and can be of several kinds. Some involve limited resources. That is, any plan you devise must stay within your budget and not use more raw materials than you have at your disposal. Constraints can also involve meeting performance criteria. For example, you must have at least three people on duty during the 9 o'clock shift. Or, your portfolio must be composed of at least 20% AAA bonds.

Linear and Nonlinear Programming

Optimization problems fall into two major categories: linear and nonlinear. If all the formulas defining an optimization model are linear, it is known as a linear programming (LP) problem and is susceptible to very powerful solution techniques. As discussed later, linearity is a serious restriction. However, many problems in manufacturing, transportation, scheduling, finance, and other areas have been formulated to be solved with linear programming. Some of these problems involve hundreds of thousands of variables.

If any of the formulas defining the problem are not linear, it is known as a nonlinear programming (NLP) problem. Nonlinear problems allow any continuous (smoothly changing) relationships between variables. They can arise in the fields of engineering and finance. These problems are more difficult to solve than linear ones. Nonlinear optimization solution techniques typically handle much smaller numbers of variables than linear programming techniques and can require good initial guesses at a solution for dependable results. The distinction between linear and nonlinear problems will be discussed further in the next chapter.

Spreadsheet Optimization Software

There are two primary spreadsheet optimization packages:

- *The Excel Solver.* The Excel Solver ships with Excel and is specified under the add-in options.
- What's*Best!*. Included with INSIGHT.xla is a small version of What's*Best!*. This package, introduced in 1985, was the first widely marketed spreadsheet optimization software (Savage, 1985).

All optimization examples in this book have been included in formats to run with both of these packages. A brief comparison of these packages appears in the following table.

	The Excel Solver	What's*Best!*
Model Specifications	Input through a dialog box. Can be stored to or retrieved from a range in the worksheet.	Stored directly into the worksheet model as formulas and cell properties.
Formula Interpretation	Interprets formulas through differencing. All Excel formulas recognized.*	Interprets formulas algebraically.
Linear versus Nonlinear solutions	Type of model must be specified in Options dialog box.	Type of model automatically detected.
Advantages	Universally available, allowing small models to be shared widely throughout organizations. Special formulas* allow elegant model formulation in certain situations. See, for example, the use of DSUM in NETWORK.xls.	Because models can be merged without losing optimization specifications, large integrated models can be created from smaller sub-models. See SUPPLYW.xls and SUPPLYUW.xls. Models can be built across multiple worksheets within a workbook. Automatic linear versus nonlinear solutions are provided.
Upgrades	Available through Frontline Systems at www.frontsys.com.	Available through LINDO Systems, Inc., at www.lindo.com.

*Note: although discontinuous functions such as IF statements will not result in error messages, they may not yield reliable results.

Tutorial: Maximum Profit

How Many Boats to Produce?

We start with a common type of a linear programming problem known as a product mix model. A manufacturer of fiberglass boats must produce during the winter in preparation for the spring selling season. The manufacturer wants to maximize its profit given its limited raw materials. The product line is shown in the following figure in order of decreasing profit per unit.

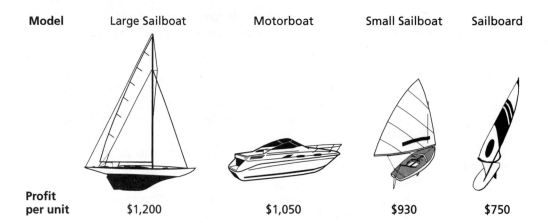

Model	Large Sailboat	Motorboat	Small Sailboat	Sailboard
Profit per unit	$1,200	$1,050	$930	$750

Although numerous raw materials are required to manufacture the boats, only five items are in short supply and might limit production. These are sailcloth for the sails on all but the motor boat, glass fiber for all the boats' hulls, epoxy resin for molding the glass fiber, aluminum for masts and other trim, and engines for the motor boat only.

The raw materials required for each boat and the units on hand are summarized in the following table. For example, a large sailboat requires 4 units of sailcloth of which 700 units are on hand.

Raw materials	On hand (units)	Requirements by Product			
		Large sailboat	Motorboat	Small sailboat	Sailboard
Sailcloth	700	4	0	3	1
Glass fiber	1,380	8	4	3	2
Epoxy resin	1,280	3	3	3	2
Aluminum	1,100	4	2	2	2
Engines	120	0	1	0	0

The Workbook: BOATS.xls

Load BOATS.xls and inspect the model. This is an expansion of the BOAT model discussed in the first chapter.

■ *The Profit Calculation.* The total profit is the production quantity of large sailboats times the profit per unit of large sailboats plus the production quantity of motorboats times profit per unit of motorboats, and so on for the remaining boat types.

- *The SUMPRODUCT formula.* Total profit can be conveniently calculated using the SUMPRODUCT formula. The SUMPRODUCT is an important building block for optimization models and was discussed in Chapter 1, "Analytical Modeling in Spreadsheets."

A6		=SUMPRODUCT(C2:F2,C3:F3)			
	A	B	C	D	E	F
1			Large Sailboat	Motor Boat	Small Sailboat	Sailboard
2	Production Quantity		0	0	0	0
3	Profit Per Unit		$1,200	$1,050	$930	$750
4						
5	Total Profit					
6	$0					

- *Raw Material Utilization.* Each raw material's usage is also calculated using SUMPRODUCT formulas in which the first argument uses absolute referencing (denoted by $ signs). This ensures that when the formulas are copied, they continue to refer back to the production quantities in cells C2:F2.

G10		=SUMPRODUCT(C$2:F$2,C10:F10)						
	A	B	C	D	E	F	G	H	I
8			Large Sailboat	Motor Boat	Small Sailboat	Sailboard			
9	Raw Materials		Requirements by product				Usage		On Hand
10	Sailcloth		4	0	3	1	0		700
11	Glass Fiber		8	4	3	2	0		1,380
12	Epoxy Resin		3	3	3	2	0		1,280
13	Aluminum		4	2	2	2	0		1,100
14	Engines		0	1	0	0	0		120

- *Maximizing Profit by Hand.* Try experimenting with the values in cells C2:F2 to maximize profit without having any of the usage formulas exceed the amounts on hand. The large sailboat has the highest profit margin, so a logical place to start is to produce as many of these as you can until you run out of a raw material. You will see that if you produce 172 large sailboats, yielding a total profit of $206,400 you will use all but 4 units of glass fiber which is not enough for an additional sailboat. The next most profitable product is the motorboat. You can produce only one of these for a total profit of $207,450 before completely exhausting the supply of glass fiber. Because every boat uses glass fiber, you are now out of production. Before we optimize this model, see if you can do better through experimentation. Be sure to write down your highest profit figure.

The ABC's of Optimization

We will now apply the ABC's as discussed earlier.

A. What can you adjust?   In this case, it is the quantity of each boat to produce. Such controls are known as the *decision variables* of the model. They are referred to as *changing cells* in the Excel solver and as *adjustable cells* in What'sBest!.

B. What do you mean by best?   We will start out by maximizing profit as the optimization's *objective*. This is known as the *target cell* in the Excel Solver and the *best cell* in What'sBest!.

C. What constraints must be obeyed?   This model has two types of constraints:

- The production quantities must not be negative. Negative production would mean buying boats, disassembling them, and storing the raw materials in inventory, which we won't allow.

- The total usage of each raw material must not exceed the quantity on hand.

Optimizing BOATS.xls

The following steps show how to use either the Excel Solver or What'sBest! to find production figures that maximize profit from the resources on hand. Be sure that your optimization package is installed and that BOATS.xls is loaded.

STEPS: USING CHANGING OR ADJUSTABLE CELLS

Excel Solver

1. Invoke **Tools Solver** to open the solver dialog box.

2. With the cursor in the **Changing Cells** field of the dialog box, select cells C2:F2.

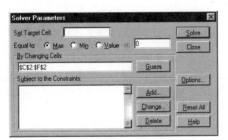

What's*Best!*

1. Highlight the adjustable cells C2:F2 in the worksheet, then invoke the **WB! Adjustable** command.

2. Click **OK**. The adjustable cells are colored blue. You can also use the adjustable cell icon as shown by clicking **Help**.

STEPS: FINDING TOTAL PROFIT

Excel Solver

1. With the cursor in the **Target Cell** field of the dialog box, select the "Total Profit" cell, A6.

2. Be sure the radio button is set to **Max**.

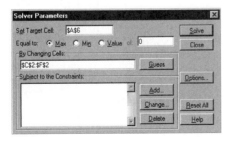

What's*Best!*

1. With the cursor in the "Total Profit" cell of the worksheet, A6, invoke the **WB! Best** command.

2. Be sure the radio button is set to **Maximize**. Click **OK**. You can also use the Maximize icon as shown by clicking **Help**.

STEPS: USING CONSTRAINTS

Usage constraints ensure that raw materials used do not exceed those on hand.

Excel Solver

1. Click the **Add constraint** button.

2. With the cursor in the left constraint field, highlight "usage" cells G10:G14.

3. With the cursor in the right constraint field select the "on hand" cells.

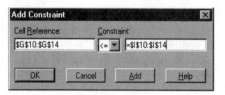

4. Make sure constraint type is < =.

5. Click **Add** to add the next set of constraints.

What's*Best!*

1. Select the range H10:H14 separating the "Usage" and "On Hand" columns. Then invoke the **WB! Constraint** command.

2. Make sure constraint type is < =.

3. Because of the way this model was intentionally laid out, the left, right, and constraint fields default to the correct ranges. Click **OK**. You can also use the < = icon as shown by clicking **Help**. Constraints don't have to be laid out in any particular format on the worksheet except for convenience.

Constraint formulas should appear as shown below. Notice that constraint formulas and their associated ranges can be either rows or columns.

H10	▼		=WB(G10,"<=",I10)		
	G	**H**	**I**	**J**	**K**
9	Usage		On Hand		
10	0	<=	700		
11	0	<=	1,380		
12	0	<=	1,280		
13	0	<=	1,100		
14	0	<=	120		

STEPS: USING NONNEGATIVITY CONSTRAINTS

Excel Solver

If you are using Excel 97, check the Assume Non-Negative box in the Options dialog box. In earlier versions of Excel, these constraints must be specified explicitly as follows.

1. With the cursor in the left field of a new constraint dialog, select the "changing" cells C2:F2.

2. Type 0 (zero) in the right constraint field as shown below.

3. Change the constraint type to > = .

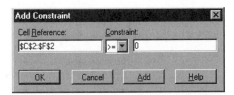

4. Click **OK**. The Solver dialog box should now appear as shown below:

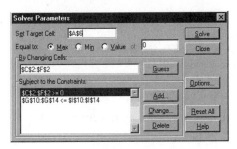

What's*Best!*

Nonnegativity constraints are not needed for adjustable cells. These default to nonnegative. If you want adjustable cells to go negative, they must be designated as **Free** in the Adjustable Cell dialog box.

STEPS: OPTIMIZING

Excel Solver

1. Although you could click the **Solve** button at this point, you will get better results on this example if you first click the **Options** button and check **Assume Linear Model**.

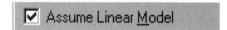

This will be explained in the next section.

2. Now click **Solve**.

3. In a few seconds you should see the Solver Results dialog box.

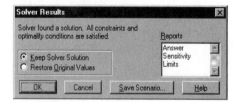

4. Click **OK** to save the results.

5. Save your optimized version of BOATS.xls as BOATSOPT.xls.

What's*Best!*

1. Invoke the **WB! Solve** command. Or, you can use the solve icon as shown under **WB! Help**.

2. A screen will display the status of the optimization.

3. Save your optimized version of BOATS.xls as BOATSOPT.xls.

The Results

The optimization results are shown in the following figure.

	A	B	C Large Sailboat	D Motor Boat	E Small Sailboat	F Sailboard
1						
2	Production Quantity		0	100	80	370
3	Profit Per Unit		$1,200	$1,050	$930	$750
4						
5	Total Profit					
6	$456,900					

Notice that

■ Total Profit is $456,900, more than twice as great as the $207,450 that resulted from starting with the highest profit large sailboat and working down.

■ The optimal production has *no* large sailboats!

Also notice that all the production figures are integers (whole numbers). This will not generally be the case, as discussed later.

Interacting with the Model: What's Best If

Once an optimization model has been created, you can explore it from various points of view.

Hierarchical Objectives

The previous optimized production plan leaves 20 remaining engines unused. Suppose these remaining engines become obsolete after the current production run. You might consider maximizing the usage of engines instead of profit.

Try this with either the Excel Solver or What's*Best!*:

1. Specify that cell G14 be maximized.

2. Re-optimize the model.

Engine usage will now be maximized without regard to the former objective of maximizing total profit. The resulting production of 120 motor boats completely exhausts the obsolete inventory, but profit has dropped significantly. We cannot expect the full $456,900 in profit obtained earlier if we want to use all the engines. However, we might want to see how many engines can be used if we require a $456,000 profit (within $900 of the maximum possible). Try this with either the Excel Solver or What's*Best!* as follows:

1. Create a new > = constraint with cell A6 on the left, and $456,000 on the right.

2. Re-optimize the model.

Re-optimization results in a $456,000 profit and five remaining engines. This process of alternatively selecting new objectives while imposing constraints on old ones allows a great deal of managerial flexibility in using optimization.

Market Limitations

Suppose it turns out that the engines will not become obsolete after all. However, the marketing department points out that the demand for the various boat types are limited as shown in the following table.

	Large sailboat	Motorboat	Small sailboat	Sailboard
Market limit (units)	160	130	170	150

Recall that the current optimal production involves 370 sailboards, far more than can be sold.

EXERCISE 7.1

Boat Market Limitations

Retrieve BOATSOPT.xls, the optimized production plan saved before the experiment of maximizing engine usage.

a. Place these market limits in row 4 of the BOATSOPT worksheet.

b. Add constraints to the current model to ensure that each boat's production figures do not exceed their associated market limits.

c. What are the new production figures and total profit?

d. Re-save BOATSOPT.xls.

The D's of Optimization: Dual Values

The Economic Value of Limited Resources

Looking at the optimized model with market constraints, you should see the following usage of scarce resources.

Raw materials	Usage	On hand
Sailcloth	700	700
Glass fiber	1370	1380
Epoxy resin	1200	1280
Aluminum	920	1100
Engines	120	120

The sailcloth and engines have been completely exhausted. How much would you profit from additional units of each resource? The answer lies in what are known as *dual values,* or *shadow prices*. Proceed as follows to find them.

STEPS: FINDING DUAL VALUES

Excel Solver

1. Re-optimize the model by clicking the **Solve** button.

2. When the Solver Results dialog appears, select the **Sensitivity** report.

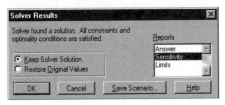

3. Click **OK** to generate the report that will be found on a separate worksheet of the workbook.

Name	Final Value	Shadow Price
Sailcloth Usage	700	300
Glass Fiber Usage	1,370	0
Epoxy Resin Usage	1,200	0
Aluminum Usage	920	0
Engines Usage	120	1,050

The column labeled "Shadow Prices" displays the economic value of additional units of each resource. If the **Assume Linear Model** option had not been used with the solver, this column would have been labeled "Lagrange Multipliers."

What'sBest!

1. Select blank cells J10:J14 in which to store the dual values.

2. Invoke the **WB! Dual** command. A dialog box appears.

3. With the cursor in the Report … field, select the constraint cells H10:H14 then click **OK**.

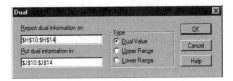

4. Formulas with values equalling 0 will appear in cells J10:J14. Re-optimize the model with the **WB! Solve** command. The dual values will appear in cells J10:J14 as shown.

J10	▼		=WBDUAL(H10,300)	
	A	**G**	**H**	**I**	**J**
9	**Raw Materials**	**Usage**		**On Hand**	
10	Sailcloth	700	=<=	700	300
11	Glass Fiber	1,370	<=	1,380	0
12	Epoxy Resin	1,200	<=	1,280	0
13	Aluminum	920	<=	1,100	0
14	Engines	120	=<=	120	1050

What the Dual Values Mean

Notice that you have not run out of glass fiber, epoxy resin, or aluminum. Because you have enough already, you can't increase profit by getting more. Hence they have a dual value equal to 0. Sailcloth and engines, on the other hand, are both in short supply. Additional supply of either of these items taken one at a time would increase profit by $300 or $1,050 per unit. This is very valuable information if you are planning to purchase additional raw materials to continue production. Taken in this context, the quote from Mother Goose that began this chapter says, in effect, that a horseshoe nail's dual value was one kingdom. We will discuss dual values further in the next chapter.

EXERCISE

7.2 **Determining the Profitability of a New Boat Type**

Suppose the marketing department thinks it can sell as many as 100 sailing dinghies at $850 profit per unit, where each sailing dinghy requires two units each of sailcloth, glass fiber, and epoxy resin.

a. Would it be profitable to add the sailing dingy to the product line? Why or why not?

b. Add the sailing dingy to the lineup and find the new optimal production.

c. Now what are the dual values of the resources?

Basic Optimization Examples

Since its introduction shortly after World War II, there have been literally thousands of linear programming applications. Although those in the following list represent a small fraction of problem types to which this technique can be applied, a few important classes have been covered. The associated worksheets can be expanded, tailored, and combined to encompass a wide variety of real-world applications. The models discussed include the following:

- *Product Mix.* Allocating limited raw materials into various products for maximum profit.

- *Blending.* Mixing ingredients to meet blend requirements at minimum cost.

- *Staff Scheduling.* Meeting staff needs at minimum cost.

- *Transportation.* Shipping goods from sources to demand points at minimum cost.

- *Network Flow Models.* A generalization of the transportation model in which material flows through complex networks or pipelines.

The files are supplied in formats for the Excel Solver and for What's*Best!* The Solver versions use the Assume Linear Model option[1] and have inequality signs entered in place of the What's*Best!* inequality formulas for clarity. The What's*Best!* versions have "W" appended to the file

---

1. The Excel Solver defaults to nonlinear optimization. If you know that your model is linear, you should always select Assume Linear Model from the Options dialog box to take advantage of the LP algorithm. If the model turns out to be nonlinear, you will get an error message. What's*Best!* detects whether or not the model is linear, then automatically applies the appropriate algorithm. The error screen will optionally display a warning for nonlinear formulas in case they are not intentional.

names. For most small problems the Excel Solver and What'sBest! perform similarly, but each has its own advantage in some cases. These will be pointed out as they arise.

Product Mix

In product mix problems, the objective of optimization is to find a most profitable allocation of a set of limited resources over a set of desired products or activities. The BOATS model discussed in the tutorial earlier in this chapter is an example of this problem type. Industrial LP software can now solve such models involving tens of thousands of products and resources.

EXERCISE 7.3

Manufacturing Athletic Shoes

A firm manufactures three types of athletic shoes: Basketball with a $10 per pair profit, Running with a $9 per pair profit, and Tennis with a $7.50 per pair profit. The resources consumed per pair of shoes and the quantities available are shown in the following table.

Resources	Basketball	Running	Tennis	Available
Canvas	2	1	1	12,000
Labor hours	4	2	2	21,000
Machine hours	2	3	2	19,500
Rubber	2	1	2	16,500

a. What production quantities maximize profit?

b. What is the economic value to the firm of each of the resources given optimal production?

Blending

Blending problems are an important class of linear programs. They occur in the refining of gasoline and other petroleum products, chemicals, paints, alloys, fertilizers, and processed foods. Unlike the product mix problem in which a single set of raw materials could be combined into many different types of products, here a single type of product can be produced from many different combinations of raw materials. In blending problems, the objective is generally to minimize cost per unit of final product, and the constraints are to enforce correct proportions of ingredients.

In the following example, various constituents are blended to form a metal alloy. The chemical requirements are that the alloy must contain at least 9% of element A and between 6.5% and 11% of element B.

The raw materials that can be used in this alloy are three ores (with chemical analysis shown in the following figure) and the element A in its pure form.

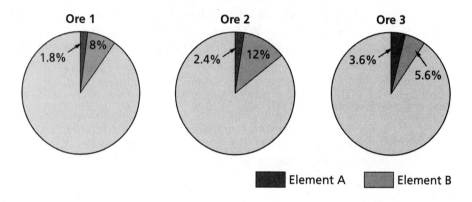

The costs of the raw materials are shown here. Notice that element A is far more expensive than any of the ores. The objective is to meet the chemical requirements at the minimum cost per ton.

Raw material	Cost per ton
Ore 1	$50
Ore 2	$60
Ore 3	$40
Element A	$8,000

Exploring the Blending Model. Retrieve BLEND.xls for the Excel Solver or BLENDW.xls for What's*Best!*. The key elements of the model are as follows:

- The percentage of each raw material used is stored in the range C3:F3.

- Cost per ton of each raw material are in C4:F4.

- The total cost per ton of the blend in cell F10 is the SUMPRODUCT of C3:F3 and C4:F4.

- The sum of C3:F3 is in C12. This must total 100% to ensure we have accounted for all raw materials in the blend.

- The percentage of element A in the blend in cell C15 is the SUMPRODUCT of C3:F3 and C6:F6.

■ The percentage of element B in the blend in cell C19 is the SUMPRODUCT of C3:F3 and C7:F7.

■ A pie chart displays the percentage of each of the raw materials in the blend.

The ABC's of the Blending Model

A. The adjustable cells, C3:F3 represent the percentage of each raw material used in the alloy.

B. The best solution is that which minimizes total cost per ton in cell F10.

C. The constraints are

• The percentages must sum to 100%.

• The blend must contain at least 9% Element A.

• The blend must contain between 6.5% and 11% Element B.

• The adjustable cells are constrained to be greater than or equal to zero. This must be done explicitly with the Solver[2] but is the default in What's*Best!*.

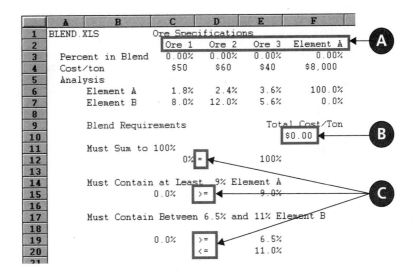

---

2. In Excel 97, it is convenient to use the Assume Non-Negative option to impose this constraint.

**EXERCISE
7.4**

Optimizing a Blending Model

a. Optimize the blending model that has already been set up. What are the proportions of raw material that will yield minimum cost?

b. Find the dual values on the constraints, and interpret their meaning. See Chapter 8 for further discussion of dual values.

Blending models are used extensively in the petroleum and chemical industry, and also in the production of fertilizers and animal feed as in the following example.

**EXERCISE
7.5**

Blending Feedmix

An animal feed is to be blended from four types of grain. The final blend must have sufficient quantities of three nutrients as shown in the following table.

	Nutrient A	Nutrient B	Nutrient C
Units required per bushel	5	8	35

Each grain has a different concentration of these nutrients as shown in the following table.

Grain type	Nutrient units per bushel			
	1	2	3	4
Nutrient A	2.2	3.4	7.2	1.5
Nutrient B	2.3	5.6	11.1	1.3
Nutrient C	12.0	11.9	41.8	52.1

If the four grains cost $25, $40, $75, and $80 per bushel respectively, what blend will result in the lowest cost feed that meets the nutritional requirements?

Staff Scheduling

In staff scheduling problems, the objective of optimization is to meet specified manpower requirements at minimum cost. The schedule must generally meet certain conditions, such as those imposed by regulations or union contracts involving shift length, number of work breaks, or maximum overtime hours.

This example involves a business with daily staff requirements that range from 120 to 190 people, depending on varying work loads each day of the week as shown in the following figure:

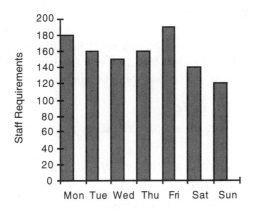

In addition, a labor union requirement must be met that employees work a five-consecutive-day workweek followed by two days off. Thus, the allowable shifts are Monday through Friday, Tuesday through Saturday, Wednesday through Sunday, and so on. Each employee earns $500 per week.

Exploring the Scheduling Model. Retrieve STAFF.xls for the Excel Solver or STAFFW.xls for What's*Best!*.

The model's key elements are as follows:

■ The number of people hired to start on each day is shown in cells F8:F14.

■ The number of people on duty each day of the week (cells C8:C14) is the sum of the number of employees starting that day and the previous four days.

■ The total number hired is the sum of F8:F14 in cell F15.

■ The total cost is the total number hired times the cost per week, in cell F19.

■ A graph shows both the staff needs and staff size.

Because 180 people are needed on Monday, enter 180 in cell F8 (the number starting Monday). You will see that cells C8:C12 now all contain 180, reflecting the union requirement that employees work a five day shift. The formula in column C for any given day is simply the sum of the number of employees starting that day and the previous four days.

The graph now shows just the right number of employees on Monday, but a few too many on Tuesday through Thursday. Friday is understaffed by 10, and Saturday and Sunday are unstaffed. Enter 10 in cell F12 (the number starting Friday). You should now have adequate coverage on Monday through Friday, but will still be short 130 on Saturday and 110 on Sunday. Next, enter 130 in cell F13 (the number starting Saturday), and view the graph.

The good news is that the staff needs have been met each day of the week. The bad news is that the employees hired to start Saturday would work until the following Wednesday. You can see from the graph, this solution is so over-staffed Monday through Wednesday that people would be sitting on each other's laps! Also notice that the total cost is $160,000.

The ABC's of the Scheduling Model.

A. The adjustable cells, F8:F14 are the number of employees starting each day.

B. The best solution is that which minimizes total cost, cell F19.

C. The constraints are as follows:

- Daily staff size is constrained to be at least as great as the staff need.

- The adjustable cells are constrained to be greater than or equal to zero. This must be explicitly specified with the Solver[3] but is the default in What'sBest!.

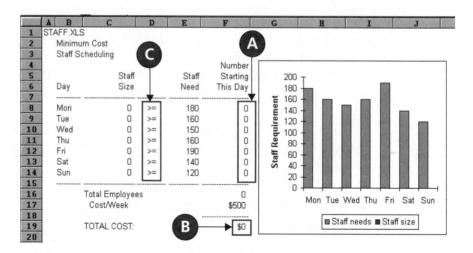

EXERCISE 7.6

Staff Scheduling

a. See if you can improve the previous solution by adjusting cells F8:F14 by hand before optimizing the model. Remember as you do so, the staff size must remain at least as large as each day's staff needs.

b. Optimize the model. How do the graph and total cost differ from the solution you found by hand?

---

3. In Excel 97, it is convenient to use the Assume Non-Negative option to impose this constraint.

EXERCISE **7.7**

Generalizing STAFF.xls: Covering Problems

The previous scheduling model provides graphic proof of the effectiveness of optimization for this kind of problem. As formulated, however, it does not generalize easily. Suppose, for example, that the union is requesting a four-day work week with three days off in a row instead of the current two. For the model to accommodate these new work rules, you would have to change all formulas in C8:C14. This exercise is to generalize STAFF.xls so that the work patterns are stored as data.

a. Modify STAFF.xls so that any allowable seven-day work patterns can be entered without changing any formulas. The work patterns will be entered as a range with a row for each day and a column for each allowable pattern. The data for the current work rules should appear as shown below in the worksheet.

	Allowable Patterns: 1 = on, 0 = off						
Pattern	1	2	3	4	5	6	7
Monday	1	0	0	1	1	1	1
Tuesday	1	1	0	0	1	1	1
Wednesday	1	1	1	0	0	1	1
Thursday	1	1	1	1	0	0	1
Friday	1	1	1	1	1	0	0
Saturday	0	1	1	1	1	1	0
Sunday	0	0	1	1	1	1	1

The 1's and 0's signify whether or not a given pattern requires working on a given day. Thus pattern 2 is off Monday, on Tuesday, and so on. Now remove the current adjustable cells and replace them with cells denoting the number hired for each work pattern. Next, you will need to replace the staff size expressions for each day with SUMPRODUCT formulas involving the number hired for each pattern and the rows of the pattern data. Test your model to make sure that it gives the same answer as before.

b. What happens to labor costs if the four-day work week is adopted without reducing the $500 per week cost? If you get fractional answers for the number of each pattern to hire, round the results up to the nearest integer.

c. Suppose the union agrees that the pay for a four-day work week should only be 4/5ths the pay for a five-day work week. How would labor costs differ from the original five-day work week?

Problems of this type in which a set of patterns is used to cover a demand are known as *covering problems*. They are useful in many different optimization settings, such as the following example.

EXERCISE
7.8

The Cutting Stock Problem

A supplier of sheet steel cuts stock in various widths from 100" rolls. Current demand in feet is shown below by width.

Width in Inches	15	18	25	35
Demand in Feet	1450	967	3000	1020

The rolls can be cut using any of the four patterns shown in the following figure.

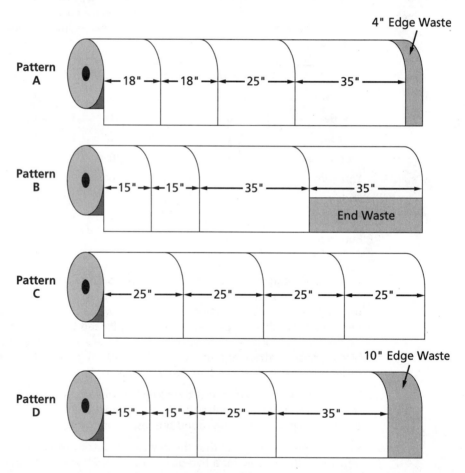

In the process of cutting, two kinds of waste can occur as shown; edge waste, at a cost of $1.50 per inch foot, and end waste at a cost of $0.75 per inch foot.

a. Build an optimization model to determine the quantity of each pattern to cut to meet demand with minimum total (edge plus end) waste cost. Assume that the rolls are much longer than the total quantities being cut, so you won't run out of material with any pattern.

b. Come up with a new pattern, which when added to the current four, results in an improved optimum cost. **Hint:** Look at the dual values from part a.

Transportation

This problem is the simplest of a class known as network problems. These generally involve the shipping of goods through transportation networks, or of oil or gas through systems of pipelines.

In this model, two steel mills supply three manufacturing plants. Each plant has a demand for steel that must be met, and each steel mill has limited manufacturing capacity as shown in the schematic below.

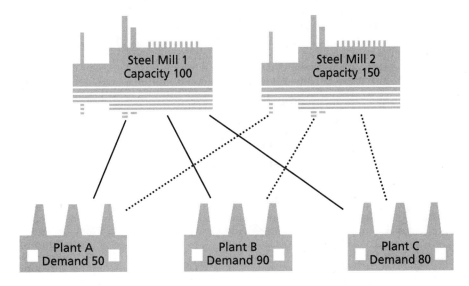

The unit shipping costs from both mills to each plant are shown in the following table.

To:	From: Steel Mill 1	Steel Mill 2
Plant A	$200	$500
Plant B	$300	$400
Plant C	$500	$600

The objective is to minimize shipping cost while meeting all demand without exceeding steel mill capacity.

Exploring the Transportation Model. Retrieve TRANS.xls for the Excel Solver and TRANSW.xls for What's*Best!*.

The model's key elements are as follows:

■ The amount shipped from each mill to each plant is stored in the range B6:C8.

■ The shipping costs per unit are stored in the range B16:C18.

■ The total shipping cost in cell G14 is the SUMPRODUCT (B6:C8,B16:C18).

■ The total shipments by plant are calculated in cells E6:E8.

■ The total production by mills are stored in cells B10:C10.

The ABC's of the Transportation Model.

A. The a̲djustable cells, B6:C8 represent the amount shipped from each mill to each plant.

B. The b̲est solution is that which minimizes total shipping cost, cell G14.

C. The c̲onstraints are as follows:

• The total shipped to each plant is at least as great as the demand.

• The total shipped from each mill does not exceed capacity.

• The adjustable cells are constrained to be greater than or equal to zero. This must be done explicitly with the Solver[4] but is the default in What's*Best!*.

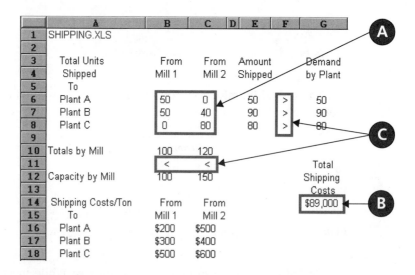

---

4. In Excel 97 it is convenient to use the Assume Non-Negative option to impose this constraint.

EXERCISE **Transportation Between Steel Mills and Plants**

7.9   Optimize the transportation model that has already been set up. What is the minimal shipping cost that meets demand without exceeding steel mill capacity?

EXERCISE **Disaster Relief**

7.10   A major earthquake has hit a developing nation leaving thousands of people homeless. They are located in four refugee camps with the following immediate requirements for food, medicine, and other emergency supplies.

	Camp A	Camp B	Camp C	Camp D
Tons Required	10	5	10	20

Supplies are available in two neighboring countries, with 25 tons in country 1 and 20 tons in country 2.

The shipping cost per ton from the two countries to each of the four camps is shown in the following table.

	From:	
To:	Country 1	Country 2
Camp A	$100	$150
Camp B	$150	$200
Camp C	$200	$300
Camp D	$300	$400

Determine the most cost effective allocation of emergency supplies to camps.

Network Flow Models

Network flow models are a generalization of the transportation model discussed earlier. Intermediate nodes are allowed between the sources of supply and the demand points. There may be capacity constraints on individual arcs within the network that limit the hourly or daily flow. Also, flow can be permitted in either direction over the arcs. Network models have the useful property that if the source flow and the capacity constraints are integers, then the LP optimized flow along all arcs will be integers.

The following figure is a schematic representation of an oil pipeline network. There is a supply or *source* of oil at oil field (1) and a consumption point or *sink* at the refinery (6). The following figure shows each pipeline's distance in miles, hourly capacity, and cost per unit flow that can differ in each direction.

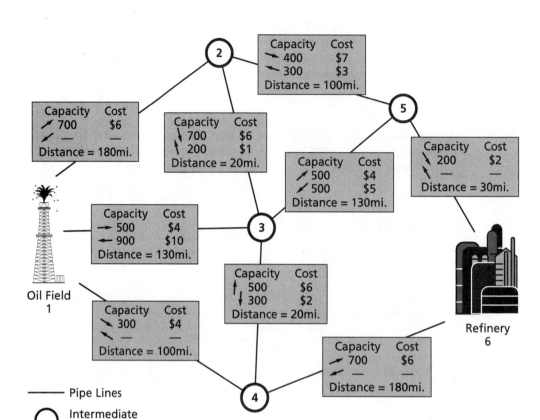

At each network node, four things can happen:

■ There can be a source of oil coming into the network, such as an oil field.

■ There can be a sink, a place where oil gets consumed, such as a refinery.

■ There can be flow to that node from other nodes.

■ There can be flow from that node to other nodes.

You could have several objectives in using such a model. We will start by determining the network's overall capacity. That is, the maximum flow possible from the source to the sink.

Exploring the Network Flow Model. Retrieve NETWORK.xls for the Excel Solver. This model formulation uses the DSUM formula, which is interesting in its own right. As What'sBest! does not handle DSUM, an alternate formulation is provided in NETWORKW.xls. However, you are encouraged to explore the Excel model first in any event.

The model has two major sections: the arc data and the node summary.

Arc data is specified in cells A3:F20. This range contains one row for each arc in the network. The key elements are the following:

■ The node the arc comes from, column A.

■ The node the arc goes to, column B.

■ The amount of oil flowing per hour through the arc, column C.

■ The maximum hourly flow capacity through the arc, column E.

■ The unit pumping cost of flow through the arc, column F.

■ The distance in miles of the arc, column G.

■ The hourly cost of the current flow in cell C1, calculated as SUMPRODUCT ($C$3:$C$20,F3:F20).

	A	B	C	D	E	F	G
1	Total Cost		$0				
2	From	To	Flow		Capacity	Cost/Unit	Distance
3	1	2	0	<=	700	$6	180
4	1	3	0	<=	500	$4	130
5	1	4	0	<=	300	$4	100
6	2	1	0	<=	0	$0	180
7	2	3	0	<=	700	$6	20
8	2	5	0	<=	400	$7	100
9	3	1	0	<=	.900	$10	130
10	3	2	0	<=	200	$1	20
11	3	4	0	<=	300	$2	20
12	3	5	0	<=	500	$4	130
13	4	1	0	<=	0	$0	100
14	4	3	0	<=	500	$6	20
15	4	6	0	<=	700	$6	180
16	5	2	0	<=	300	$3	100
17	5	3	0	<=	500	$5	130
18	5	6	0	<=	200	$2	30
19	6	4	0	<=	0	$0	180
20	6	5	0	<=	0	$0	30
21	Insert New Arcs Here						

The Node Summary is specified in cells I25:O37. This range contains one column for each node in the network. Each column contains the following:

■ The flow entering the node from a source (if one is present at that node), row 28.

■ The flow coming to the node from other nodes, row 29.

■ The total flow entering the node, row 30.

- The flow leaving the node through a sink (if one is present at that node), row 35.
- The flow leaving the node to other nodes, row 36. This is similar to the formula in row 29.
- The total flow leaving the node, row 37.

Excel Solver: These values are calculated using formulas of the form = DSUM(ArcData,"Flow",L26:L27). See your Excel documentation or help file for an explanation of DSUM.

What'sBest!: The DSUM function is not supported, so this model follows an approach suggested by Donald Plane (Plane, 1994). Although more cumbersome, it reproduces the functionality of the DSUM in a form that can be handled by What'sBest!.

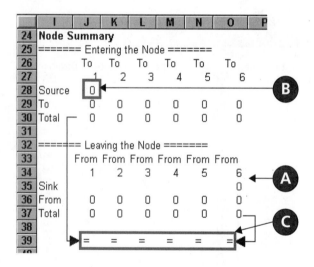

The ABC's of the Network Flow Model.

A. The adjustable cells are the following:
- The flow through each of the arcs, cells C3:C20.
- The source at node 1, cell J28.
- The sink at node 6, cell O35.

B. The best solution is that which maximizes either the source at node 1, or the sink at node 6, we have used cell J28. Note that the objective function is an adjustable cell, not a formula.

C. The constraints are the following:

- The total flow down the arcs, C3:C20, must not exceed the capacities, E3:E20.
- The total flow into each node, J30:O30, must equal the total flow out of that node, J37:O37, to prevent the pipes from bursting. These are known as *conservation constraints*.
- The adjustable cells are constrained to be greater than or equal to zero. This must be done explicitly with the Solver[5] but is the default in What's*Best!*.

Three Related Network Flow Problems

Network flow models form the basis of a number of interesting optimization problems, three of which follow:

- *Maximum Flow Problem.*   What is the overall capacity of the network? The objective is to determine the maximum flow possible from the source to the sink.
- *Minimum Cost Problem.*   What is the cheapest way to achieve it? The objective is to determine how much oil to flow down each arc to achieve the maximum flow?
- *Shortest Path Problem.*   What is the shortest path between the source and the sink? The objective is to find the shortest set of arcs that connect the source to the sink, for example, for laying a communication line.

The network flow problem presented earlier is an example of the maximum flow problem. Minor modifications are needed for the minimum cost and shortest path problems, as demonstrated in the following exercises.

EXERCISE
7.11

Maximum Flow Through a Network

Optimize the network flow model to find the maximum hourly flow of oil that can be supported over the network between the field and refinery. This information is critical in planning for future oil field development.

Explore the flow through the various arcs. What is the total hourly flow through the network from source to sink? You should see a total hourly flow through the network from source to sink of 800 units. What is the hourly cost?

---

5. In Excel 97, it is convenient to use the Assume Non-Negative option to impose this constraint.

EXERCISE 7.12 **Minimum Cost at Maximum Flow**

Modify the maximum flow model to determine whether the solution found in Exercise 7.11 represents the lowest cost way to flow 800 units through this network. If not, what is the minimum cost solution?

EXERCISE 7.13 **Shortest Path Problem**

Suppose it is necessary to lay a phone line from the oil field to the refinery. The line is to be laid over the pipelines because the land is already leased. We require the shortest path along the arcs, which starts at node 1 and ends at node 6. *Hint:* Start with the minimum cost problem and limit the flow from the source to the sink to 1 unit, then create a new cell to calculate total distance.

EXERCISE 7.14 **The SUMIF Formula**

Cliff Ragsdale of Virginia Polytechnic Institute has an alternate formulation of this model that uses the SUMIF formula instead of DSUM to calculate the node summaries. Modify NETWORK.xls to use the SUMIF formula.

Conclusion

This chapter has introduced some important classes of linear optimization models. Once these are understood, they may be modified or expanded to solve a wide variety of problems. In the next chapter, we will explore some extensions of optimization and show how small models may be combined to form larger ones.

8

Extensions of Optimization

The final test for a theory is its capacity to solve the problems which originated it.

GEORGE DANTZIG, FATHER OF LINEAR PROGRAMMING

The technique of linear programming was developed in 1947 by George Dantzig. He first came up with a simple characterization that brought a tremendous class of problems under a single roof. He also devised the powerful simplex algorithm to potentially solve them all in one fell swoop. The quote is from the preface of his book *Linear Programming and Extensions*.

As you attempt to solve real-world problems with linear programming, additional complications arise for which the theory of optimization has been extended. For example:

■ Optimization might not give integer answers. No one would produce 5.75 large sailboats and 1.5 motorboats. The good news is that variables can be specified to take on integer values. The bad news is that the optimization process may be greatly slowed down.

■ Real-world problems are seldom solved in isolation. You would not decide how to produce sailboats at a factory in a single time period without also being concerned about what you would do in future time periods.

■ Many aspects of the problem might be uncertain. Optimizing for "average" conditions might not be optimal under *any* conditions. Stochastic optimization attempts to optimize over a set of uncertain scenarios.

■ Some important problems, particularly those in financial portfolio optimization, are not linear and require nonlinear programming.

OVERVIEW

Extending the Application of Optimization

We extend the concepts of the last chapter to cover:

- **Integer Models:** Models in which fractional solutions cannot be tolerated.
- **Combining Optimization Models:** Simple optimization models can be viewed as objects that can be combined to form more complicated ones. Examples include multi-time period and vertically integrated models.
- **Optimization Under Uncertainty:** Problems with uncertain inputs are solved with stochastic optimization.
- **Nonlinear Optimization:** An important class of financial portfolio problems require nonlinear optimization as do certain data-fitting techniques.

Common Errors in Optimization Models

A few of the most common errors in model formulation are discussed for linear and nonlinear problems.

The Basics of Optimization Theory

To discuss the theory behind optimization, we examine a very small model in some detail.

Extending the Application of Optimization

Integer Variables

As mentioned in the last chapter, network optimization models return integer (whole number) answers when the sources and sinks are integers. This is not true of optimization in general. In many cases, if you get fractional answers, rounding to the closest integers that do not violate the constraints can provide a good solution. However, there are situations, especially when the desired number is a small integer, when rounding might not give satisfactory results. The good news is that there are techniques that force optimization to give integer answers. The bad news is that these techniques can greatly slow down the solution process. Thus, it is generally not practical to solve problems with a large number of integer variables.

As an example of a situation where you would want only integer answers, suppose you have decided to run away from home and can take only those personal possessions that will fit in your knapsack. You have ranked all the items according to both value and size. The problem of selecting the most valuable set of items that will fit is known as the *knapsack problem*.

This is not such an easy problem because if you take the most valuable thing, your portable TV, there isn't room for anything else. And obviously, you require an integer answer. No one wants to hit the road with half a portable TV and two-thirds of a teddy bear!

Similar problems arise in stocking limited shelf space in a store with items of various sizes and profit margins, or, as in the next example, loading a truck.

Optimal Truck Loading

A firm is loading six types of items of different weights and values into a truck with a 10,000 pound load capacity. Management wants to know the most valuable set of cargo that can be loaded without exceeding the weight limit. In this example, we will assume that there is a large number of each item, so you can load as many as you like of any one.

Exploring the Model. Retrieve TRUCK.xls for the Excel Solver and TRUCKW.xls for What's*Best!*.

The model's key elements are as follows:

- The value of each item that can be loaded, B6:B11.

- The weight of each item that can be loaded, C6:C11.

- The number of each item to load on the truck, D6:D11.

- The total value of the load in cell A15 is SUMPRODUCT (B6:B11,D6:D11).

- The total weight of the load in cell C15 is SUMPRODUCT (C6:C11,D6:D11).

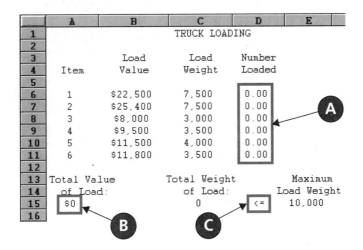

The ABC's of the Truck Loading Model.

A. The <u>a</u>djustable cells, D6:D11 represent the number of each type of item loaded.

B. The <u>b</u>est solution is that which maximizes the total value of the loaded items A15.

C. The <u>c</u>onstraints are as follows:

- The total weight of the items loaded must not exceed the capacity of the truck.

- The adjustable cells are constrained to be greater than or equal to zero. This must be done explicitly with the Solver[1] but is the default in What's*Best!*.

STEPS: **OPTIMIZING TRUCK.XLS/TRUCKW.XLS**

Optimize this model with the Solve command and you will get a fractional solution that suggests loading 1.33 of item 2, yielding a $33,867 value. Round this down to one unit of item 2 and the value drops to $25,400. There is an integer load with a significantly higher value. Can you find it by hand? To specify that the adjustable cells take on integer values, proceed as follows:

Excel Solver

1. Bring up the Solver dialog box, and add a constraint.

2. Select D6:D11 for the left hand side of the constraint, and **Int** for the type of constraint, then click **OK**.

What's*Best!*

1. Select cells D6:D11, then invoke the **WB! Integer** command. The following dialog box appears. A name is required for each integer. Type a name in the **Integer Names in Workbook** field.

2. **General** specifies that any number of each item can be loaded on the truck (**Binary** would have implied 0 or 1). Click **OK**.

---

1. In Excel 97, you can use the Assume Non-Negative option to impose this constraint.

Now re-optimize the model. You should see a completely new set of items loaded with a higher value than the $25,400 that was found through rounding.

The Fixed-Cost Problem

An area in which integer variables are even more important is that of *Yes/No decisions*. This is summed up by the old adage that there is no such thing as being "a little bit pregnant." Undoubtedly there are parents who wish they could have had 1/3 of a baby, heard 1/3 of the crying, bought 1/3 of a crib, changed 1/3 the number of diapers, and so on.

Similar Yes/No decisions arise in business when you must incur a fixed cost of some kind before engaging in some activity. This is known as a *fixed-cost problem*.

Let's return to the boat manufacturing problem but introduce a new wrinkle. Suppose it has just been determined that to produce any large sailboats, it is necessary to replace a piece of manufacturing equipment for $14,000. Thus, if any large sailboats are produced at all, $14,000 must be subtracted from the profit cell.

FIXCOST.xls models an activity for which there is a fixed cost when the activity is undertaken and a variable cost per unit of activity thereafter as follows:

Total Cost = Fixed Cost + Variable Cost × Number of Units of Activity

The contents of FIXCOST.xls can be copied into any desired worksheet.

Exploring the Model

Retrieve FIXCOST.xls if you use the Excel Solver and FIXCOSTW.xls if you use What's*Best*.

The model's key elements are described in the following list. The cell names given are for the FIXCOST file itself. Actual cell names depend on where the module is copied into other worksheets.

■ Fixed Cost: G7. This is the fixed cost incurred if the activity is undertaken.

■ Variable Cost Per Unit: G8. You can also input a variable or marginal cost associated with the activity.

■ Maximum: G9. This should contain an upper limit on the level of the activity. It is most effective to enter a number somewhat higher than the maximum level of activity you believe to be possible.

■ Activity: G10. This cell must be equal to the level of the activity on which the fixed cost is being imposed. It should contain the formula = CELL, where CELL is the adjustable cell containing the activity in the worksheet to which FIXCOST has been copied.

Program cells that force the fixed cost to be incurred are as follows:

- Yes/No Cell: G14. This is a changing or adjustable cell. It must be forced to take on the values of 0 (No) or 1 (Yes).

- Cell G15 calculates Max Activity * Yes/No, or = G9 * G14.

- Cells E16 and G16 are set up to constrain Activity < = Max * Yes/No. Thus, if the Yes/No cell is 0, the activity must be 0. If the Yes/No cell = 1 then the activity can be as great as Max.

Module output is as follows:

- Cell G18 contains a formula for the total cost associated with the activity, that is,

  Fixed Cost * Yes/No + Variable Cost * Activity, or = G7 * G14 + G8 * G10.

  This cell must be subtracted from the formula in your profit cell to make sure the economic impact of the fixed cost impacts the optimization.

Combining FIXCOST.xls with BOATSOPT.xls

We will now combine this module with BOATOPT.xls (the optimized boat production model saved earlier) to model the $14,000 fixed cost for producing large sailboats. We will complete the following four procedures in this process: paste a copy of FIXCOST.xls into BOATSOPT.xls; link input cells in the copy of FIXCOST to cells in the BOATSOPT model; respecify the ABC's of optimization; and optimize the model.

If you want to save the fixed-cost version of this model, use a different file name, as we will use BOATOPT.xls again further on.

STEPS: **COPYING THE FIXED-COST MODULE**

1 Retrieve FIXCOST.xls (FIXCOSTW.xls if you are using What'sBest!).

2 Select the entire contents of cells A1:G20, and copy it to the clipboard with the **Edit Copy** command.

3 Retrieve BOATSOPT.xls and paste the clipboard with the cursor in cell J1.[2]

---

2. When used with What'sBest!, it is more convenient to paste FIXCOST.xls into its own worksheet.

STEPS: **SPECIFYING THE INPUTS**

1 Enter the $14,000 fixed cost in cell P7. We are not concerned with variable cost in this model, so P8 should be left at 0.

2 We will assume that the production of large sailboats will not exceed 200 under any conditions. Enter 200 in cell P9.

3 Place the cursor in cell P10 and type " = ". Move the cursor to C2, the number of large sailboats to be produced, then click **Enter**. Cell P10 should now contain = C2.

STEPS: **MODIFYING THE ABC'S**

Excel Solver

1. In the Solver dialog box, add the Yes/No cell to the changing cells as shown below.

2. Constrain the Yes/No cell to integer.[3]

3. Constrain the Yes/No cell not to exceed 1.

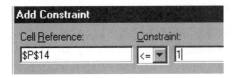

What'sBest!

1. Select the Yes/No cell, P14 then invoke the **WB! Integer** command. Don't forget to put a name in the **Integer Names in Workbook** field.

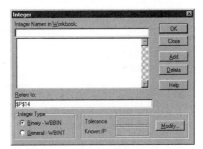

2. Click **Binary** to specify that the Yes/No variable can only take on the values 0 or 1. Click **OK**.

3. Edit the total profit in cell A6 by subtracting the fixed cost. The formula should now read: = SUMPRODUCT (C2:F2, C3:F3) − P18.

---

3. In Excel 97, steps 2 and 3 can be replaced by specifying the Bin constraint type.

Excel Solver (continued)

4. Constrain cell N16 not to exceed P16. This constraint ensures that there will be no activity if the Yes/No variable = 0.

5. Edit the total profit in cell A6 by subtracting the fixed cost. The formula should now read: = SUMPRODUCT (C2:F2, C3:F3) − P18

> ***Optimize the Model.*** Re-optimize the model and you should find the following production and profit figures. Notice that it is no longer optimal to produce large sailboats.

	Large sailboat	Motorboat	Small sailboat	Sailboard
Production quantity	0	120	170	150
Profit per unit	$1,200	$1,050	$930	$750
	160	130	170	150
Total Profit $396,600				

EXERCISE 8.1   Using Binary Integer Variables for Boolean Logic

In the previous example we modeled an *if* A *then* B situation: *If* you produce large sail boats *then* you must incur a fixed cost. Unfortunately you cannot simply use an Excel =IF formula for this purpose as neither the Excel Solver or What's*Best!* will interpret this correctly. Instead we used a binary (0,1) integer variable and a constraint to do the same thing. Use binary integer variables to model *if* A *and* B *then* C, *if* A *or* B *then* C, and *if* A *exclusive or*[4] B *then* C. This is a difficult but rewarding exercise.

---

4. Exclusive Or is A or B but not both.

Combining Optimization Models: An Object Oriented Approach

Traditionally, optimization models have been developed and described in terms of algebraic representations. This has often led to an *algebraic curtain* separating management from management science. In contrast, all the classes of optimization models presented so far have been expressed in terms of small fully functioning spreadsheet models that I refer to as the *developmental necessities of applications,* or DNA for short. They can be expanded and modified to fit a wide array of small, real-world situations.

A practical way to create complex models is to combine and modify the DNA of simpler models (dare I call this recombinant DNA?).

In the last chapter, we saw that the Excel Solver allowed a more elegant formulation of the network model because it could interpret the DSUM formula. When it comes to the technique of combining models, What's*Best!* is more convenient for two reasons:

- All variables and constraints are part of the model itself instead of being defined in a dialog box. Thus, when two or more models are combined it is not necessary to respecify them.

- Models can be built across different worksheets within the same workbook. This keeps the combined model from getting difficult to manage.

We now present two situations in which it makes sense to combine models.

Multiperiod Models

With the exception of the scheduling model, all optimization examples addressed so far have modeled a single period in time. Most important management decisions, however, must consider the effect of actions in one time period on future periods. Models of this type are known as multi-period models and often have their basis in simple one-period models. We will describe how the boat production model introduced earlier can be replicated to reflect two time periods.

STEPS: **BUILDING A TWO-PERIOD MODEL**

If you completed the boat production tutorial, then the results were saved as BOATSOPT. This contains a single time period of production, say the first half of the year. We will now split this one time period into a distinct first and second quarter. This version of BOATSOPT will reflect two refinements:

■ The total demand for the various boats is the same, but differs by quarter as shown in the following table:

Market limit	Large sailboat	Motorboat	Small sailboat	Sailboard
Q1	80	65	85	45
Q2	80	65	85	105

■ Additional sailcloth can be ordered in the first quarter at $50 per unit that will arrive in time for second quarter production.

Create two quarters by following the these steps:

Retrieve BOATSOPT.xls.

1

Copy A1:I14 to the clipboard with the **Edit Copy** command.

2

With the cursor in cell A16, paste the clipboard. The original copy of the model represents the first quarter. This second copy represents the second quarter. *Note:* If you are using What's*Best!* you will get a more manageable model if you paste the second model into cell A1 of a new worksheet. Now each worksheet represents a different time period. You will, of course need to modify some of the following cell references.

3

Change labels in cells A5 and A2 to Q1 Profit and Q2 Profit respectively.

Make the necessary changes to each quarter by following these steps:

4

Change market demands in rows 4 and 19 to reflect the Q1 and Q2 figures in the previous table.

5

Inspect the formula for the total usage of sailcloth in the second quarter, cell G25. Notice that because of the absolute ($) addressing, it still refers to first quarter production (C2:F2). Change this formula to = SUMPRODUCT (C$17:F$17,C25:F25) to reference second quarter production. If you are using What's*Best!* and build your model across two worksheets you will not have this problem.

6

7

Copy cell G25 to G26:G29 to complete usage formulas for the other raw materials.

8

The raw materials on hand in the second quarter must equal those originally on hand in the first quarter minus those used in the first quarter. Change the amount On Hand in I25 to = I10–G10.

If you have built your model across two worksheets, then the On Hand formula in cell I10 on the second sheet is = Sheet1!I10–Sheet1!G10. You do not need to type "Sheet1! Etc.". Simply type " = " into the cell to start the formula, then tab to sheet 1 and click on cell I10, then "-" and so on to complete the formula.

9

Copy the formula just created down for the remaining raw materials.

Now, model the sailcloth purchase by following these steps:

10

Place a 0 in cell J10 to represent the amount of sailcloth to purchase in the first quarter.

11

Enter 50 in cell K10 for the cost per unit of sailcloth.

12

Edit the formula for the sailcloth On Hand in the second quarter to add in the first quarter purchase of sailcloth (J10).

And finally, create a new total profit formula by following these steps:

13

In cell B1, enter total profit equal to first quarter profit plus second quarter profit minus the cost of the first quarter sailcloth purchase. The formula should be = A6 + A21– J10*K10 for the single sheet model. For the two-sheet model, this formula will be = A6 + Sheet2!A6 –J10*K10.

Specify B1 as the objective to maximize.

14

Next we will specify variables and constraints then optimize the model.

STEPS: SPECIFYING VARIABLES AND CONSTRAINTS

Excel Solver

1. In the Solver dialog box, add the second quarter production and Sailcloth purchase to the changing cells as shown below.

2. Add nonnegativity constraints for both the second quarter production (C17:F17) and sailcloth purchase (J10).

3. Constrain the second quarter usage not to exceed the amount on hand.

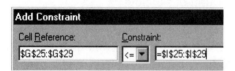

What's*Best!*

1. Select J10, the quantity of sailcloth to purchase in first quarter, then invoke the **WB! Adjustable** command.

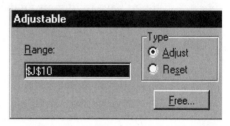

2. All other adjustable cells and constraints were preserved when the second copy of the model was pasted into place.

Optimize. When you optimize, you should get a total profit of $409,850, with a purchase of five units of sailcloth. But if you look at the second quarter production you will see 11.25 large sailboats. Round this down to 11, and you will have a profit of $409,550. Is this the optimal integer solution?

EXERCISE 8.2 **Integer Production Amounts**

Specify that both first and second quarter production take on integer values and re-optimize.

EXERCISE 8.3 **Additional Motors**

Suppose you could purchase additional motors for $500 in the first quarter for second quarter delivery. What would the profit be?

Two-Period Supply Chain Model

This problem is a generalization of the transportation problem modeled in TRANS.xls. Instead of two steel mills supplying three plants, we now have three warehouses supplying four customers. More important, you must make decisions in two time periods. In period one, we must decide how much to stock at each warehouse. In period two, we must decide how much to ship from each warehouse to each customer. This problem's schematic is shown in the following figure.

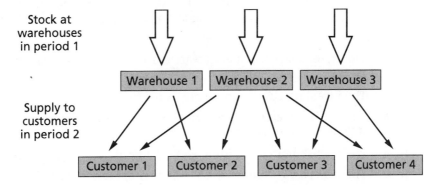

Stock at warehouses in period 1

Supply to customers in period 2

For each unit stocked at a warehouse in period one, there is an inventory cost shown in the following table.

	Warehouse 1	Warehouse 2	Warehouse 3
Inventory Cost per Unit	$1.00	$1.25	$1.00

The unit shipping cost from the warehouse to the customers is shown in the following table:

	Shipping Cost/Unit		
	Warehouse 1	Warehouse 2	Warehouse 3
Customer 1	$2.00	$2.50	
Customer 2	$1.00	$1.50	
Customer 3		$1.50	$1.00
Customer 4		$2.00	$1.50

The objective is to find stocking levels in period 1 and shipping routes in period 2 that minimize total cost (inventory plus shipping) while meeting customer demand, and without shipping more from any warehouse in period two than was stocked in period one.

Exploring the Model. Retrieve SUPPLY.xls for the Excel Solver or SUPPLYW.xls for What's*Best*.

SUPPLYW.xls takes advantage of the fact that What's*Best!* can optimize across worksheets. It has one sheet for each time period. SUPPLY.xls, formatted for the Excel Solver, is similar in structure, but stored on a single sheet. SUPPLYW is described here. The model's key elements are the following:

Period 1

- The amount stocked at each warehouse in period 1 appears in the range B4:D4.

- The inventory costs per unit are stored in B5:D5.

- The total inventory cost in cell B9 is calculated as SUMPROD-UCT(B4:D4,B5:D5).

- The total shipping cost from period 2 in cell D9 is 'Period 2'!F17.

- The total cost (inventory plus shipping) appears in cell C11.

Period 2

- The amount shipped from each warehouse to each customer is stored in the range B6:D9. Note that blank cells denote nonexistent routes.

- The shipping costs per unit appear in the range B19:D22.

- The total shipping cost in cell F17 is the SUMPRODUCT (B6:D9,B19:D22).

- The total shipments by warehouse are calculated in cells B11:D11.

- The stocks available at each warehouse from period 1 appear in cells B13:D13.

- The total shipments to each customer are stored in cells F6:F9.

The cell row references will be different on SUPPLY.xls (the Solver version.)

The ABC's of the Supply Chain Model.

A. The a̲djustable cells

   1. B4:D4 in period 1 represent the amount stocked at each warehouse.

   2. B6:D9 in period 2 are the quantities shipped between warehouses and customers.

B. The b̲est solution is that which minimizes total cost (inventory plus shipping), in cell C11 of period 1.

C. The c̲onstraints are the following:

   1. The total shipped to each customer is at least as great as the demand.

2. The total shipped from each warehouse in period 2 does not exceed that stocked in period 1.

3. The adjustable cells are constrained to be greater than or equal to zero. This must be done explicitly with the Solver[5] but is the default in What's*Best!*.

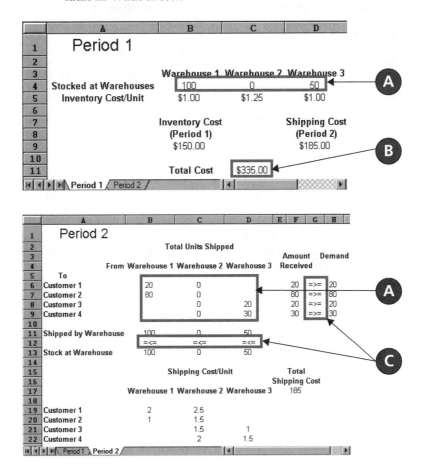

Vertically Integrated Models

We saw in the two-period boat manufacturing example how worksheet BOATSOPT.xls can be recombined with itself to create a multiperiod model. In the next exercise, you will combine BOATSOPT.xls and TRANS.xls to cre-

---

5. In Excel 97, it is convenient to use the Assume Non-Negative option to impose this constraint.

ate a vertically integrated model that addresses both profit from manufacturing and the cost of transporting resources.

EXERCISE 8.4 Combining a Production and Transportation Model

Suppose the boat manufacturer has plants in three countries, each producing the same line of boats. The unit profit and demand vary by country as shown in the following table.

Country		Large sailboat	Motorboat	Small sailboat	Sailboard
A	Profit/unit	$1,200	$1,050	$930	$750
	Demand	160	130	170	150
B	Profit/unit	$1,100	$1,000	$900	$500
	Demand	120	120	180	160
C	Profit/unit	$1,400	$1,000	$950	$800
	Demand	50	80	180	140

The corporation orders all its aluminum from two mills. The combination of shipping cost and tariffs between the two mills and three countries is shown in the following table with the mills' capacities.

		From:	
		Mill 1	Mill 2
To:	A	$100	$75
	B	$90	$80
	C	$70	$50
Capacity by Mill		1000	1500

Each plant's starting inventories are shown in the following table:

	A	B	C
Sailcloth	700	720	800
Glass Fiber	1380	1400	1200
Epoxy Resin	1280	1300	1100
Engines	120	130	90

Model this situation by combining TRANS.xls with three copies of BOATSOPT.xls in the same worksheet.

Hints:

■ Your objective should be to maximize the sum of the profit from the three plants minus the shipping cost.

■ If you build the model in a single worksheet for the Excel Solver, remove the absolute ($) references from the usage formulas before copying BOATSOPT. If you are using What's*Best!,* keep the transportation model and each of the production models on its own sheet.

■ You no longer need constraints requiring that a given amount be shipped to each plant. The model will decide how much to ship to maximize profit.

A possible single sheet layout is shown in the following figure where Excel's auditing tools have been used to show how the models have been tied together.

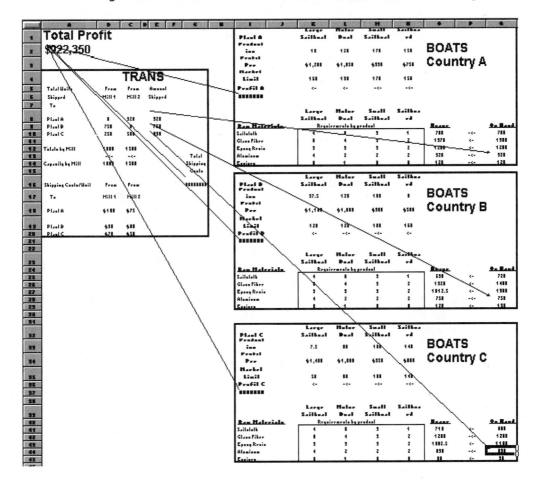

Optimization Under Uncertainty

This next example revisits the two-period supply chain model. This time, however, the demand in period 2 is not known with certainty. A linear program that incorporates uncertainty, such as this one does, is known as a *stochastic linear program*. This model was jointly developed with Gerd Infanger. For a thorough explanation of stochastic linear programming, see Infanger [1994].

Retrieve SUPPLYU.xls for the Excel Solver or SUPPLYUW.xls for What's*Best!*. Recall that in this model we are uncertain about the quantity of demand. Specifically, the marketing department is fairly certain about overall demand, but does not know whether it will be heavier among West Coast customers (1 and 2) or East Coast customers (3 and 4).

The two contingencies are referred to as scenario 1 and scenario 2 as outlined in the following table.

	Demand by Scenario		
	Scenario 1	Scenario 2	Average
Customer 1	10	30	20
Customer 2	70	90	80
Customer 3	30	10	20
Customer 4	40	20	30

The average demand is simply that used in the previous (deterministic) version of the supply chain problem. As discussed in the chapters on simulation, it is a common, but usually erroneous, practice to use averages of uncertain numbers in place of distributions.

Here we have approximated the complete distribution of demand with only two scenarios. This is quite simplistic, but we can conceptually extend this approach to much larger numbers of scenarios. In the defense of simplicity, however, don't forget that Paul Revere only needed two scenarios (one if by land or two if by sea) to adequately prepare the colonial forces for the British offensive.

In general, the scenarios used in stochastic linear programming can simply be states of the world that management believes are likely. Scenarios can also be generated by Monte Carlo simulation or other automated means.

SUPPLYU differs from SUPPLY in the following respects:

■ In period 1, we must now decide how much to stock at each warehouse without knowing what the customer demands will be in period 2.

■ In period 2, we will now make different shipping decisions depending on which scenario occurred.

■ We must allow for the fact that given certain stocking decisions in period 1, it might not be possible to supply all customers under both scenarios. Therefore, we will introduce cells to measure lost sales in that case.

■ We will also introduce formulas that calculate the average shipping costs and lost sales across both scenarios.

We now have conflicting objectives of minimizing average cost and average lost sales. Our approach will be to explore the trade-offs between these two, by minimizing one while constraining the other.

Exploring the Model. SUPPLYUW.xls again takes advantage of multiple worksheets. It has one sheet for time period 1 and a separate sheet for each of the two scenarios of period 2. SUPPLYU.xls, formatted for the Excel Solver is similar in structure, but is stored on a single sheet. SUPPLYUW is described in the following lists. Key differences from the deterministic supply model are as follows:

Period 1

■ The total shipping cost from period 2 in cell D9 has been replaced by the average shipping cost over both scenarios: ('Period 2 – Scenario 1'!F17 + 'Period 2 – Scenario 2'!F17)/2.

■ The average lost sales over both scenarios appears in D13, as

('Period 2 – Scenario 1'!E13 + 'Period 2 – Scenario 2'!E13) / 2.

Period 2

■ Period 2 is now represented by two sheets, one for each scenario.

■ Cells E6:E9 have been added to track lost sales for each customer under that scenario.

■ Total lost sales for the scenario appear in E13.

■ In the event that a customer's entire demand is not met by the warehouses, the remainder of the order will be lost to competitors. Thus the totals received by each customer (F6:F9) are now expressed as the sum of those delivered from the warehouses plus lost sales. In the case of customer 1, for example, this is SUM(B6:E6).

■ The only difference between the scenarios in this example is the customer demand in cells H6:H9. However, it would have been possible for anything, such as shipping costs or even whether or not a particular shipping route was open, to vary across scenarios.

Changes to the ABC's.

A. The a̲djustable cells

The lost sales E6:E9 must be made adjustable so they will automatically take up the slack left by unfulfilled demand.

B. and C.

There are two potential objectives for this model: the minimization of costs or lost sales. Load the model and optimize it to minimize total average cost. The good news is that you should get a cost of zero, the bad news is that you have lost all your sales. Next try minimizing average lost sales. This time the good news is that there are no lost sales, but the bad news is that costs are quite high. As you can see there is a trade-off between average cost and average lost sales. Either of these can be chosen as an objective with the other limited by a constraint.

EXERCISE **Generating a Trade-Off Curve**

8.5

How do we deal with these conflicting objectives? Cost, of course, is measured in money. Lost sales are measured not only in money, but also good will on which it is difficult to place monetary value. In such situations, it is useful to perform repeated optimizations on one of the two objectives while increasingly constraining the other. This creates a trade-off curve between the two that can assist management in making a final decision. Proceed as follows:

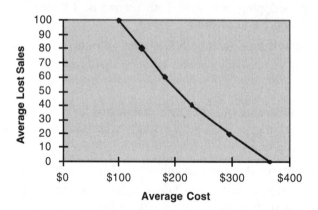

a. Constrain average lost sales to be <= 100 and then minimize average cost. Copy the resulting values of cost and lost sales into blank cells at the bottom of the worksheet using **Paste Special Values**.

b. Repeat this experiment, tightening the constraint on lost sales to 80, 60, 40, 20 and finally 0, copying the results below those of part a.

c. Move the column of lost sales results just to the left of the cost results, then create a scatter plot of the data. Use the second scatter plot format, which connects the points with a line, to display the trade-off curve between lost sales and cost.

d. What expected cost and lost sales would have resulted from using the stocking levels specified by the deterministic model?

Nonlinear Optimization

Financial Portfolio Optimization

In the 1950s, Harry Markowitz pointed out that there are generally trade-offs between the expected return and the risk (often measured in variance) of an investment portfolio. He went on to develop a method to determine the least risky portfolio that met a required rate of return.[6]

By *investment instrument,* we mean a single stock or other investment with known statistical behavior. By *investment portfolio,* we mean a mix of investment instruments. We will start our discussion with a portfolio containing only two instruments and then describe a worksheet model with three instruments.

An investment's *expected return* is the percentage return you would expect on average from that investment. For example, an expected 10% return would imply an average return of $1.10 for each dollar invested. The expected returns of our two hypothetical instruments will be denoted by r_1 and r_2.

Let x_i denote the percentage of the portfolio in instrument i. Because these are percentages, the sum of x_1 and x_2 must total 100%, that is, $x_1 + x_2 = 1$. The expected return of the portfolio as a whole is

$$E_p = x_1 r_1 + x_2 r_2$$

The contours of E_p are shown in the following figure for the three possible orderings of r_1 and r_2. A contour is a line along which the expected return is constant. In this figure, the heavier the line, the greater the expected value. That is, all combinations of x_1 and x_2 lying on a thin line yield the same low expected return, and all those combinations lying on a thicker line yield the same higher expected return.

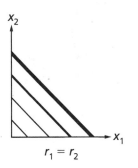
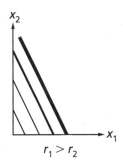
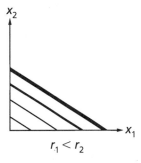

6. This discussion assumes some familiarity with statistical dependence, for which you might want to review Chapter 3.

An investment's *risk* is often measured by its variance. Variance turns out to be a nonlinear function of the elements in the portfolio, hence the need for nonlinear optimization.

The variance of the two instruments under discussion are denoted by σ^2_1 and σ^2_2 respectively. The covariance of the two returns, a measure of the degree to which one return goes up or down when the other goes up or down, is denoted by σ_{12}, and can be found using the COVAR function in Excel. See Chapter 3 for more information on covariance.

The variance or risk of the portfolio as a whole can be shown to be

$$\sigma^2_p = x^2_1\sigma^2_1 + x^2_2\sigma^2_2 + 2x_1x_2\sigma_{12}$$

The risk contours as measured by σ^2_p are shown in the following figure under several conditions. Because this is a nonlinear function, the contours are curves rather than straight lines. The heavier the line, the greater the risk. All combinations of x_1 and x_2 lying on a thin line result in the same low risk, and all those combinations lying on a thicker line result in a higher risk.

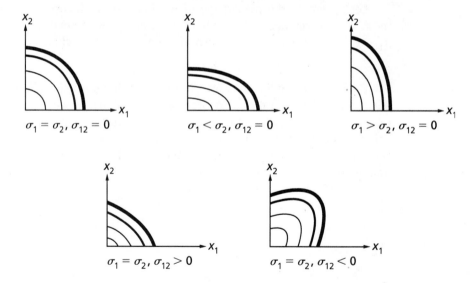

Consider a case in which $r_1 < r_2$, and $\sigma_1 < \sigma_2$, $\sigma_{12} = 0$. The following figure superimposes both the expected return contours (black straight lines) and risk contours (shaded curved lines). Because $x_1 + x_2 = 1$, our choices of portfolio are limited to the thick textured line.

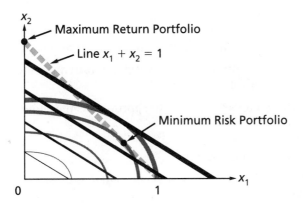

The portfolios yielding maximum return and minimum risk are marked. Any point on the line between these two portfolios will yield intermediate values of return and risk, which could reasonably be favored by people with different preferences for risk. Note that any portfolio to the southeast (that is down and to the right) of the minimum risk portfolio offers *decreased* return at *increased* risk and is therefore not sensible regardless of one's risk preference. For an arbitrary number of instruments, the variance of the portfolio is $\sigma^2_p = x \bullet Q \bullet x^T$, where Q is the covariance matrix, x is the vector of investment percentages, and x^T is x transpose.[7]

Exploring the Model. Retrieve MARKWTZ.xls for the Excel Solver or MARKWTZW.xls for What's*Best*.

The model's key elements are the following:

■ Cells A10:C10 contain x, the vector of percentages of the three investment instruments to be included in the portfolio.

■ Cells A13:C13 contain r, the vector of expected returns of reach instrument.

■ The covariance matrix Q in cells A16:C18 is defined as follows:

$$Q = \begin{array}{ccc} \sigma^2_1 & \sigma_{12} & \sigma_{13} \\ \sigma_{21} & \sigma^2_2 & \sigma_{23} \\ \sigma_{31} & \sigma_{32} & \sigma^2_3 \end{array}$$

---

7. You can run the model without understanding what this means. See Luenberger (1997) for a further explanation.

- Cells E16:G16 contain **x·Q**.
  Excel Solver: The calculation uses the MMULT array formula.
  What's*Best!*: The calculation uses addition and multiplication.

- Cells E5 and G5 contain the actual expected return and required expected return of the portfolio.

- Finally cell E7 contains the risk of the portfolio as measured by the variance, **x·Q·x**.

The ABC's of the Portfolio Model.

A. The adjustable cells, A10:C10, are the percentages of each instrument in the portfolio.

B. The best solution is that which minimizes the risk of the portfolio, cell E7.

C. The constraints are as follows:

1. Because the adjustable cells represent percentages, their sum must equal 1.

2. The expected return is required to be at least a specified minimum.

3. The adjustable cells are constrained to be greater than or equal to zero. This must be done explicitly with the Solver[8] but is the default in What's*Best!*.

Additional constraints can be added to limit the percentage of the portfolio devoted to any particular instrument or class of instruments.

The Efficient Frontier: Parameterized Optimization

Every possible investment opportunity, including individual instruments as well as portfolios, has both an expected return and a risk. In theory, we could plot all investments relative to these two measures. Suppose that each plotted investment opportunity were the head of a nail. Imagine stretching a piece of string across the nail heads as shown in the following figure. Let x be any investment opportunity that touches the string.

---

8. In Excel 97 it is convenient to use the Assume Non-Negative option to impose this constraint.

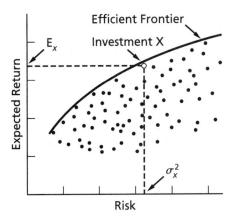

Its expected return and variance are labeled E_x and σ^2_x. It should be apparent from the figure that no other investment with expected return greater than or equal to E_x has risk lower than σ^2_x and that no other investment with variance less than or equal to σ^2_x has an expected return higher than E_x.

Thus, an investment such as x is said to be efficient, and the line formed by the string is known as the *efficient frontier*. Depending on an investor's willingness to trade higher risk for a higher expected return, an investment at any point on the efficient frontier might be reasonable, whereas an investment away from the frontier is generally not reasonable. An efficient investment can be found at any point on the frontier by combining other investments.

An optimal solution of the portfolio model yields one point on the efficient frontier. By repeatedly solving the model while incrementally changing the constraint on expected return, the frontier can be plotted out. This is known as parametric or parameterized optimization.

**EXERCISE
8.6**

Parameterized Portfolio Optimization

Repeatedly optimize the portfolio model for required returns of 10%, 12%, 14%, 16%, 18%, and 20%. After each optimization, copy the expected return and variance to a blank range in the worksheet (*Hint:* Use **E**dit Paste **S**pecial **Values**). Then graph all five values with an XY plot to display the efficient frontier.

**EXERCISE
8.7**

Visual Basic Macro for Parameterized Portfolio Optimization

Write a Visual Basic macro to perform the parameterized optimization and graphing.

Curve Fitting

A common nonlinear problem involves fitting a curve to data. As an example, consider the time series extrapolation technique of Exponential Smoothing discussed in Chapter 5, "Forecasting."

Exponential Smoothing involves adjusting one or more parameters in a forecasting model to minimize the mean squared error between the model and the actual data. Exercise 5.5 describes how to apply nonlinear optimization to the exponential smoothing models to minimize mean squared error. Use the built-in solver in Excel to change alpha and beta to minimize the MSE. *Note:* Alpha and beta must be constrained to be between 0 and 1.

Common Errors in Optimization Models

Two common problem areas in formulating linear programming models involve nonlinear formulas and improper constraints.

Linear and Nonlinear Formulas

The great problem-solving power of linear programming, as the name suggests, is based on linear formulas. As discussed earlier, the Excel Solver defaults to nonlinear optimization. If you know that your model is linear, you should select Assume Linear Model from the Options dialog box to take advantage of the LP algorithm. If the model turns out to be nonlinear, you will get an error message. What's*Best!* detects whether or not the model is linear, then automatically applies the appropriate algorithm. The What's*Best!* error screen will optionally display a warning for nonlinear formulas in case they are not intentional.

What Are Linear Formulas?

In their simplest form, linear formulas are "straight line" relationships. For example, suppose you are buying tomatoes at $1.50 per pound. The formula for your bill (B) for the amount of tomatoes purchased (T) is B = 1.5*T. This formula's graph is a straight line and shown in the following figure. Hence, the name "linear."

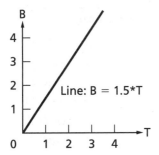

In this example, there is only one input value, the pounds of tomatoes purchased, but the concept of linearity also applies to more than one input variable. For instance, suppose that in addition to tomatoes we purchased potatoes at $0.75 per pound and apples at $1.25 per pound. The corresponding formula for the bill (B) is: $B = 1.5*T + .75*P + 1.25*A$, where T, P, and A are the pounds purchased of tomatoes, potatoes, and apples, respectively. This formula is also said to be linear because it is the sum of three linear relationships. because this formula has three input values, however, it is not possible to visualize as a straight line graph.

Rules for Writing Linear Formulas

Linear formulas can be built from simpler linear formulas according to the following rules:

- Adjustable cells can be multiplied or divided by numbers to form linear formulas.

- Two or more linear formulas can be joined together by +, - , or **SUM** to form a new linear formula.

- Linear formulas can be joined to *any* formula that does **not** depend directly or indirectly on an adjustable cell, by +, -, *, /, or **SUM** to form a new linear formula.

- If A is a range of adjustable cells and B is a range of constant numbers, then = SUMPRODUCT (Range A, Range B) is a linear formula.

- DSUM, SUMIF, and some other formulas can be linear depending on which arguments are adjustable cells. These will be interpreted correctly by the Excel Solver but not necessarily by What'sBest!.

Examples of Linear and Nonlinear Formulas

A few examples of both linear and nonlinear formulas are shown in the following table. Cells A1 through A3 are adjustable cells. Cells B1 through B3 are nonadjustable (fixed) cells.

Linear Formulas	Nonlinear Formulas
= A1*B1	= A1*A2
= A1/B1	= B1/A1
= A1*B1 + A2*B2	= A1^2
= A1*SQRT(B1)	= SQRT(A1)
= SUM(A1:A3)	= LOG(A1)
= SUM(A1:A3)*SQRT(B1)	= EXP(A1)
= SUMPRODUCT(A1:A3, B1:B3)	

When in doubt about a formula, try optimizing. If it is nonlinear and the Solver Option is set to Assume Linear Model, you will get an error message. What's*Best!* will return a warning message unless warnings are turned off.

Improper Constraints

Too many constraints create infeasible solutions. Suppose you add a constraint that contradicts one or more of the existing constraints. In the BOATS problem, for example, if you add the requirement that the number of large sailboats to be produced must be greater than 200, you will get a message that the problem is *infeasible*. This is because the new constraint violates both the market limit and usage constraints.

In contrast, too few constraints create unbounded solutions. Suppose you forget to include usage or market constraints in the BOATS production planning problem. Then there is no limit on the production and profit can also be increased without limit by producing an infinite number of boats. In such cases, you will get an error message indicating that the problem is *unbounded*. This message may also indicate that you maximized the wrong cell or incorrectly maximized the objective cell, when in fact you really wanted to minimize it.

Local Maxima or Minima in Nonlinear Optimization

Unlike linear optimization, which nearly always gets an optimal solution if there is one, nonlinear optimization often gets stuck at local maxima or minima. It is therefore important to test your solution by making several runs, with different starting values of the adjustable or changing cells.

The Basics of Optimization Theory

To discuss the theory behind optimization, we will examine a very small model in some detail.

Optimizing a Simplified BOAT Problem

Consider a simplified version of the BOATS problem with only two possible products and three raw materials. This is stored in BOAT.xls as discussed in Chapter 1. Recall that the production was optimized in Chapter 1 using a data table to maximize profit without exceeding the usage of raw materials.

EXERCISE
8.8

Optimizing BOAT.xls

Optimize this model using the Excel Solver or What's*Best!*. The results should appear as shown in the following figure.

	A	B	C	D	E	F	G
1			Large Sailboat	Motor Boat			
2	Production Quantity		65	120			
3	Profit Per Unit		$1,200	$1,000			
4	Market Limit						
5	Total Profit						
6	$198,000						
7							
8			Large Sailboat	Motor Boat			
9	Raw Materials		Requirements by product		Usage		On Hand
10	Sailcloth		4	0	260	<=	400
11	Glass Fiber		8	4	1,000	=<=	1,000
12	Engines		0	1	120	=<=	120

The Algebraic Expression of the BOAT Model

Traditionally, linear optimization problems have been expressed algebraically. The BOAT model can be expressed as follows, where L and M denote the number of large sailboats and motor boats produced respectively. The defining elements in this representation are as follows:

- The objective coefficients
- The constraint coefficients
- The constraint limits

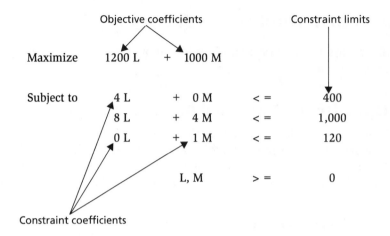

Tableau Representation

Remarkably, every linear optimization problem can be expressed in this same form. The only thing that varies from model to model are the number of variables, objective coefficients, constraint coefficients, and constraint limits.

Because of this, linear programming problems were traditionally expressed as the coefficients only in a representation known as a *tableau* as shown in the following table. Although it is possible to create a tableau for any linear problem, it is not an intuitive notation for use by managers. Today, spreadsheets and specialized optimization languages [AMPL, GAMS, LINGO] are most commonly used to express optimization problems.

Tableau for BOAT

1200	1000	
4	0	400
8	4	1000
0	1	120

A Geometric View of Optimization: TABLEAU.xls

TABLEAU.xls provides a geometrical interpretation of the simplified production problem modeled by BOATS_2.

■ **FUNDAMENTALS 8-1** ■ ■ ■ ■ ■ ■ ■ ■ ■ ■ ■ ■

Tableau

Every linear problem can be expressed as a *tableau* that consists of the objective coefficients, constraint coefficients, and constraint limits.

■ **FUNDAMENTALS 8-2** ■ ■ ■ ■ ■ ■ ■ ■ ■ ■ ■

Feasible Region

The set of values that satisfy all constraints is known as the *feasible region*.

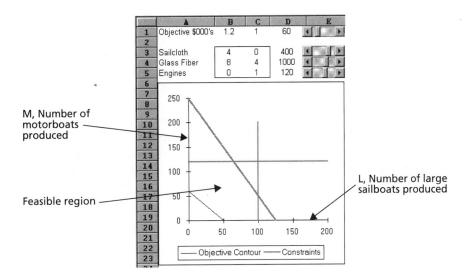

The Constraint Contours and Feasible Region. The thick lines (in green in the worksheet) denote *constraint contours*. That is, each line represents a production combination along which one of the resources would be completely exhausted. Specifically,

- The vertical line at L = 100 means that 100 large sailboats would consume all 400 units of resource 1, sailcloth.

- The diagonal line running from L = 125 to M = 250 indicates that all 1000 units of resource 2, glass fiber, would be consumed by production anywhere on the line.

- The horizontal line at M = 120 means that 120 motorboats would consume all of resource 3, motors.

■ **FUNDAMENTALS 8-3** ■ ■ ■ ■ ■ ■ ■ ■ ■ ■ ■ ■ ■ ■

Contours

■ A **contour** is a line in the plane over which a function takes on a constant value.

■ For linear functions, the contours are straight.

■ In a linear program with two variables, combinations of values that exactly meet constraints define contours.

■ **FUNDAMENTALS 8-4** ■ ■ ■ ■ ■ ■ ■ ■ ■ ■ ■ ■ ■ ■

Corner Solutions

If a linear problem has an optimal solution at all, there will always be one in a corner.

The Feasible Region. The region bounded by the axes and these solid lines represents the only feasible combinations of production and is known as the *feasible region*.

By moving the slide bars, you can see how the feasible region is effected by changes in the quantity of raw materials. If you make large changes to the numbers in the worksheet, you may need to adjust the scale factor in cell C26 to properly adjust the graph. Be sure to return numbers to their original values before proceeding. Compare the feasible region to the data table generated in the tutorial of Chapter 1.

The Objective Contour. The thin line on the graph (in blue in the worksheet) denotes the *objective contour*, that is, the combinations of large sailboats on the horizontal axis and motorboats on the vertical axis that result in the objective value displayed in $000's in cell D1. In the example shown, the line runs from 50 on the L axis to 60 on the M axis. This means that 50 units at $1,200 or 60 units at $1,000, or any linear combination in between will result in $60,000.

Corner Solutions. The optimal solutions to linear problems are at corners where constraint contours intersect.

Use the slide bar to increase the objective value to $120,000 and observe how the contour moves out while staying parallel with the original line. Now move it all the way to $300,000. The objective contour has moved outside of the feasible region. This objective cannot be achieved with the raw materials on hand.

How high can you raise the objective before you leave the feasible region? At 198,000, the objective just intersects the corner of the feasible region where the motor and glass fiber constraints intersect as shown in the following figure. It is not possible for any contour to take on higher value without leaving the feasible region, hence this corner is the optimal solution.

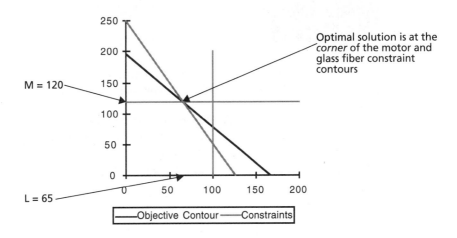

EXERCISE 8.9 Corner Solutions for Large Sailboats

To test your understanding of corner solutions, answer the following questions by observing the graph in TABLEAU.xls. Start with the original coefficients in the worksheet, but with the objective set to $198,000.

a. Increase the profit per unit for large sailboats beyond $1,200.

b. What happens to the angle of the objective contour?

c. For what profit per unit does another corner also become optimal?

d. Approximately what value of profit can be obtained with this profit per unit for large sailboats?

e. How many optimal solutions are there now?

f. Approximately what production figures does the new corner represent?

g. How many optimal solutions are there if you increase the profit per unit of large sailboats a little further?

More Variables and Constraints

Variables Correspond to Dimensions. The number of decision variables (adjustable cells) corresponds to the dimension of the feasible region. In the BOAT model, there are two decision variables and, hence, a two-dimensional feasible region. If a third boat type were added to the model, the feasible region would be three dimensional and might look like the following figure.

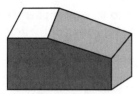

If there are more than three decision variables, then the feasible region cannot be visualized directly. But the concept is still useful.

Constraints Correspond to Boundary Lines. Each boundary line of the feasible region corresponds to a constraint as shown in the graph in TABLEAU.xls. If more linear constraints were added, the feasible region would be bounded by more straight lines, perhaps like the following figure.

Linear versus Nonlinear Problems

These geometrical concepts illuminate some of the important differences between linear and nonlinear optimization problems.

Linear Problems

For *linear* problems, the *boundary* lines of the feasible region and *contours* of the objective function are *straight lines* (or flat planes in three dimensions, or hyper planes in higher dimensions).

There are always *solutions* to linear problems in corners of the feasible region. This is a generalization of the fact that a ball-bearing in a tilted cardboard box rolls to the lowest corner. For certain angles of the box, there might be two corners and an edge or even a whole side of the box that is lowest.

The famous linear programming simplex algorithm developed by George Dantzig in 1947 in effect rolls a mathematical ball bearing from corner to corner of a high-dimensioned box.

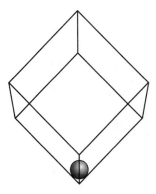

Nonlinear Problems

For *nonlinear* problems, some of the *boundary* lines of the feasible region or the *contours* of the objective function, or both, are *curved lines* (or curved planes in three dimensions, or curved hyper planes in higher dimensions).

The *solutions* can be anywhere in the feasible region. This is because nonlinear problems can take many forms, unlike linear problems that are always generalizations of a ball bearing acted on by gravity within a card-board box. For example, a problem with a nonlinear objective formula and linear constraint formulas would be more like a ball-bearing in a box acted on by one or more magnets.

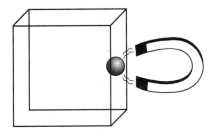

A problem with a linear objective formula but nonlinear constraints would be analogous to a smooth bowl in which the bearing slowly spirals to the bottom, or worse yet, like a rubber glove in which the bearing gets trapped in the thumb and never gets to the lowest point at all. The bowl represents a *convex* problem, whereas the glove is an example of a *nonconvex* problem.

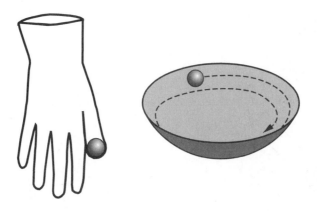

More on Dual Values

As we have seen, optimization can help you *maximize* profit or *minimize* cost given your *current* resource limitations and performance requirements. Dual values help you plan beyond the current environment, by indicating *rewards* or *penalties* associated with *changes* in your resource limitations and performance requirements.

Specific types of dual values for linear problems are *shadow prices* and *reduced costs*. The dual values for nonlinear problems are called *Lagrange multipliers*.

We can output the ranges over which shadow prices and reduced costs are valid. In general, it is not possible to determine the ranges over which Lagrange multipliers are valid.

Dual Value of a Constraint Cell—Shadow Price. Loosely stated, dual values let you assess the impact on your objective cell of tightening or relaxing a constraint in your model. For example, in the BOATS tutorial we found that the limit on sailcloth created a binding constraint. Additional sailcloth would increase profit by $300 per unit. That is, the shadow price of sailcloth was $300. The shadow price of a constraint that is not tight must always be 0 because loosening it further would have no effect.

Dual Value of an Adjustable or Changing Cell—Reduced Cost. Dual values can be found for adjustable cells in the same manner as for constraint cells. Remember that adjustable cells are usually constrained to be greater than or equal to zero. Therefore, an adjustable cell forced to 0 during optimization is a tight constraint. Tightening this constraint further by one unit corresponds to constraining the adjustable cell to be at least +1. In other words, we engaged in one unit of the associated activity even though it was not optimal to do so. The penalty of this non-optimal activity is reflected in the dual value, which in this context is referred to as a ***reduced cost***.

■ FUNDAMENTALS 8-5 ■ ■ ■ ■ ■ ■ ■ ■ ■ ■ ■ ■

Dual Values

- A *dual value* is the reward associated with relaxing a constraint or, equivalently, the penalty associated with tightening a constraint.

- For linear problems, a dual value associated with the nonnegativity constraint of a variable is called a *reduced cost,* any other dual value is called a *shadow price*.

- For nonlinear problems, a dual value is called a *Lagrange multiplier.*

Dual Values for Models Containing Integer Variables. Dual values do not give dependable information with models containing integer variables. The Excel Solver will not display them at all if integer constraints are present.

EXERCISE 8.10

Reduced Cost on Large Sailboats

Before market limits were imposed on the BOATS problem, no large sailboats were produced. The reduced cost on large sailboats indicates the amount that the profit per unit needs to be increased before they could be profitably produced. Remove the market limit constraint from BOATSOPT and find all the reduced costs.

Reward/Penalty Interpretation of Dual Values

We are now ready to state more generally the interpretation of dual values. Dual values pertain to all adjustable cells and to all constraint cells in models that do *not* contain integer ranges. There can be a non-zero dual value associated with each constraint that is tight, that is, met exactly, after optimization. Remember that adjustable cells are usually constrained to be greater than or equal to zero. In this case, any adjustable cell that equals zero after optimization is also considered to be a tight constraint.

The dual value can be interpreted either as a *reward* for relaxing a constraint or *penalty* for tightening a constraint.

Under the first interpretation, the dual value is the *amount* by which the objective cell would change if the constraint in question is relaxed by one unit. Examples include the increase in profit given one additional unit of a limited resource, or the decrease in cost given a unit reduction of a performance requirement.

Under the second interpretation, the dual value is the *negative amount* by which the objective cell would change if the constraint in question is tightened by one unit. Examples include the decrease in profit given one less unit of a limited resource, or the increase in cost given a unit increase in a performance requirement.

Valid Ranges for Dual Values

Going back to BOATSOPT, recall that each additional unit of sailcloth contributed $300 to profit. How many additional units could be purchased before this number changed? This is known as the dual value's upper range or allowable increase.

Conversely, if sailcloth currently in stock were lost, how many units would it take before the penalty for lost cloth changed from $300 per unit. This is known as the dual value's lower range or allowable decrease.

With the Excel Solver, the ranges can be read from the sensitivity report. With What's*Best!*, range information can be requested from the Dual dialog box.

EXERCISE
8.11
Dual Value Ranges

Find the upper and lower ranges for the dual values of BOATSOPT.

Conclusion

As we have seen, the possibilities for optimization are endless. However, with complex situations, there is a danger that the problem you are trying to solve might change before you finish the optimization model. Such models, although intellectually satisfying, fail George Dantzig's test that began this chapter.

Queuing Equations: QUEUE.xla and Q_NET.xla

User Inputs

The following variables and formulas apply to both QUEUE.xla and Q_NET.xla. However, with Q_NET.xla, much of the structure is repeated for each station in the queuing network.

Maximum Run Time. The simulation will run until time equals the max run time.

Mean Interarrival Time and Mean Service Time. The simulation assumes exponential distributions. ***Note:*** Mean interarrival time must be greater than mean service time or the queue length will eventually become infinite.

Initial State. This screen contains the values used to initialize the simulation, there are no formulas. To reach stability more quickly, you can enter any starting values in the current screen after initialization and before running. To specify permanent changes in the initial conditions, you can edit the initial screen.

Formulas

The following formulas appear in the *next state* sheet of QUEUE.xls. Multiple columns of these formulas appear in Q_NET.xls. They are quite complex and need not be understood in detail to run simulations. However, if you want to modify the models as suggested in some of the exercises, you will need to understand at least some of these.

Queue Statistics

Time. Time is determined from the next event, a system arrival or a departure. The next event is generated by taking the minimum of the next arrival time and the next service time. These appear in the section labeled Next Event Times.

Time = MIN(SRVC_TIM_NXT,ARIVL_TIM_NXT).

Queue Length. The queue length increases by one when the server is busy and an arrival occurs. It decreases by one when there is a departure unless the length is already 0. (see Status Indicators below).

Queue Length = (Q_LENGTH + (BUSY*ARIVL_NXT)) −
((DEPRTR_NXT*Q_LENGTH)<>0)

Number Served. The total number served increases by one for a departure from the system (see Status Indicators below).

Number Served = SERVED + DEPRTR_NXT

Total Wait Time. The total wait time is the current total wait time plus the queue length multiplied by the time between the current and the next events.

Total Wait Time = TTL_WAIT_TM+Q_LENGTH*(TM_NXT-TM)

Average Wait Time. The average waiting time in the queue is the total waiting time divided by the number served.

Avg Wait Time = IF(OR(TM = 0,SERVED = 0),0, TTL_WAIT_TM / SERVED)

Average Queue Length. The average queue length is calculated by dividing the total wait time by time.

Avg Queue Length = TTL_WAIT_TM /TM_NXT

Average Through-Put. The average through-put equals the total number served divided by the time.

Avg Through-Put = SERVED_NXT/TM_NXT

Maximum Queue Length.   The maximum queue length takes the maximum of the current maximum queue length and the queue length in the next state.

Max Queue Length = MAX(MAX_L,Q_LENGTH_NXT)

Status Indicators

The Status Indicators signify a true or false statement. A "1" indicates the statement is true, and a "0" indicates the statement is false.

Server Busy.   This formula defines the status of the server in the next state. If there is an arrival in the next state, then the server *is busy* (= 1). If there is no arrival in the next state, and if there is a departure and the queue length is 0, the server is *not busy* (= 0). In any other case, the busy indicator in the next state is the same as that in the current state (= BUSY).

Server Busy = IF(ARIVL_NXT = 1,1,IF(AND(DEPRTR_NXT = 1,Q_LENGTH = 0),0,BUSY))

Arrival.   An arrival occurs if the next *arrival* time equals the next time. This is a Boolean formula that equals 0 or 1 depending on the truth value of the equality.

Arrival = TM_NXT=ARIVL_TIM_NXT

Departure.   A departure occurs only when the next service time equals the next time and the server is busy. This is a compound Boolean expression.

Departure = ((TM_NXT = SRVC_TIM_NXT) * BUSY)<>0

Next Event Times

The service and system arrival times determine when the next event will occur. These are drawn from an exponential distribution with mean inter-arrival time and mean service time set by the user.

The exponential random variable is generated by evaluating the inverse cumulative distribution function with a uniformly distributed random argument. Thus

–M * LN(RAND())

yields an exponentially distributed random variable with mean M (Bratley, Fox, and Schrage, 1987, or Law and Kelton, 1991). This expression appears in both the service time (M = SERVICE_MEAN) and arrival time (M = SYSARRVMEAN) formulas. It can be replaced by other random number generators if appropriate.

Service Time.   Service time refers to the time at which the customer presently being served will depart the system, allowing the queue length to be reduced. If the server in the current state is not busy, the next service time is set to 10^8. Otherwise, if the current service time is 10^8 or there is a current departure, then the next service time is set to the current time plus an exponential random variable with mean = SERVICE_MEAN. In all other cases, the next service time is replaced with the current service time.

$$\text{Service Time} = \text{IF(BUSY} = 0,10\wedge8,$$

$$\text{IF(OR(SRVC\_TIME} = 10\wedge8,\text{DEPRTR} = 1),$$

$$\text{TM} + (-\text{SERVICE\_MEAN} * \text{LN(RAND()))},\text{SRVC\_TIME)})$$

System Arrival. The system arrival time refers to the time at which the next customer arrives. If the current arrival time is less than the current time or the queue length is 0, the next system arrival time is set to the current time plus an exponential random variable with mean = SYSARRVMEAN. In all other cases, the next system arrival time is replaced with the current system arrival time.

$$\text{System Arrival} = \text{IF(OR(ARIVL\_TIME} <= \text{TM},\text{Q\_LENGTH} = 0),$$

$$\text{TM} + (-\text{SYSARRVMEAN} * \text{LN(RAND()))},\text{ARIVL\_TIME)})$$

Traffic Flow Equations

Q_NET.xls has a column of these formulas for each station plus formulas to control the flow of traffic between stations. Following are summaries:

Transition Matrix. The probability of going to station *j* after leaving station *i* is found in the *ith* row and *jth* column. Station *0* denotes system arrival, the final station denotes system exit. You can input these probabilities directly as either numbers or formulas that depend on the current states of the various queues. ***Note:*** The rows of this matrix must always sum to 1.

From and To Calculations. Cells B13 and B14 on the *next event* sheet contain formulas giving the station the next event is coming *From* and going *To*. The *From* formula depends on cells in row 19, which indicate which station has triggered the current event. The *To* formula involves a lookup table based on the cumulative probability distribution across the rows of the transition matrix. This is stored on its own sheet.

FIRE.xls

FIRE.xls and its macros can be modified to simulate a wide variety of simple situations. However, numerous commercial packages are available to perform discrete event simulation on a much larger scale. Some of these contain graphics depicting the current state of the simulation.

Two-Parameter Exponential Smoothing for Estimating Trends

One-parameter exponential smoothing does not accurately track time series with a trend. For time series with either a *constant* or *slowly varying trend*, two-parameter exponential smoothing is appropriate.

The Formulas

One-parameter exponential smoothing uses a single parameter to smooth random fluctuations in a series that is assumed to have a constant or slowly changing mean. In two-parameter exponential smoothing, of which there are several kinds, a second parameter is added to smooth random fluctuations in the *trend* of a series that is assumed to be constant or slowly changing. The parameters are referred to as α (alpha) and β (beta). The approach used in FORECAST.xla is modeled after Gardner (1985, 1992).

The two-parameter smoothing routine in FORECAST.xla makes its initial estimate of the trend by performing linear regression on the data, then the smoothing proceeds to adapt the trend to fluctuations in the data. As with one-parameter smoothing, the data is divided into a warm-up and forecast period.

Linear regression is performed on the warm-up period with the resulting Y-intercept and slope used as the initial level and trend. α and β can be adjusted to minimize the Mean Square Error (MSE) over the period. *Note:* This model is much more sensitive to changes in β than it is to changes in α. Good starting values for α and β are 0.1 and .01 respectively.

Remember that the forecast for period t in one-parameter exponential smoothing is

$$F(T) = F(T-1) + \alpha E(T-1),$$

where

$$E(T-1) = Y(T-1) - F(T-1)$$

is the error of the forecast at time $t-1$.

Two-parameter exponential smoothing models $F(t)$ as the sum of two parts, a level $S(t)$, and a trend $T(t)$. This is based on the following formulas:

$$F(t) = S(t-1) + T(t-1)$$

where

$$S(t) = F(t) + \alpha * E(t),$$

$$T(t) = T(t-1) + \beta * E(t),$$

$$E(t-1) = Y(t-1) - F(t-1)$$

and where α and β are smoothing parameters between 0 and 1.

To get the model started, linear regression is performed on the sample, whereupon $S(0)$ and $T(0)$ are set to the Y-intercept and slope of the regression line respectively.

Future Forecasts

If you have n data points, then using these formulas, the forecast for period $n + 1$ is

$$F(n+1) = S(n) + T(n)$$

Because $Y(t)$ is assumed to have either a constant or slowly changing trend, we would expect the series to increase by the trend amount for each time period. Hence, for all future periods the formula is

$$F(t) = F(t-1) + T(n), t > n + 1$$

Note: Because both a level and a derivative are being forecast, you should not rely on a forecast many periods into the future.

The Effect of Changes in α and β.   If α and β are both set to 0, then for each t, $S(t) = F(t)$ and $T(t) = T(0)$. In this case, this model reduces to a linear regression of Y against t. Because β has a significant effect on the slope of the above model, it is much more sensitive to this parameter than it is to changes in α. Good starting values of α and β are 0.1 and .01, respectively.

Seasonal Data

When a time series displays repeating seasonal fluctuations, the data should be deseasonalized or seasonally adjusted before other forecasting techniques are applied. A forecast based on the deseasonalized data can then be made using exponential smoothing. Finally, this forecast is reseasonalized to get the desired result.

Deseasonalization is generally not performed unless you have at least three full seasons of data. FORECAST.xla assumes that one full season is 12 months. Deseasonalizing and reseasonalizing are accomplished as follows:

1. Calculate seasonality factors for each month, indicating that month's percentage of the average monthly total for the series, as follows:

$$S_j = \frac{12}{N} \sum_{i=1}^{N} \frac{Y_{ij}}{A_i}, \ j = 1 \dots 12$$

where N is the number of complete years worth of data, Y_{ij} is the value of the time series $Y(t)$ in month j of year i, and A_i is the annual total of the series in year i. **Note:** A perfectly average month will have a seasonality factor of 1.0.

2. Calculate the deseasonalized data by dividing the data in each month by its corresponding seasonality factor. Use the following formula:

$$D_{ij} = \frac{Y_{ij}}{S_j}, \ i = 1 \dots N, j = 1 \dots 12$$

Notice that if some month j of the time series data consistently had very small or zero values, that the S would be very small or zero and lead to instabilities in this equation.

3. A 12-month forecast, f_j is made of the D's, using one- or two-parameter exponential smoothing.

4. Find the final forecast F_j by multiplying each month of the future forecast by its corresponding seasonality factor, as specified in the following equation:

$$F_j = S_j f_j, \ j = 1 \dots 12$$

C

Software Command Reference

Outline of Reference

SIM.xla

QUEUE.xla and Q_NET.xla

FORECAST.xla

TREE.xla

OPTIMIZATION SOFTWARE

SIM.xla

SIM.xla requires Excel 5.0 or higher. Run Excel and open SIM.xla from the **File** menu. A **Simulate** menu will appear.

Auto Load Option. If you want SIM.xla to load every time you launch Excel, follow these steps:

1. Select **Add-ins** from the **Tools** menu in Excel.
2. Select SIM.xla from list of add-ins and click **OK**.
3. You can later go back and deselect SIM.xla from the **Add-in** menu to prevent Excel from loading it automatically.

A **Simulate** menu will be added to the Excel menu bar. *Note:* While SIM.xla is loaded, the Excel Edit Undo command will be disabled. When you close SIM.xla, this feature will be restored.

Menu and Dialog Boxes

Once SIM.xla is loaded, the **Simulate** menu will appear.

- **Run Simulation** initiates a simulation run with as many as five output cells.

- **Parameterized Sim** repeatedly runs the same simulation of a single output cell with as many as five different parameter values.

- **Save Results** saves a simulation's results.

- **Close Simulation** closes SIM.xla and removes the **Simulation** menu.

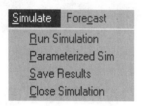

Run Simulation

The following dialog box will appear when you select **Run Simulation**.

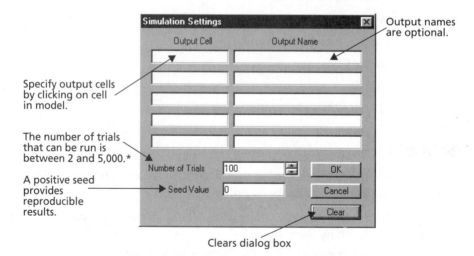

Output names are optional.

Specify output cells by clicking on cell in model.

The number of trials that can be run is between 2 and 5,000.*

A positive seed provides reproducible results.

Clears dialog box

*A larger version of SIM.xla is available from AnalyCorp. Inc. (www.Analycorp.com).

Parameterized Sim

The following dialog box will appear when you select **Parameterized Sim.**

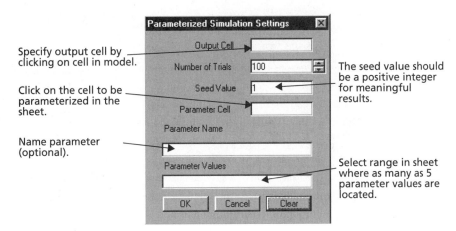

Specify output cell by clicking on cell in model.

Click on the cell to be parameterized in the sheet.

Name parameter (optional).

The seed value should be a positive integer for meaningful results.

Select range in sheet where as many as 5 parameter values are located.

Simulation Results

SIM.xla can produce the following outputs: statistics, histograms, cumulative graphs and parameterized graphs. All outputs are Excel cells and graphs and can be edited with standard Excel commands.

Statistics

After completion of the simulation, statistics are displayed for each output cell. For **Run Simulation**, statistics appear as shown in the following figure:

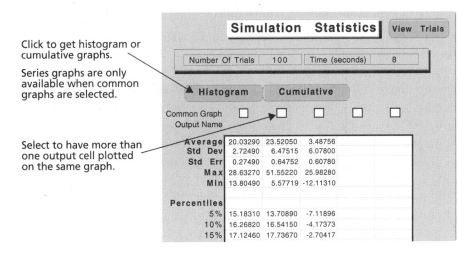

Click to get histogram or cumulative graphs.

Series graphs are only available when common graphs are selected.

Select to have more than one output cell plotted on the same graph.

For **<u>P</u>arameterized Simulation**, statistics will be displayed for each parameter value in the following figure:

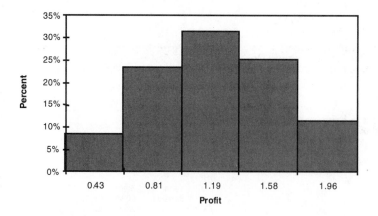

Histogram

Histograms are available after <u>R</u>un Simulation and are created by clicking the Histogram button on the statistics sheet.

Individual Histograms. A separate histogram is created for each output cell that has not been designated for inclusion in a common graph. The *x* axis labels represent the right edge of the bins. When you click the histogram button, a dialog box allows you to request the number of bins you want. For histograms of discrete random variables, you should use a large number of bins even with a small number of trials.

Common Histogram. A common histogram is created for all output cells designated for inclusion in a common graph.

To aid in viewing multiple histograms on the same graph, a smoothed line format has been used. However, the numbers on horizontal axis are not accurate when used with a small number of bins. The common histogram should be used for qualitative results only. For common numerical results, use the common cumulative graph.

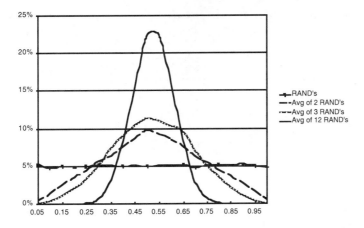

Cumulative Graph

Cumulative Graphs are available after **Run Simulation** and are created by clicking the **Cumulative** button on the statistics sheet.

Individual Cumulative Graphs. A separate cumulative graph is created for each output cell that has not been designated for inclusion in a common graph. A vertical line marks the mean.

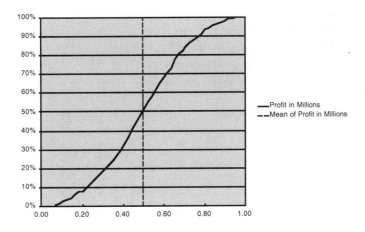

Common Cumulative Graph. A common cumulative graph is created for all output cells designated for inclusion in a common graph. Vertical lines mark the means for each graph.

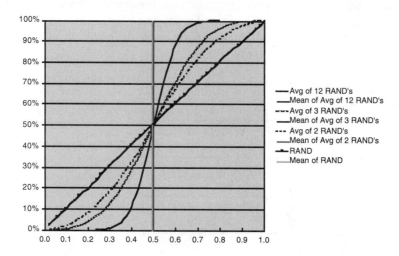

Parameterized Graph

The Parameterized Graph is available after **Parameterized Simulation** has been run and is accessed by clicking the **Parameterized Graph** button.

This graph displays the mean and an upper and lower percentile of the single output cell for each of as many as 5 parameter values.

By clicking on **Settings**, you can change the percentiles.

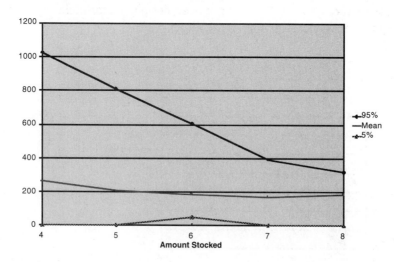

Simulation Trials

The trials sheet lists the model's outputs. Click the **View Trials** button on the **Statistics** sheet to create the trials sheet. By using Excel's Chart Wizard, you can view scatter plots of the trials to gain insight into the model's sensitivity to its random inputs.

Rate of Convergence

Click **Rate of Convergence** on the trials sheet to produce a graph of the running average of the output cell(s) versus trial number.

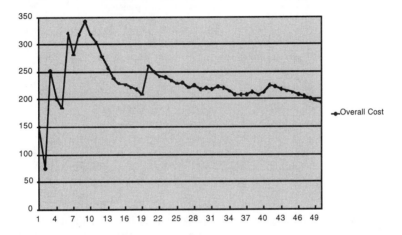

Random Number Generators

Make sure that SIM.xla is open before entering random number generating functions or opening an Excel workbook which uses these functions.

Note: When models using add-in functions are moved between computers, occasionally #**NAME?** will appear. This means that the random number generation formula has not yet been recognized by the worksheet. Edit the formula by clicking in the formula bar, removing any reference to a path name if present, then click on the check mark. Save the file now and you won't have to bother with this again.

Using the Function Wizard

To place a random number generating function in the spreadsheet, place the cursor in the desired cell, then click on the function icon (shown on the left below). You should see the following screen. Select **Statistical** from the left menu and the desired function name from the right menu.

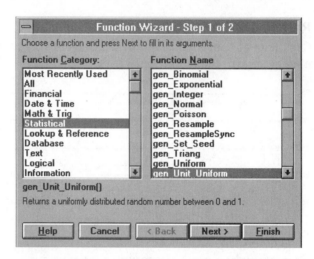

Click on **Next**, and you will be prompted for the distribution's parameters. If, for example, you selected **gen_Normal**, you will be prompted for the Normal distribution's mean and standard deviation as shown in the following figure.

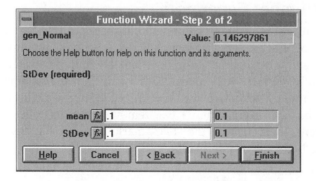

Fill in the requested parameters, and click **Finish**. Each time you press the calculate key—the F9 key in Windows and **Command =** in Macintosh—you should see a new random number generated in the cell. ***Note:*** Although a Help button appears on this screen, Help is not available for these add-in functions. See the next section for a complete list of the functions supplied with SIM.xla.

Random Number Generating Functions

The following list shows random number generating functions available in SIM.xla and their parameters:

- *gen_Binomial* (Number of Trials,Probability of Success)
- *gen_Cumulative* (Range of Cumulative Probabilities,Range of Associated Values)
- *gen_Discrete* (Range of Discrete Probabilities,Range of Associated Values)
- *gen_Exponential* (Mean)
- *gen_Integer* (Lower Integer,Upper Integer) returns integers uniformly distributed between Lower Integer and Upper Integer.
- *gen_Normal* (Mean,Standard Deviation)
- *gen_Poisson* (Mean)
- *gen_Resample* (Data Range) samples with replacement from the Data range.
- *gen_ResampleSync* (Data Range) samples with replacement from the Data range in synchrony with all other entries of this function. Thus, if gen_ResampleSync(Data_1) returns the kth element of the range Data_1, then gen_ResampleSync(Data_2) will return the kth element of range Data_2. This is useful for maintaining correlation in multivariate samples.
- *gen_Triang* (Low,Most Likely,High)
- *gen_Uniform* (Lower,Upper) returns a continuous random variable uniformly distributed between Lower and Upper.
- *gen_Unit_Uniform* (No Arguments) returns the same distribution as Rand(), but is subject to SIM.xla's seed.

Software Limitations

SIM.xla provides an introduction to Monte Carlo Simulation for spreadsheet users. Although intended to solve real problems, the emphasis has been on ease of use rather than on computational power. A 25,000 iteration version of SIM.xla is available through AnalyCorp, Inc. (www.Analycorp.com). In addition, two commercial spreadsheet add-ins, @RISK (www.Palisade.com) and Crystal Ball (www.decisioneering.com), provide greater Monte Carlo performance in several areas, although at higher costs and steeper learning curves.

If you believe that you have a spreadsheet model to which Monte Carlo simulation can be applied, you should make a prototype using SIM.xla. One of the following will generally occur:

1. You find that the problem is more complicated than you thought, and you do not get useful results. In this case you might want to explore discrete event simulation or decision trees.

2. You find that SIM.xla provides valuable insights and that nothing more is needed.

3. You are convinced that further Monte Carlo analysis could have a great impact. In this case, you should consider upgrading to more powerful software.

The primary areas of increased performance available through upgrading to more powerful software are as follows:

1. Larger number of trials allowed. SIM.xla is limited to 5,000.

2. Larger number of idealized distributions. SIM.xla is limited to those shown under the Function Wizard.

3. Unlimited number of output cells. SIM.xla allows a maximum of five.

4. Latin hypercube sampling. This sophisticated method of generating random numbers can speed the rate of convergence of a simulation.

5. Correlations can be directly specified between random inputs.

6. Sensitivity of specified output and input cells is provided as R^2 values.

QUEUE.xla and Q_NET.xla

QUEUE.xls

QUEUE.xla is used with QUEUE.xls to model a simple queue. Q_NET.xla is used with Q_NET.xls to model a queuing network. *QUEUE.xla and Q_NET.xla should not both be loaded at the same time.* Both QUEUE.xla and Q_NET.xla require Excel 5.0 or higher.

Running QUEUE.xla and Q_NET.xla.   Launch Excel and open QUEUE.xla and QUEUE.xls or Q_NET.xla and Q_NET.xls from the **File** menu. QUEUE.xls and Q_NET.xls can be modified and saved under any desired file name. *Note:* Make sure your worksheet's calculation mode is set to automatic under **Tools Options** before running these add-ins.

Auto Load Option.   If you want QUEUE.xla or Q_NET.xla to load every time you launch Excel

1. Select **Add-ins** from the **Tools** menu in Excel.

2. Select QUEUE.xla or Q_NET.xla from the list of add-ins and click **OK**. You can later go back and deselect either of them from the **Add-in** menu

to prevent Excel from loading them automatically. Do not load them both at once because they will not run correctly.

You will see the worksheet shown in the following figure when you open QUEUE.xls. Make sure that QUEUE.xla is opened first.

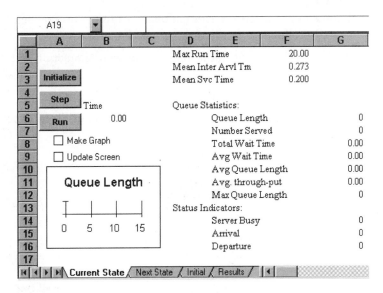

User Inputs

You must specify the maximum run time, mean interarrival time, mean service time, and initial state of the system

- *Maximum Run Time.* The simulation will run until time equals the maximum run time.

- *Mean Interarrival Time and Mean Service Time.* The simulation assumes exponential distributions. Note that mean interarrival time must be greater than mean service time or the queue length will eventually become infinite.

- *Initial State.* This screen contains the values used to initialize the simulation; there are no formulas. To reach stability more quickly, you can enter any starting values in the current screen after initialization and before running. To specify permanent changes in the initial conditions you can edit the initial screen.

Menu and Buttons

Once QUEUE.xla is loaded, the **Queue** menu will appear.

- **Initialize** sets all counters to the initial state stored in the **Initial** tab of the workbook.

- **Run Simulation** initiates a simulation run until time reaches Max Run Time and produces a graph of the queue length.

- **Quick Run** performs the same function as **Run Simulation** but does not produce a graph.

- **Single Step** advances the simulation to the next event.

- **Quit** removes QUEUE.xla from memory and **Queue** from Excel's menu bar.

- **Update Screen** toggles screen updating on and off.

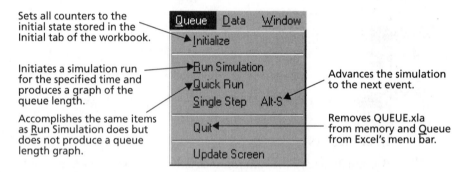

Sets all counters to the initial state stored in the Initial tab of the workbook.

Initiates a simulation run for the specified time and produces a graph of the queue length.

Accomplishes the same items as Run Simulation does but does not produce a queue length graph.

Advances the simulation to the next event.

Removes QUEUE.xla from memory and Queue from Excel's menu bar.

You can access the Initialize, Single Step, and Run Simulation or Quick Run functions through either buttons or menus.

Output and Results

QUEUE.xls and Q_NET.xls generate *Queue Statistics, Status Indicators,* and *Next Event Times.* The formulas appear in the *next state* sheet of QUEUE.xls. Multiple columns of these formulas appear in the *next state* sheet Q_NET.xls. The formulas, detailed in Appendix A are quite complex, but you don't have to understand them in detail to run simulations. However, if you want to modify the models as suggested in some of the exercises, you should understand at least some of these.

Q_NET.xls

When you load Q_NET.xls, you will see the following worksheet. Make sure that Q_NET.xla is loaded first.

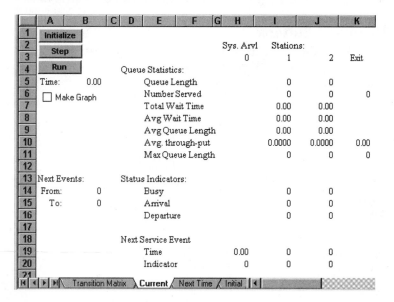

User Inputs

You must specify the maximum run time, mean inter-arrival, and mean service times for each station and the probabilities that characterize network's traffic flow in Q_NET.xls's Transition Matrix sheet, shown in the following figure:

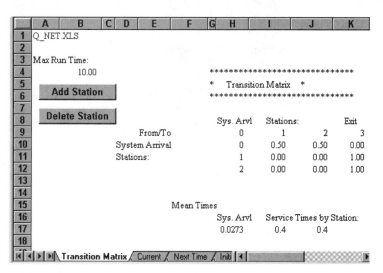

The maximum run time and mean inter-arrival and mean service times have already been described in the discussion of QUEUE.xls's inputs. The *Transition Matrix* contains transition probabilities that describe the network flow. The rows of the probabilities in the transition matrix must sum to 1.

Menu and Buttons

Once QNET.xla is loaded, the **QNet** menu will appear. Most menu selections are the same as those in QUEUE.xla. The exceptions are shown in the as following figure:

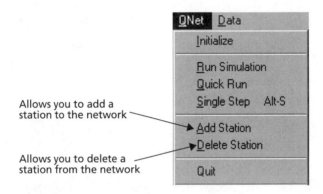

Allows you to add a station to the network

Allows you to delete a station from the network

FORECAST.xla

Menu and Dialog Box

Once FORECAST.xla is loaded, the **Forecast** menu containing the following items will appear, as shown in the following figure:

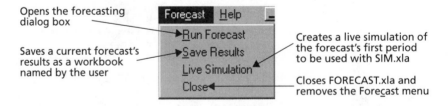

Opens the forecasting dialog box

Saves a current forecast's results as a workbook named by the user

Creates a live simulation of the forecast's first period to be used with SIM.xla

Closes FORECAST.xla and removes the Forecast menu

Run Forecast

Range containing time series ——————

Specify One Parameter Smoothing for series without a trend and Two Parameter Smoothing for series with a trend ——————

Check here for data displaying 12-month seasonality ——————

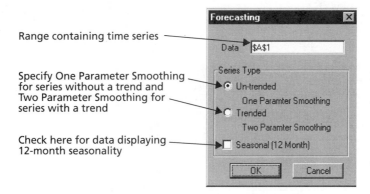

The Calculations

FORECAST.xla's calculations are discussed in the context of the motorcycle data within SERIES.xls. You should run a forecast on the motorcycle data using two-parameter smoothing with seasonality before proceeding.

The Results Sheet.   Columns B, C, and D contain the original data, the fitted "warm up" series, and the future forecast respectively. Notice that the forecast column does not have meaning until the first period into the future. For the current example, this is month 73, which is found in row 76.

The Forecast Graph.

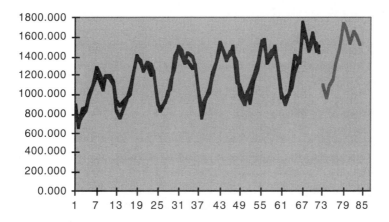

The Numbers. The month number, original series, "fitted" data, and the forecast appear in columns A through D of the results sheet where applicable. #NA appears where not applicable as in the following figure.

Month number   Historical data

	A	B	C	D	
70	67	1760.000	1622.1	#N/A	
71	68	1588.000	1581.3	#N/A	
72	69	1461.000	1448.4	#N/A	
73	70	1640.000	1561.9	#N/A	← Warm-up series
74	71	1439.000	1533.8	#N/A	
75	72	1491.000	1435.6	#N/A	
76	73	#N/A	#N/A	1100.2	← Forecast
77	74	#N/A	#N/A	965.18	
78	75	#N/A	#N/A	1096.2	
79	76	#N/A	#N/A	1162.1	

The "Deseason" Sheet. The Deseason sheet contains the seasonality factors as well as a copy of the original and deseasonalized data. The seasonality factors can be interpreted as percentages of an average month. The calculation of these factors is discussed later.

Original Data	Deseasoned Data	Seasonality Factors	
894	1097.65156	0.8145	← January sales are 81% of an average month
667	929.8396875	0.7173	← February sales are 71% of an average month, and so on
858	1054.611866	0.8136	
865	1013.686077	0.8533	
989	1087.039011	0.9098	
1093	996.9751227	1.0963	
1191	978.822955	1.2168	
1159	999.6711137	1.1594	
1046	969.701995	1.0787	
1191	1036.086388	1.1495	
1203	1095.22102	1.0984	
1121	1026.152052	1.0924	
931	1143.080092		
874	1218.410625		

The deseasonalized data is found by dividing each month of the historical data by the corresponding seasonality factor. You can use the Excel Chart Wizard to graph the original and deseasonalized data side-by-side to observe the extent to which seasonality has been removed.

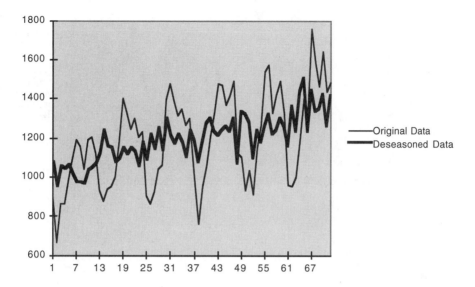

The Smoothing Sheet.   The smoothing sheet contains the formulas that calculate the nonseasonal part of the forecast. These are discussed in more detail in Appendix A. Here we will discuss only the concept of the Warm-up and Forecast data points.

	H	I	J	K	L	
5			**Warm-up**	**Forecast**	**Total Data**	
6		**Data Points**	72	0	72	

The ***warm-up data*** is used to calculate the forecast. It defaults to the entire data set, in which case the forecast is assumed to be for twelve months into the future. The ***forecast data*** is set aside at the end of the historical data as a surrogate for the future.

As an example, type 12 into cell K6 of the smoothing sheet. Cell J6 will now equal 60. This means that the forecast is now based only on the first 60 months of data. To find out how successful this forecast was for months 61 through 72, look at the Forecast graph as shown in the following figure. This shows that if we had used the first five years of data with this method to predict the sixth year, that we would have significantly underestimated May sales.

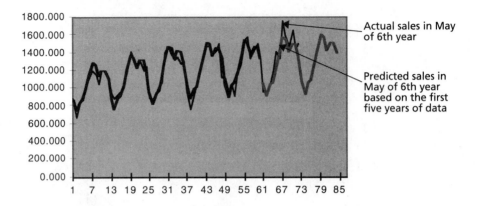

Actual sales in May of 6th year

Predicted sales in May of 6th year based on the first five years of data

TREE.xla

Menu and Dialog Boxes

Once TREE.xla is loaded the **T**ree menu will appear, with the following options:

- **N**ew opens a new worksheet, prompts user for number of state variables, and starts a new tree.

- Add **D**ecision Fork adds a specified number of decision branches to the selected node in the tree.

- Add **U**ncertainty Fork adds a specified number of uncertainty branches to the selected node in the tree.

- **R**emove Subtree removes selected subtree from current tree.

- **H**ide Variables hides state variable and joint probability columns.

- **S**how Variables shows state variable and joint probability columns.

- Cop**y** Utility copies a utility function of the state variables from the topmost leaf of a tree into all other leaves.

- **C**lose closes TREE.xla and removes the **T**ree menu.

New.   When the **New** command is invoked, the user is prompted to enter the number of state variables, if any, in the dialog box shown in the following figure. State variables, which will be discussed later, are not required for simple trees, for which the field can be left at zero. When you click **OK**, a new worksheet containing the root of the new tree will be created.

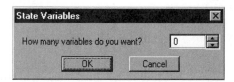

Add Decision Fork.   When you add a decision fork, the degree of branching (number of alternatives) is specified by a submenu as shown in the following figure.

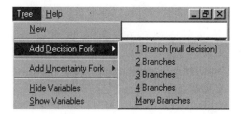

If you want more than four branches, use the **Many Branches** option, which will bring up the following menu.

Add Uncertainty Fork. When you add an uncertainty fork, the degree of branching (number of possible outcomes) is specified by a submenu as shown in the following figure.

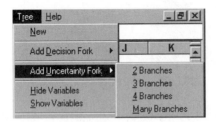

If you want more than four branches, use the **Many Branches** option, which will bring up the following menu.

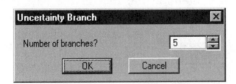

Remove Subtree. Select the entire subtree to be removed, with the node in the upper left hand corner as shown in the following figure. Then invoke the **Remove Subtree** command.

Subtree to be removed

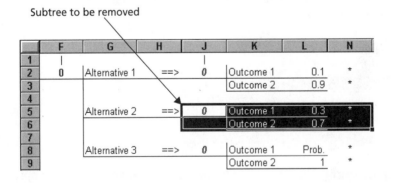

Hide Variables. When state variables are used, the **Hide Variables** command can be used to hide the columns containing state variables and joint probabilities, making the structure of the tree easier to view.

Show Variables. The **Show Variables** command un-hides the state variable and joint probability columns.

Copy Utility.   A utility function of the state variables can be entered in the topmost leaf of the tree, then the **Copy Utility** command will copy the function to the remaining leaf nodes. The tree will then evaluate automatically. *Note:* You must start with the cursor in the topmost leaf, and all leaf nodes must be in the same column to use the **Copy Utility** command. If they are not, use the 1 Branch (null decision) fork to extend leaf nodes to the same column. After the command is executed, the leaves of the tree will appear in **Bold Underlined Green** format.

Close.   The close command closes TREE.xla and removes the **Tree** menu.

State Variables

You can use state variables to simplify the calculation of utilities at the leaf nodes of the tree. For example, suppose that utility can be expressed as Profit = Revenue – Cost, where Revenue and Cost take on different values on different branches of the tree. The following steps show how the utility can be calculated directly from the state variables.

1. In creating the tree one would specify two state variables. Var1 and Var2 would then be labeled Revenue and Cost.

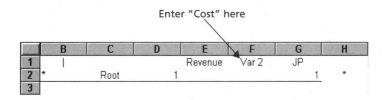

2. When a branch occurs, the associated values of the state variables are entered.

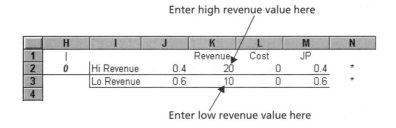

Note: All subsequent branches will inherit the appropriate values of the state variables.

3. When all branching is completed, enter a utility formula based on the state variables for the topmost leaf of the tree. In this case, it is Profit = Hi Revenue – Hi Cost.

	T2	▼	=Q2-R2			
	N	**O**	**P**	**Q**	**R**	**S**	**T**
1	I			Revenue	Cost	JP	
2	7.5	Hi Cost	0.5	20	5	0.2	15
3		Lo Cost	0.5	20	3	0.2	*
4							
5	0	Hi Cost	0.5	10	5	0.3	*
6		Lo Cost	0.5	10	3	0.3	*

4. Finally, with the cursor still in the topmost leaf, invoke the **Copy Utility** command to copy the formula in the topmost leaf to all other leaves. *Note:* All leaf nodes must be in the same column to use the **Copy Utility** command. If they are not, use the 1 Branch (null decision) fork to extend leaf nodes to the same column.

	N	**O**	**P**	**Q**	**R**	**S**	**T**
1	I			Revenue	Cost	JP	Utility
2	16	Hi Cost	0.5	20	5	0.2	15
3		Lo Cost	0.5	20	3	0.2	17
4							
5	6	Hi Cost	0.5	10	5	0.3	5
6		Lo Cost	0.5	10	3	0.3	7

Optimization Software

The two primary optimization packages available in spreadsheets are the Excel Solver, which ships with Excel, and What's*Best!*, a small version of which is included with INSIGHT. Larger versions of each product are available at www.Frontsys.com and www.Lindo.com, respectively.

The Excel Solver

The solver is included with Microsoft Excel, but is not automatically installed. If your installation of Excel has not included the solver, rerun Excel Installation and select the solver components. Once installed, the solver must be attached to Excel using the **Tools Add-Ins** command.

Menu and Dialog Boxes

Once installed and attached, the solver is invoked using the **Tools Solver** command. The following dialog box appears:

Cells that can change during optimization (decision variables); correspond to adjustable cells in What's*Best!*; can have positive or negative values.

Enter cell to be maximized, minimized, or set to a specified value here. This corresponds to "Best" cell in What's*Best!*

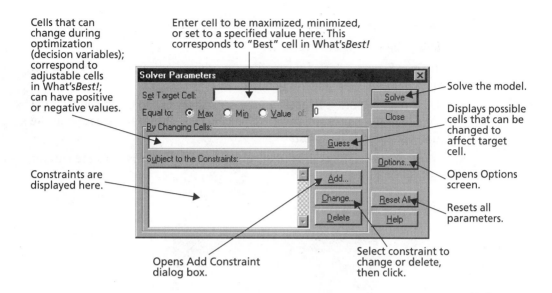

Solve the model.

Displays possible cells that can be changed to affect target cell.

Opens Options screen.

Resets all parameters.

Constraints are displayed here.

Opens Add Constraint dialog box.

Select constraint to change or delete, then click.

When you add a constraint, the following dialog box appears. Select the ranges on both sides of the inequality and the inequality itself.

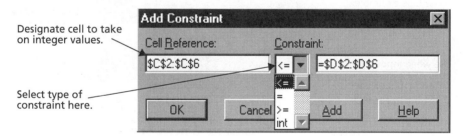

Designate cell to take on integer values.

Select type of constraint here.

Once the solver has run, the Solver Results dialog box appears. Click the appropriate radio button to either keep the solver's solution or restore the original numbers in your model. Optionally, you may select one of the three listed reports.

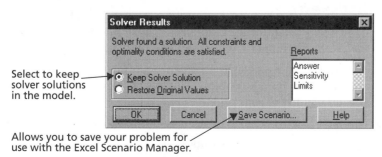

Select to keep solver solutions in the model.

Allows you to save your problem for use with the Excel Scenario Manager.

Reports

The following reports are available:

■ *Answer Report.* Lists information on original and final values of target and changing cells and constraints.

■ *Sensitivity Report.* Reports on the sensitivity of the target cell to small change in the constraint levels. This contains similar information to the dual values in What's*Best!*

■ *Limits Report.* Lists the target cell and changing cells with their lower and upper limits.

Solver Options Dialog Box

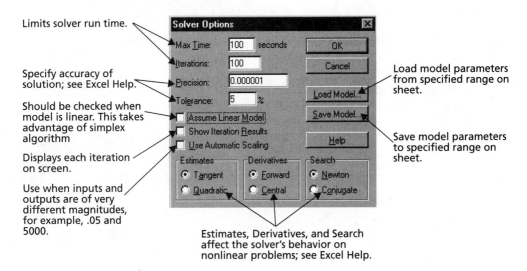

Limits solver run time.

Specify accuracy of solution; see Excel Help.

Should be checked when model is linear. This takes advantage of simplex algorithm

Displays each iteration on screen.

Use when inputs and outputs are of very different magnitudes, for example, .05 and 5000.

Load model parameters from specified range on sheet.

Save model parameters to specified range on sheet.

Estimates, Derivatives, and Search affect the solver's behavior on nonlinear problems; see Excel Help.

Note: In Excel 97, the Assume Non Negative option defaults all changing cells to be greater than or equal to zero on optimization.

What's*Best!*

Run the setup program from the INSIGHT disk and follow instructions. Once What's*Best!* is installed a **WB!** menu and tool bar will appear.

■ **Adjustable** specifies cells that can be adjusted during the optimization process (decision variables). These cells are colored blue so you can easily identify them.

■ **Best** specifies cell to maximized or minimized.

■ **Constrain** specifies constraints.

- **S**olve solves model.
- **D**ual specifies cells to contain dual values and their ranges.
- **I**nteger specifies cells to take on integer values.
- **O**ptions opens options dialog box.
- **R**eport opens report dialog box.

The icons associated with these commands are shown in the following figure:

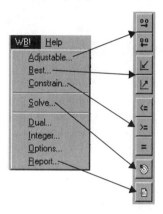

When the **A**djustable dialog box appears, highlight a range of cells that can be adjusted by the optimizer (decision variables). These correspond to the "changing" cells of the Excel solver. They are assumed to be non-negative unless designated as free.

Note: Adjustable cells are colored blue, and have their format status changed to Unlocked (see **Format Cells Protection** on the Excel menu).

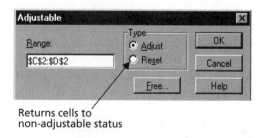

Returns cells to
non-adjustable status

When the **B**est dialog box appears, select the single cell to be maximized or minimized. This corresponds to the target cell of the Excel solver. If there is none, that is, you are merely trying to satisfy constraints, click **None**.

The constrain command opens the following dialog box. Highlight cells on both sides of the constraint type and the range used to store the constraint equations.

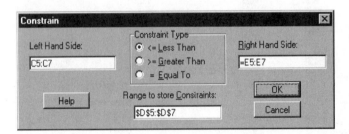

Note: If a range of columns is selected before you invoke the command, the three ranges in the dialog box will default appropriately, so that no further specification is required.

Formulas in the constraint range indicate whether the constraint is satisfied, tight, or not satisfied as shown in the following figure.

	C	D	E	F
D5		=WB(C5,"<=",E5)		
5	10	=<=	10	
6	15	<=	20	
7	20	Not <=	15	

Dual designates cells in which to store dual values and ranges associated with specified constraints and adjustable cells. This information corresponds to the sensitivity report of the Excel Solver.

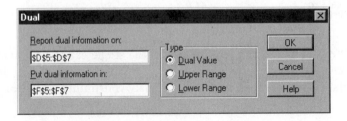

This designates cells to take on integer values in <u>B</u>inary (0,1) or <u>G</u>eneral (0,1,2,3...) format. Ranges of integer cells must be named. Tolerance and known integer solution (IP) can speed up optimization process when integer ranges are specified. See What's*Best!* help.

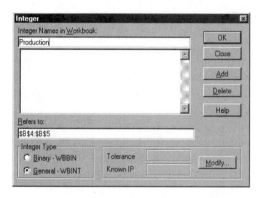

The **Options** command opens the following dialog box:

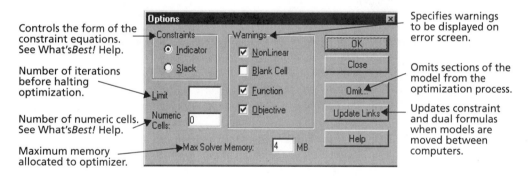

The **Report** command opens the following dialog box:

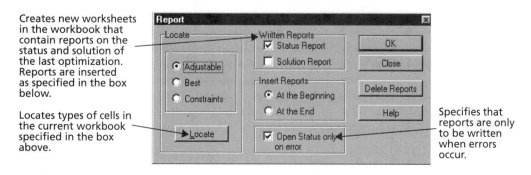

References

@RISK. Palisade Corp., Newfield NY

Bratley, P, Fox, B. L. and Schrage, L. E. *A Guide to Simulation*, Springer-Verlag. 1987.

Brightman, Harvey J. *Statistics in Plain English*, South-Western. 1986.

Crystal Ball, Decisioneering Inc., Boulder, CO.

Dantzig, George B. *Linear Programming and Extensions,* Princeton University Press, 1963.

Dyson, Freeman. *Weapons and Hope*, Harper & Row, New York. 1984.

Efron, Bradley and Tibshirani, Robert J. *An Introduction to the Bootstrap,* Chapman & Hall. 1993.

Gardner, Everette S. Jr. "Exponential Smoothing: The State of the Art," *Journal of Forecasting*, 4 (1), pp. 1–38, 1986.

Gardner, Everette S. Jr. *The Spreadsheet Operations Manager.* McGraw Hill. 1992, pp. 10–13.

Gonick, Larry and Smith Woollcott. *The Cartoon Guide to Statistics*. Harper. 1993.

Hertz, David B. "Risk Analysis in Capital Investment," *Harvard Business Review,* 57 (5), 1979.

Hillier, Frederick S. and Lieberman, Gerald J. *Introduction to Operations Research*, 1990.

Hull, John C. *Introduction to Futures & Options Markets*, Prentice Hall. 1991.

Infanger, Gerd. *Planning Under Uncertainty*, Boyd & Fraser. 1994.

Law, A. M. and Kelton, D. W. *Simulation Modeling & Analysis*, McGraw Hill. 1991.

Luenberger, David G. *Introduction to Dynamic Systems*. John Wiley. 1979.

Luenberger, David G. *Investment Science*. Oxford University Press, 1997.

Markowitz, H. M. *Portfolio Selection, Efficient Diversification of Investments*. John Wiley. 1959

Plane, Donald R. *Management Science A Spreadsheet Approach*, Boyd & Fraser. 1994.

Savage, Sam L. *The ABC's of Optimization using What'sBest!*, General Optimization. 1985.

Savage, Sam L. *Fundamental Analytic Spreadsheet Tools for Quantatative Management*. McGraw-Hill. 1993.

Savage, Sam L. "Statistical Analysis for the Masses" in *Statistics and Public Policy*, edited by Bruce Spencer, Oxford University Press, 1996.

Simon, Julian L. *Resampling: The New Statistics*. Resampling Stats, Inc. 1974–1995.

Simon, J.L., Atkinson, D.T., and Shevokas, C. *Probability and statistics: Experimental results of a radically different teaching method*, American Mathematical Monthly, 83 (9), 1976.

Tufte, Edward, *Visual Explanations*, Graphics Press, 1996.

Winston, Wayne L., Albright S. Christian, and Broadie, Mark. *Practical Management Science, Spreadsheet Modeling and Applications*, Duxbury Press. 1997.

Index

A

@RISK, 18, 89, 267
absolute $ references, 111
absolute reference, 5
advertising, 19, 123, 126
air traffic control, 108
algebraic curtain, 2
analytical model, 3
analytical modeling, 2, 3, 7, 12, 13, 15
applications
    air traffic control, 108
    assembly line, 106
    bank, 107
    bidding, 70
    blending, 197
    boat manufacturing, 3
    cash flow statement, 64
    champagne sales, 129
    commercial aircraft, 76
    cutting stock, 204
    disaster relief, 207
    drilling for oil, 173
    estimating overtime
        expenses, 65

    estimating production, 65
    feedmix, 200
    forest fire, 96
    health care screening, 116
    inventory costs, 54
    investment, 44
    machine replacement, 116
    manufacturing, 197
    market share, 109
    optimal staffing level, 70
    product introduction, 19
    product mix, 197
    production, 11
    routing, 151
    staff scheduling, 200
    stock options, 71
    toll booth, 98
    toy manufacturing, 178
    transportation, 205
assembly line, 106
average, 59
    Central Limit Theorem, 40
    covariance, 82
    cumulative, 89
    expected value, 157

    inputs, 60, 62, 63
    mean, 33, 43
    mean squared error, 140
    mode, 57
    of random variables, 36
    of two spins, 37
    of uncertain inputs, 55
    outputs, 60, 62, 63
    queue length, 99
    queue waiting time, 99
    random variables, 38, 40
    standard deviation, 35
    value of a function, 63
    variance, 35

B

Bacon, Francis, 52
bad outcomes, 28, 50
ball bearing, 246
bank application, 107
basketball example, 143
bell-shaped curve, 40
Berkson, Joe, 14, 126
best guess, 53, 55, 61, 62, 66, 92

BID.xls, 70
bidding application, 70
binary integer, 219
binomial distribution, 42
blending problems, 197
Blitzogram, 42
BOATS.xls, 3, 4, 186
BOATSOPT.xls, 192, 194
Boolean logic, 220
bootstrapping, 56

C
cash flow statement, 64
causal forecasting, 119
   regression, 120
Central Limit Theorem, 36, 40, 90
champagne sales, 129
Chart Wizard, 79
Cholesky Factorization, 86
coin toss, 128
commercial aircraft, 76
common graph option, 86
conservation constraint, 211
constraint contours, 243
contour, 233, 244
   expected return, 234
   of a linear function, 246
   of a nonlinear function, 247
   risk, 235
convergence, 61, 89
   graph, 265
   rate of, 265
convex problem, 247
corner solutions, 244, 245
correlated random variables, simulating, 88
correlation, 78, 83, 84, 137, 142, 143, 267
   positive, 79
   rank order, 89
   regression, 142
covariance, 82, 83, 85, 88, 143
   average area, 82

geometrical interpretation, 81
   linear regression, 84
covering problems, 203
Crystal Ball, 18, 89, 267
cumulative distribution, 36, 37, 80, 253
cumulative graph, 26, 34, 35, 38, 43, 48, 60, 90, 263, 264
   common, 49, 87, 88
curve fitting, 238

D
Dantzig, George, 213, 246
data analysis tools, 42, 134
data, separation from formulas, 4
data tables, 8, 166, 179
   command, 9
   creating simulations from, 42
decision analysis, 150
   basic concepts, 157
decision criteria, 162
   good decisions versus good outcomes, 151
decision forks, 163
decision tree, 149, 150, 156, 173
   decision forks, 163, 164
   leaves, 152, 155, 164, 174, 178
   node, 164
   root, 153, 164, 165, 172, 175
   subtrees, 171
   uncertainty forks, 164
decision variables, 188
Deming, W. Edward, 13
dependence, statistical, 76
dependent variable, 125, 137
developmental necessities of applications, 221
discrete-event simulation, 94, 95
   paste special method, 95

distribution, 33, 36, 40, 160, 251, 253, 254, 268, 269
   binomial, 42–43
   Central Limit Theorem, 40
   cumulative, 37
   exponential, 43
   idealized, 53
   normal, 43
   Poisson, 43, 98, 100
   triangular, 57
   uniform, 53
diversification, 36, 38, 49, 85
   and correlation, 84
domestic fund example, 46, 85
drilling for oil, 173
drug development, 152
dual values, 194, 248, 249, 250
Dyson, Freeman, 180

E
efficient frontier, 237
enlightenment, levels of, 66
equilibrium percentages of Markov chain, 112
event-incremented time, 97
Excel
   = FREQUENCY, 41
   = RAND, 22, 29, 31, 37, 41
   Analysis ToolPak, 120
   Chart Wizard, 79
   CORREL, 83
   COVAR, 82
   data analysis tools, 134
   data table, 9, 42
   range names, 6
   simulation add-in, 18, 19
   SUMPRODUCT, 6, 187
Excel 97, 191
Excel Solver, 183
expected return of an investment, 233
expected value, 33, 157, 162
exponential distribution, 43, 100, 251, 253, 269
   interarrival time, 251
   relation to Poisson distribution, 100
   service time, 251

exponential model, 128
exponential smoothing, 142
  one parameter, 146
  smoothing parameter, 147
  two parameter, 146, 255

F

fastest route, 151
feasible region, 244
FIRE.xls, 96, 254
fixed-cost problem, 217
fixed-time increments, 97
  forest fire example, 96
FORECAST.xla, 119, 122, 129, 139, 147
forecasting
  causal, 118
  errors, 133
  linear model, 126
  link to simulation, 133
  period, 138
  time series analysis, 118, 128
  using forecast errors, 132
  warm-up period, 138
foreign fund example, 46, 51, 84, 85, 87
formulas, separation from, 4
function icon, 23, 45, 56, 58, 266
function of random variables, 62
FUNDS.xls, 85

G

Gardner, Everette S. Jr., 119, 255
gen_Normal, 46, 72, 86, 89, 267
gen_Resample, 56, 57, 75, 78, 80, 88, 267
gen_ResampleSync, 75, 80
gen_Triang, 23, 57, 58, 71, 267
gen_Uniform, 65
Geoffrion, Arthur, 13

H

hedge fund example, 85

Hertz, David, 18
hierarchical objectives, 193
histogram, 26, 33, 35, 37, 38, 39, 41, 60, 90, 160, 262, 263
  common, 87
  create using the FREQUENCY function, 60
  data analysis tools, 42
  dice, 39
holding pattern example, 108
hyperscaling, 13

I

ice cream example, 149
idealized distributions, 28, 42
imperfect information, value of, 173
independent variable, 125, 137, 141
indicator, 65, 73
infeasible solution, 240
INT() function, 41
integer binary, 219
integer, general, 216
integer variables, 193, 207
  the fixed cost problem, 217
Inter Ocular Trauma Test, 14, 15, 126
international fund example, 85
inventory problem, 54
investment example, 44, 50, 53
  expected return, 233
  instrument, 233
  portfolio, 233
  risk, 234
INVNTORY.xls, 54, 89, 91
  parameterized simulation, 67

J

Johnson, Samuel, 118

K

knapsack problem, 214
Knuth, Donald, 12

L

Lagrange multipliers, 195, 248
linear formula, 238
  rules for writing, 239
linear model, 62, 92, 126
linear optimization models
  errors in, 238
linear problems, 246
linear programming, 184
linear regression, 142, 143
lognormal random variable, 72

M

M/M/1 queue, 99
machine replacement modeling, 114
management science, 2
manufacturing, 3, 178, 197, 222, 228
  two-period, 227
market share example, 109
Markov chain, 93, 109, 110, 112, 113
MARKOV.xls, 110
Markowitz, Harry, 233
MAX() function, 41
maximum flow problem, 211
McLuhan, Marshall, 93
mean, 33, 35, 36, 38, 43, 44, 72, 85, 88, 98, 101, 253, 254, 263, 264, 265
  as line on parameterized graph, 69
mean squared error, 140
median, 35
minimum cost problem, 211
MMULT formula, 111
mode, 35, 57, 223, 224
model
  auditing, 11
  checking for feasibility, 7
  development, 12
  documentation, 11
  experimenting with, 7
  scaleable, 6
  what-if analysis, 8

model-building tips, 238
modeling in spreadsheets, pros and cons, 15
Monte Carlo simulation, 18, 19, 21, 24, 29, 61, 89, 92, 151, 162, 267
multiperiod model, 221
multivariate data, 75
multivariate linear regression, 128
multivariate normal random variables, 86

N
net present value, 72
network flow model, 207
network flow problem, 211
network model, 205
nonconvex problem, 247
nonlinear error message, 240
nonlinear optimization, 233
nonlinear problems, 247
nonlinear programming, 184
normal distribution, 40, 43, 44
NORMDIST, 44
NPV, 72

O
object oriented approach to modeling, 221
objective contour, 244
operations research, 2
optimal staffing, 70
optimal stocking level, 66
optimization
  ABC's of, 183
  categories of, 184
  D's of, 194
  geometric view, 242
  under uncertainty, 230
optimization models, combining, 221
option
  call, 71
  implied volatility, 73
  put, 71
OPTION.xls, 72
output cell, 24, 31, 68

P
parallel queues, 103
parameter, 66, 260, 264, 266
parameterized graph, 74
parameterized optimization, 236
parameterized simulation, 66, 74, 78, 81
parking ticket example, 150
PAYLOAD.xls, 76
percentiles, 48
perfect information, value of, 169
Pliny, 17
point estimate, 55, 59, 60, 62, 63, 78
Poisson distribution, 43, 98
  relation to exponential distribution, 100
portfolio optimization, 237
probability
  assessing, 160
  classical approach, 160
  estimates, 166
  independent outcome, 160
  joint, 171, 178
  mutually exclusive, 160
  subjective definition, 161
probability distribution, 33, 254
probability wheel, 161
PROFIT.xls, 20, 21, 24
PROFORMA.xls, 64, 65

Q
Q_NET.xla, 94, 95, 104, 251, 268
  installation, 268
  running, 268
Q_NET.xls, 103
queues, 98
  arrival, 253
  average length, 99
  average waiting time, 99
  classification, 99
  departure, 253
  length, 251, 252, 253
  M/M/1, 99

multiple queues, multiple servers, 106, 107
  number served, 252
  parallel, 103
  serial, 105
  server busy, 253
  service time, 253
  single server, 99
  statistics, 252
  system arrival, 254
  theoretical results, 99
  through-put, 252
  wait time, 252
QUEUE.xla, 94, 95, 101, 102, 104, 251, 268
  installation, 95, 268
  operation, 101
QUEUE.xls
  explanation and formulas, 251
  operation, 101
queuing equations, 251
queuing networks, 103

R
Ragsdale, Cliff, 212
RAND, 22, 32, 37, 40, 41, 97, 253, 254
random number generators, 22, 46, 67, 265
random numbers, seeding, 67
random variable, 17, 28, 29
  average of a function of, 63
  continuous, 30
  discrete, 30, 100
  expected value, 33
  functions of, 52, 61, 62
  intuition, 30, 36
  outcome of rolling dice, 30
  stationary, 128, 129
  uniform, 32, 41
random walk, 72
range names, 6
rank order correlation, 89
rate of convergence, 265
reduced cost, 248
regression, 120, 142
  analysis tools, 122

errors, 134
Excel, 119, 126
formulas, 143
intuitive explanations, 119
linear, 142
linest and trend functions, 123
multivariate linear, 128
scatterplot, 123
resampling
historical data, 56, 81
multivariate data, 75
residual plot, 136
resource allocation, 182
resources
economic value of, 194
scarce, 182, 194
risk management, 50
rolling dice example, 39

S
Savage, Sam L., 15
scaleable, 6
scatterplots, 123, 125
seasonal data, 257
seasonality, 122, 129, 133, 147
seasonality factor, 257
seed, 67
sensitivity analysis, 90, 152, 156, 179
graphical approach, 166
in decision analysis, 166
two way, 179
serial queues, 105
shadow price, 194, 195, 248
shortest path problem, 211
SIM.xla, 19, 20, 44, 54, 64, 66, 72, 91, 101, 122, 138, 151, 260, 265, 267, 268
commands, 267
simplex algorithm, 246
SIMSTATS.xls, 25
simulation
discrete event, 95
event-incremented, 100
fixed-time increment, 100

link to forecasting, 133
output, 25, 31, 37, 47, 68, 87
parameterized settings, 68
settings, 24, 31, 47, 59
statistics, 25, 31, 59, 87
slope of regression line, 142
smoothing parameter, 147
software limitations, 267
specialized optimization languages, 242
Spetzler, Carl, 161
spinner, 29, 30, 32, 36, 39, 53
SPINNER.xls, 29
staff scheduling problem, 202
standard deviation, 35, 36, 38, 43, 44, 83, 85, 90, 137, 237
standard error, 36, 89, 90
startup effect, 102
state variables, 150, 173, 179
stationary random variable, 129
statistical dependence, 75, 81, 82
stochastic linear program, 230
stock, 71
subtrees, 171
SUMPRODUCT, 6, 13, 15, 154, 165, 187, 203, 215, 219, 222, 226, 239, 240

T
tableau representation, 242
time series, 143
confidence intervals, 141
errors, 138
time series analysis, 119, 121, 128, 140
toll booth example, 98
trade-off curve, 232
traffic flow equations, 254
transient effect, 102
transition matrix, 104, 110, 113, 114
transition probability, 110

transportation model, generalization of, 207
transportation problem, 205
two-period supply chain, 224
TREE.xla, 149, 151, 152, 159, 164, 165
trend, 122, 129, 139, 147
significance of linear, 123
triangular distribution, 22, 57
Tufte, Edward, 14
tutorial
estimating inventory costs, 54
estimating profit, 19
experimental drug development, 152
machine replacement, 114
manufacturing, 3
maximum profit, 185
sales based on advertising, 123
two-period supply chain, 224

U
umbrella problem, 150
unbounded, 240
uncertain numbers, 28, 29, 36, 42, 50, 61, 75
average, 36
bad outcomes, 28
diversification, 28
important classes of, 28
risk management, 28
uncertainty
advantage, 71
building blocks of, 28
buildings of, 61
modeling, 28
over time, 74
uniform random variable, 41
utility, 157, 158, 163

V2
value
of imperfect information, 173
of perfect information, 169

value at risk (VAR), 50, 51, 70, 87
variance, 35, 36, 38, 85, 88, 137, 233, 234, 235, 236, 237
vector inner product, 7
vertically integrated models, 227
Visual Basic, 24, 97
voices of experience, 2, 12

W

waiting lines, 98
"What If" analysis, 8
What'sBest!, 183, 193
wildcatter problem, 173
Woolsey, Gene, 13
worksheet model
    elements of, 4, 61
    PROFIT.xls, 20

Y

Yes/No decisions, 217
yield management, 76
y-intercept of regression line, 142